BRANDING
IN A
COMPETITIVE MARKETPLACE

BRANDING
IN A
COMPETITIVE MARKETPLACE

RAJAT K. BAISYA

$SAGE | Response Business Books

www.sagepublications.com

Los Angeles • London • New Delhi • Singapore • Washington DC

First published in 2013 by

SAGE | Response Business Books

SAGE Response
B1/I-1 Mohan Cooperative Industrial Area
Mathura Road, New Delhi 110 044, India

SAGE Publications Inc
2455 Teller Road
Thousand Oaks, California 91320, USA

SAGE Publications Ltd
1 Oliver's Yard, 55 City Road
London EC1Y 1SP, United Kingdom

SAGE Publications Asia-Pacific Pte Ltd
33 Pekin Street
#02-01 Far East Square
Singapore 048763

Published by Vivek Mehra for SAGE Publications India Pvt Ltd, typeset in 10/13 pt Goudy Old Style by Diligent Typesetter and printed at De Unique, New Delhi.

Library of Congress Cataloging-in-Publication Data

Baisya, Rajat K.
    Branding in a competitive marketplace/Rajat K. Baisya.
        pages cm
    Includes bibliographical references and index.
    1. Branding (Marketing) 2. Brand name products. 3. Strategic planning. I. Title.
    HF5415.1255.B35   658.8'27—dc23   2013   2013011444

ISBN: 978-81-321-1059-0 (PB)

The SAGE Team: Sachin Sharma, Dhurjjati Sarma, and Nand Kumar Jha

I dedicate this book to my two uncles,
Amitabha Chaudhuri and late Nalini Kumar Baisya,
and also to the fond memory of my daughter,
Deepanwita Baisya.

Thank you for choosing a SAGE product! If you have any comment,
observation or feedback, I would like to personally hear from you.
Please write to me at contactceo@sagepub.in

—Vivek Mehra, Managing Director and CEO,
SAGE Publications India Pvt Ltd, New Delhi

Bulk Sales

SAGE India offers special discounts for purchase of books in bulk.
We also make available special imprints and excerpts from our
books on demand.

For orders and enquiries, write to us at

Marketing Department
SAGE Publications India Pvt Ltd
B1/I-1, Mohan Cooperative Industrial Area
Mathura Road, Post Bag 7
New Delhi 110044, India
E-mail us at marketing@sagepub.in

Get to know more about SAGE, be invited to SAGE events, get on
our mailing list. Write today to marketing@sagepub.in

This book is also available as an e-book.

————ೞೞ————

Contents

List of Tables

List of Figures

List of Abbreviations

AIK	All Insect Killer
AMUL	Anand Milk Producers' Union Ltd
AMI	Asia Market Intelligence
ATL	Above the Line
BBC	British Broadcasting Corporation
BCL	Bombay Chemicals Ltd
BRIC	Brazil, Russia, India, China
BSE	Bombay Stock Exchange
BTL	Below the Line
CAGR	Compound Annual Growth Rate
CBBE	Customer-Based Brand Equity
C&F	Clearing and Forwarding
CII	Confederation of Indian Industries
CIK	Crawling Insect Killer
CLV	Customer Lifetime Value
CRM	Customer Relationship Management
CSA	Consignment Selling Agent
CSE	Center for Science and Environment
CSR	Corporate Social Responsibility
CST	Central Sales Tax
CTC	Central Technical Centre
EBITDA	Earnings Before Interest, Tax, and Depreciation
EPS	Earning Per Share
ECR	Efficient Consumer Response
EU	European Union
F&V	Fruit and Vegetable
FDI	Foreign Direct Investment
FICCI	Federation of Indian Chambers of Commerce and Industry
FIK	Flying Insect Killer

FMCG	Fast Moving Consumer Goods
GBU	Global Business Unit
GCPL	Godrej Consumer Products Ltd
GDP	Gross Domestic Product
GE	General Electric
GSK	GlaxoSmithKline
GSSL	Godrej Sara Lee Ltd
GST	Goods and Service Tax
HUL	Hindustan Unilever Ltd
HVO	Hydrogenated Vegetable Oil
IPO	Impact Per Opportunity
IPO	Initial Public Offer
IPR	Intellectual Property Right
JLL	Jyothy Laboratories Ltd
KAL	Kingfisher Airlines Ltd
M&A	Merger and Acquisition
MIS	Management Information System
MNC	Multinational Corporation
NCR	National Capital Region
NCAER	National Council of Applied Economic Research
NSAID	Non-Steroid Anti-Inflammatory Drug
OOH	Out of Home
OTC	Over the Counter
OTS	Opportunity to See
P/E	Price Earnings Ratio
P&G	Procter and Gamble
PIE	Potential Industry Earning
PIL	Public Interest Litigation
PR	Public Relations
QSR	Quick Service Restaurant
R&D	Research and Development
ROCE	Return on Capital Employed
ROE	Return on Equity
ROI	Return on Investment
SBU	Strategic Business Unit
SEBI	Securities and Exchange Board of India
SHG	Self-Help Group
SKB	SmithKline Beecham
SKU	Stock Keeping Unit
SME	Small and Medium Enterprises

SMS	Short Messaging Service
VAT	Value Added Tax
UBL	United Breweries Ltd
UID	Unique Identification Device
USP	Unique Selling Proposition
UN	United Nations
VC	Venture Capitalist
WTO	World Trade Organization

Foreword

I have known Dr Rajat Baisya for over 20 years. He had earlier worked in the industry (Herbertsons, Reckitt and Coleman), and then moved into academics. He is one of the few, who (after the shift) has still kept a connection with the industry, with the consultancies, and been on the Board of Directors of many companies across India. For many years, he has also been an elected member of the Council of the Institute of Management Consultants of India.

I am glad that he has written this book on BRANDING—which I must say, is a very complete book on the subject, covering the entire spectrum. In addition to compressing much of the knowledge on the subject into about 250 pages, he has been able to include a large number of cases from India, and shown the application of theory to practice in the local context. It makes the book particularly valuable to students of Marketing in India, and to all those from the industry in India or overseas, who are interested in the marketing scenario in this vast and complex subcontinent.

In the 21st century, BRANDING occupies a very special place in the practice of Marketing. It is sometimes said that Branding is Marketing; or even that Marketing is Branding!! This may not be entirely true. But suffice it to say that Branding is a key factor in Marketing. The stronger the Brand, the lesser the dependence on lower price, provided of course, that all the other factors of product or service quality, effective distribution, and promotion are taken care of. There are still some exceptions, like Angustura Bitters, that defy even this qualification.

Many attempts have been made to describe Branding. Sometimes it has ended up like the attempt to describe the elephant by the five blind men. Each described the elephant, based on the "feel" he got from the part of the elephant that he touched. Branding is a nebulous element. You know what it is, when you see it. You also know when and where it is absent. In some ways, it is like CHARACTER or REPUTATION. You know it when it is there and you also know when it is not there. But you cannot really define it in very real terms. And like Character, it takes a long time to build a brand, and it takes a very short time to kill it.

For consumers, Brands do not lend themselves to clinical examination. The Brand says it all. The brand VOLVO immediately projects the image of safety; the brand WALMART projects the image of low prices and good value for money; the brand GUCCI projects the image of style at a premium price; the brand DETTOL projects the image of a powerful antiseptic. And the list goes on. Those who try to change the perceived image of the established brand have often met with failure, because they have tried to ride two different horses at the same time. The examples are legend, too many to name.

Many have tried to fight the tyranny of brands, on the plea that consumers are being taken for a ride. They say that consumers are made to pay more because of their brand loyalty, which makes them blind to the realities of the marketplace. There are the pharmaceutical companies who have introduced generics and have succeeded only partly, because generic products have got branded with the name of the manufacturer. The consumer wants paracetamol tablets of Company X only. This is where the whole movement of generics has failed to achieve the stated objective.

It is possible that the Brand may be a country: German engineering products, French wines, Japanese electronics, Indian silk, Chinese green tea, and Dutch cheese. Or a company could be a brand: Westinghouse, Ford, Canali, or Channel. And this could be for a refrigerator, a car, a suit, or a perfume. Or it could be for a single product itself: a Parker Gold pen, an iPhone 5, or Hush Puppy shoes. This can be a great advantage and sometimes, a disadvantage. Or a brand could even be an individual. Richard Branson is a brand, and so is Amitabh Bachchan, and so are many celebrities in the field of arts, culture, and other fields.

Since brand building takes so many years and is a long and tortuous process, there is the great temptation to spread the brand and gain mileage from it. Sometimes it works and sometimes it does not. The goodwill of Virgin Airlines has been transferred to Virgin Music and Virgin Communications and there seems to be no great harm done. Kingfisher has transferred the goodwill from the beer to the airlines, but the airline has been in problems. Will this affect the Kingfisher brand? Only time will tell.

Spreading the goodwill of the brand name is a very delicate business. It is a great temptation, and requires a lot of restraint and the use of good judgment. And it is the same with endorsements. Does a famous movie actor endorsing a brand of cement add credibility to the cement brand? Is he able to transfer his credible personal brand image to the cement product? Consumers will best answer this question, by showing an increase in cement sales!!

Dr Baisya has dealt with a complicated subject of valuation of a brand with complexity made simple or as simple as it can be made. It is one of the most valuable chapters in the book, which will be very useful to managers who have to grapple with this subject (more often now than in the past) with the spate of mergers, acquisitions, and buyouts. There have been the Piramals, the Ranbaxys, the Parles, and the Gujarat Ambujas, who have been bought out—and who seem to have managed brand valuation extremely well. Looking at these examples, one can say that in this area, India has come of age!!

I would wish that this book is in the library of every management institute in India, and on the bookshelves of every marketing manager in the country, who has built brands or is in the process of doing so, and read by every overseas manager who intends to enter the complex marketplace, which is India.

Walter Vieira
President, Marketing Advisory Services Group, India;
and Former Chairman, International Council of
Management Consulting Institutes (World Apex Body)

Foreword

We live in a world of brands. The idea of branding has now traveled way beyond its origins and is used today to describe people, political parties, cities, states, countries, and even ideas. At a time like this, it becomes imperative to understand this concept in its fullness. Traditional approaches to this subject need to be updated and a measure of rigor needs to be practiced when working with brands. The context in which we live too is evolving rapidly thanks to changes in technology and the resulting relationship between brands and human beings. Business no longer holds the upper hand in its interactions with consumers; the consumer of today is empowered and sophisticated, and has the means to express herself assertively. As a market, India brings to branding an additional layer of complexity thanks to its diversity, and to its tendency to live simultaneously in different eras.

The timing is just right for an updated academic consolidation on branding drawn from Indian examples as most categories are now witnessing rapid growth. While being largely an under-branded market so far, Indian consumers are on their way to becoming highly brand conscious as brand choice proliferates. Brand managers and branding experts have an opportunity to conceive new brands across categories and consumer segments. Indian entrepreneurs are keener than ever to create, grow, and protect the economic value of business with brands. More global brands have evolved in India with specific brand strategies. This book comprehensively discusses key branding concepts in eight chapters from new brand conception to brand valuation. Written in a lucid and accessible style, the academic body of the text has a marketer's soul. Appropriately punctuated with relevant cases from fast moving consumer goods (FMCG), it offers an inside view of the applied world of branding.

I had an opportunity to work with Dr Baisya when he led businesses at Reckitt Benckiser in early 1990s. His current academic success and intellect suitably leverage his past experience in FMCG marketing and subsequent consulting practice.

Reflective of this expertise, this scholarly work will not only provide a strong foundation to young students of branding but will also be a valuable reference for future academic projects.

Santosh Desai
Managing Director and Chief Executive Officer,
Futurebrands Limited

Preface

Manufacturers produce quality products using best ingredients, best technology, and engaging best people that they can get. But consumers buy those depending on their own perception. This perception is created by the concerted effort of the brand marketers. It is the perception which lies in the consumers' mind that makes all the difference and not the physical product which exists only to support the perception. It is, therefore, considered that perception is the only reality and rest are all illusion. Brand is, therefore, considered the most valuable asset to the business. Same product produced under different brand names will create different perceptions in consumers' mind and, therefore, their demand and sales would also be different. It is the brand that makes all the difference in terms of product's performance in the marketplace. A name does not, however, simply become a brand. A lot of marketing resources and efforts go behind the product to become a brand over a period of time.

The forces of globalization have removed the typical trade barrier and we have now a plethora of brands in any product categories available in the market fighting for their brand share. The traditional marketing effort, traditional brand-building strategies seem to be not delivering the expected result any longer. Marketers have to think radically different now. This has resulted into much higher failure rate. And the cost of failure is very high these days. The success rate of new launches has now reduced to about 10 percent. In spite of best efforts of businesses why brands still fail? In a fiercely competitive environment, old ball games, old methods and approaches, and old strategies are not working. Marketers are now trying many new strategic initiatives.

This book starts with the issues concerning how a simple name graduates to a brand and ultimately to a power brand. It then continues to deal with other strategic issues in brand building such as brand identity, brand equity, brand extension, brand valuation, and most importantly what the marketers are now doing to build a strong brand in a competitive environment. The book attempts to illustrate every lesson from the real-life marketing environment supported by case studies of successful brands which stood the onslaught of competitive actions.

This book also traces the reasons for failures in a competitive environment studying relevant cases and analyzing numerous examples from both domestic as well as international market to distill the key lessons from both failures and successes. And finally, it attempts to provide strategic directions and lessons for creating and developing brands that last the test of time and competitive forces. It is expected that brand marketers will have some key lessons that can really have practical implications in their own businesses.

Rajat K. Baisya

Acknowledgments

I have been working on this book for last three years. The book has undergone many reviews and after each of them some additions and modifications and inclusions have been done. The book that has now finally been published is significantly an improved version enriched by the review process. Even the title of the book has been changed by SAGE with whom I have worked earlier. SAGE has been closely associated with this review process and I am very thankful to them. The book got delayed for case studies to be included as originally planned were not ready. I would like to thank my friend Chander Sethi, former CMD of Reckitt Benckiser India Ltd, and Rahul Kumar Singh, Marketing Manager of the same company, for helping me in completing the Mortein Case study. Similarly, I am grateful to Kalyan Ganguly, President, United Breweries Ltd; Sekhar Ramamurthy, Deputy President; Perry Goes, Senior Vice President; and Mr Deepak Jain, Senior Manager Strategic Planning & Business Analysis of United Breweries Ltd for providing a lot of information which helped me to develop the case study on Kingfisher Beer brand. I would like to thank Mr Walter Vieira, President, Marketing Advisory Services Group and a well-known management consultant and Mr Santosh Desai, MD & CEO of Futurebrands and a well-known social commentator for writing the Forewords for the book.

One of my research scholars, Pankaj Priya, working for his PhD under my guidance and currently a faculty at Birla Institute of Technology & Management at Noida, has helped me in writing the case study on Nirula's Fast Food Restaurant Chain. I would like to take this opportunity to thank him for rendering this support. Atul Patil, Category Manager of Booker India Pvt. Ltd, did help me with the drawing of some figures included in this book. I also would like to acknowledge the support that I got from my two research students Dr Somnath Chakraborti and T. Vijaykumar, faculty at IMT Ghaziabad and IGNOU, respectively, for collecting some information while writing this book.

I would like to acknowledge the unstinted and unconditional support that I had received from my family members, namely my wife Susmita, my daughter

xxvi BRANDING IN A COMPETITIVE MARKETPLACE

Deepshikha, and my son Rishabh. They closely followed-up with me to know the progress I am making with the manuscript. In fact my daughter Deepshikha has helped me in editing the book as well as in drawing many illustrations. My son Rishabh always asked me when my book will be out in the market and whether I am working on a new title or not. Rishabh also takes keen interest to know how my earlier books are doing in the market. I gratefully acknowledge their support. Whenever I venture on some new initiatives including writing and other academic work I always remember my elder daughter Deepanwita, who is no more. Her fond memory gives me lot of energy and enthusiasm. I also acknowledge the blessings of my parents, Late Rabindra Kumar Baisya and Vidyut Prova Baisya, without which I would not have been able to complete this work. My mother-in-law, Shefali Dey, showed interest in my academic work and I am grateful to her for her support. My younger brother, Arup Baisya, takes a lot of interest in my academic and social activities and I wish him well.

Lastly, I would like to thank my publisher SAGE for closely working with me and helping me to improve upon the text and, in the process, added additional value to it.

Introduction

Brand is the most important and most valuable asset in the business to be preserved and supported to grow in order to deliver the targeted business performance and create shareholders' wealth and that is the primary purpose of the existence of any business organization. Shareholders make the business managers as custodians of their investment and expect to reap the harvest which is the result of prudent business decisions and effective implementation of the action plans by the management team. Businesses are set up to exploit the opportunities in the marketplace. But these days too many business ventures are pursuing too few opportunities. Take any product category, and you will find how many players are struggling to get a portion of the cake in terms of total market opportunity. For example, earlier we had only Maggi noodles in the market from Nestle who had in fact created this category and was enjoying over 80 percent share and only other brand was Top Ramen from Indo Nissin having about 15 percent market share. Seeing that the category growing at over 15 percent annually, Hindustan Unilever Limited (HUL) introduced Knorr Soupy noodles, ITC introduced Sunfeast Yuppie, GlaxoSmithKline (GSK, maker of Horlicks) also has introduced Foodles—all fighting in the same market with a hope to take away and be a part of the growing segment. It can be noted here that all players are multinationals with deep pockets and enormous resources in their command. Hence, there is keen competition, each one trying to outsmart the other. Of course, all may not emerge winner at the end. But the task of brand managers handling these brands is no doubt becoming increasingly difficult. Traditional marketing efforts are no longer seem to be working now. Brand managers normally attempt to design the marketing plan around the 4Ps of the marketing mix and in the days of tough competitions simple plan around the basic marketing mix are not delivering anything. As a result we see more failures than successes. We also see established brands are losing the market share to even the new entrants. Regional and local brands have given formidable competition to the well known national brands and succeeded in terms of taking away the market share.

Holding on to the market share and building the brand equity are the primary tasks of the brand marketers. But this task seems to be increasingly becoming difficult. Traditional marketing approaches thus are fast becoming irrelevant particularly because results are not forthcoming through such approaches. Traditional marketing management of marketing mix is only the part of the exercise that we need to do in the business, but to create success stories or to deliver the targeted performance against stiff competition, we need to do much more. Businesses are to be managed now in a much more dynamic environment. Everything seems to be changing fast, familiar goal posts are no longer able to guide the business decisions. Even in terms of basic marketing mix, changes have to be incorporated more frequently. Earlier brand managers were scared to make any changes as long as things are working well for them. For example, Dettol, a hardworking product, an antiseptic liquid, used to be sold in traditional glass bottle with equally traditional looking paper label and metal cap. The product was the market leader. Everything was working well for the brand with typically old-fashioned packaging when modern packaging system were already available and many products in consumer segments were using state of the art packaging material and system. Dettol was delivering results and hence there was no need to upgrade. Even its variant, Dettol Soap, was also having a traditional look. Subsequently when competition surfaced and Savlon was introduced, Dettol started changing its look and appearance and even many new variants including Dettol Fresh was introduced which was unthinkable one decade ago. In the face of competition, thus, product, packaging, technology, promotion, price, etc., need to be revisited often to remain contemporary with the changing expectations of the consumers. Competitive actions often redefine the consumers' expectation and brand marketers have to ensure that their brand's response to these emerging changes are meeting changing customers demand and expectation. If the brand fails to imbibe those changes in its presentations and total offering, it is likely to lose out in the market due to intense competitive pressure. Pricing is another key strategic tool. Many new products have been seen to fail due to wrong pricing. Pricing has to match the perceived value of the total offering. Technology also plays a very important role in determining the price. One can observe that while cost of everything goes up with time, some of our technology products cost less even with increased and better features. Computers are well-known examples of that category.

Smaller manufacturers including local and regional players are taking big players head on only on price front being more efficient and cost-effective producers. Big players like Britannia and Parle lost out to local players like Priya Foods in north and Bisk Farms in East. They produce and sell locally almost equally good products at a lower price and offer much higher trade margins to channel partners. Lipton and Brooke Bond, the two leading global brands of tea, also lost out to small local players like Society brand of tea in the west India market.

Brands are being acquired now for astronomical price because creating a new brand is not that easy any longer and, therefore, acquiring an established brand is a preferred route to deliver growth. There are well-known companies which are constantly eying for new acquisition for the growth as they are not able to deliver organic growth exploiting the current portfolio. Reckitt Benckiser, an Anglo-Dutch multinational corporation, can be named as one of those types of organizations which are in constant lookout for the promising brands which have a strategic fit with their portfolio. The acquisition of brands paying exorbitant price also create severe cost pressure in the business which the organization has to absorb. Most often than not it was seen that corporations have gone for heavy borrowing to acquire a rival brand which subsequently triggers many other actions within the business in terms of restructuring, selling some of the nonstrategic but otherwise profitable brands to generate cash, drastic reduction in advertising spend in the short run, etc.—all in the name of cost reduction. Absorbing and integrating a newly acquired brand with the business and then managing the brand for the growth is not an easy task. Still many businesses prefer this route to deliver shareholders' expectation rather than deliver growth organically.

Consumers are increasingly becoming unpredictable and they are more discerning as well as more demanding. Consumer loyalty can no longer be taken for granted and, as a result, current consumers need special attention so that they don't switch to other brands for which enough provocation and inducement are already there from competition. To keep competition at bay, marketers have to constantly design and redesign new promotional campaigns, provide extra services, upgrade the product to remain contemporary, imbibe new technology, create variants and innovation around the product. It also pays to have a unique position for the brand to claim unique benefits for the targeted consumers. Look at how the three leading shampoo from HUL (All Clear), P&G (Head & Shoulders), and Garnier (Fructis) are fighting against each other. Each of them are trying to occupy a unique position in the consumers' mind.

Advertisement and promotions are no longer delivering expected results. Too many brands trying to draw the attention of the consumers to motivate and influence them are not working as well, as before. While cost of television advertisement has gone up many fold, its impact has reduced drastically. To get noticed one has to give several insertions in press media and slots in television advertisement, costing a fortune and then not knowing whether it will work. Only companies with enormous resources can afford to play those upfront advertisement games. Others will have to find out more tactical and strategic approach to be affordable. Both opportunity to see (OTS) an advertisement as well as the impact per opportunity (IPO) of each exposure are much lower these days as a result of huge clutter and multiple channel, in the media, and more particularly in television media. It is, therefore, a key strategic decision for the brand marketers to decide how to spend the limited marketing budget that they have to spend to support a brand. Resource allocation is a key strategic issue in brand marketing. Portfolio management and issues related to investment, divestment of brands have to be taken after careful analysis of the business, environment, and competition.

To create a successful portfolio it is necessary to know your customers' requirements better than the competitors and then also deliver their expectations through the product and services that the business has to offer better and faster than competitors. Knowing customers better require acquiring customer-specific information. Customer relationship management and organizing customer loyalty program and managing the customer lifetime value require intense knowledge of the customers to build intimacy with them. Marketing, therefore, is no longer simply a set of activities to bring in or attract customer toward your product and services. The subject has now developed to a level that these days a lot of analytical tools are available to guide the marketers in the decision-making exercises.

Portfolio management, new product launches, deciding on a brand name, using and extending an existing brand or to use a new brand name for the launch of a new product require strategic thinking. Under what circumstances launching a new product giving a new brand name will depend on numerous factors to be carefully analyzed. Managing multiproduct business in a diversified group poses serious challenges to the marketers in terms of complexity that exists in such decision areas. Normally, a portfolio of products will have all types of brands with varied degree of success, potential, performance, in a given environment and brand managers' task is to understand the brand's promise, potential, competition and take direction.

Businesses now need radical thinkers as marketers. Heads of businesses and CEOs need to be marketers now, taking the marketing decisions themselves and leading from the front. Involvement of heads of business or CEOs directly in marketing functions is what we require now. Creating a success story from a new product launch or even creating a business from just an idea requires the radical thinkers who can perform as radical marketers. Customers have wide choice now; they are also more knowledgeable and, therefore, customers now make judicious choices before taking a purchase decision. Simply a well-known brand will no longer be the only criteria for buying a product. Marketers thus have all the more challenges to face to keep customers loyal to their brands and to retain the market share. Brand managers these days depend a lot on the support of the outsourced independent research agencies as well as marketing analytics. A new set of companies in the space of Marketing Analytics have come up which acts as the think tank for the businesses and offers valuable advice to the brand marketers by analyzing the business data regarding what marketing action will deliver what kind of results in which geographical locations. But ultimately the responsibility of marketing actions still remains with the brand managers.

This book is intended to discuss some of those issues that brand marketers face in challenging times. The book starts with the discussion of the core strategic issues in brand management and then goes on to clarify the concept of brand, its value and strategic brand management.

The book has eight chapters that deal with the issues of brand extension, brand positioning, brand equity, brand acquisition and brand divestment, brand valuation, and new business models in managing brands for success in a competitive business environment.

The book attempts to provide numerous examples to illustrate a point, taking examples from the real-life market in the current context. Finally, the book discusses some live cases to illustrate the elements of branding that made those brands successful and how marketers systematically tried to project brand's superiority amongst its own competitive set and succeeded to plant that perception in the consumers' mind. This requires not only strategic thinking but also formulation of strategic actions and implementation. The contents of the book have been designed in a manner to provide systematic lessons of strategic thinking, strategic planning, and strategic actions for the brand marketers in today's challenging environment.

CHAPTER 1

Brand Management in Competitive Environment

The marketer's task is becoming increasingly difficult and challenging with the competition triggered by forces of globalization. And when there is competition, marketers need strategies to overcome the competitive forces and challenges and still perform and deliver shareholders' value. Traditional marketing plan seems to be no longer working when it means fierce competition in the market. The key imperative for any business is to grow. Growth can come through organic exploitation of the brand potential or even inorganic growth through acquisition and diversification. Organic growth can come either through increased and deeper brand penetration in existing market or through geographical expansion. Most of the markets are now becoming saturated and matured. When market or category growth is low or limited, brand can only grow by taking away the market share from competition.

Brand marketing plan essentially deals with taking key decisions on the marketing mix and delivering those decisions by designing appropriate, integrated marketing communication and advertising plan with tactical and strategic elements to support. When brand marketing plan is designed with respect to specific target market, we call it a strategic marketing.

Kotler (2004) feels that marketing is definitely not fulfilling its potential and strongly believes that marketing must become the driver of business strategy and that companies need to adopt a more holistic view of the new marketing challenge. In today's competitive world, if a product does not maintain differentiation and can't graduate to a brand, then it remains a commodity and competes only on the basis of price. A strong brand improves and enhances the demand by providing the benefits of increased sales volume, higher price (premium), lower churn, and the prospect of more brand stretching. It also improves supply by imparting favorable supplier terms, greater trade acceptance as well as trade support, lower staff acquisition and retention costs, lower cost of capital, and better economies of scale through higher sales volume.

Today, key brands have to be managed keeping in mind that technology is changing very fast and there is a plethora of new product introductions all the time in the market. The number of trademarks and patents are increasing and customers are getting more and more fragmented. These days retail stores are getting crowded with multiple brands and stock-keeping units (SKUs). The number of SKUs in an average store has increased by more than 50 percent in last three years (Banga 2004). Category definitions and competitor sets are changing rapidly. Major fast moving consumer goods (FMCG) marketer Hindustan Unilever Ltd. (HUL) realized that rather than competing in the shampoo category where it has a market share of 50 percent, it is competing in the much broader hair wash category where it has only 6 percent market share. In the broader category definition, it needs conversion from people using water, soap and other natural ingredients for hair wash.

Kotler and de Bes (2003) observes, "The most basic marketing strategies—segmentation and innovation—are in a crisis. Marketers are obliged to increase sales and market share in markets and categories that are saturated." This is affecting some major marketers like Unilever which has failed to adjust its plans quickly enough to react to a more difficult business environment. In recent times, on worldwide basis, it has thus failed to achieve sustained top-level growth. Clancy and Stone (2005) indicate that effectiveness of marketing is not up to the mark and identify some of the ills plaguing marketing programs for consumer and business-to-business (B2B) programs and services (Table 1.1).

Table 1.1   Key Indicators of Inefficiency of Marketing Programs

Efficiency Indicators	Current Status
Brand equity and market share	84 percent of the programs resulting in decline
Sales promotion program	Most of the programs unprofitable
Maximum success rate of new products	Success rate only 10 percent
ROI of advertisement campaign	Below 4 percent

SOURCE: Clancy and Stone (2005).

Clancy and Stone (2005) go on to add:

In the short term, advertising returns in consumer-packaged goods is only 54 cents for every dollar invested. A recent A. C. Nielsen BASES and Ernst & Young study put the failure rate of new U.S. consumer products at 95 percent. It is no better even in India. A 2004 Deutsche Bank study of packaged goods brands found that just 18 percent of television advertising campaigns generated a positive ROI in the short term.

These are strong challenges for any marketer. Strong brands may come in handy in such a scenario as they can provide both functional and emotional benefits to their consumers. Despite being intangible assets, strong brands are often valued at a higher level compared to the total value of the tangible assets of an organization. There is a link between building a stronger brand and generating stock returns and return on investment (ROI) (Raman 2002) as long as the entire brand management system is in line and geared to the right business strategy of the organization. McKinsey research shows that companies with strong brands have shareholder returns of 1.9 points more than their industries' average (Court et al. 1999). But creating a strong brand in a highly competitive environment, as it exists today, is in itself a big challenge to the marketers which we would like to address.

Hence, consistent consumer delight for existing base and expansion of the consumer base through brand creation and sustenance may provide the necessary stimulus for sustainable growth. But the question is how brands will reach that status whereby they can regularly delight the consumers. There is clarity that without differentiation, the core of any brand and its associated business (a loyal customer base) cannot be created or sustained (Aaker 2003). Aaker also thinks that the solution to the brand-building question lies in the branded differentiator, a new tool that can help companies maintain a competitive advantage over others in the marketplace. It can be a feature, functions, benefits, service, program, or ingredient, but it must be meaningful to consumers and must also be actively managed over an extended period so that it does not become stagnant.

In India, major environmental changes in recent times are creating both opportunities and threats for global brand marketers. These days, access to capital has become much easier which in turn is helping Indian manufacturers in capacity acquisition and expansion as well as for generating resources for building brands and competing effectively in the marketplace. This is leading to a situation where many of the entry barriers in key FMCG categories are crumbling. Changing attitudes toward debt and toward recreation, entertainment, and lifestyle expenditure are leading to a scenario where a basic product like soap or detergent has started competing with products like credit card, cell phone, or digital camera (Banga 2005). Consumers now are more open and willing to take loan or even buy the recreation, entertainment, and consumer durable items on credit. These factors and additional factors like poor monsoon and low growth in agricultural sectors (rural markets) and pressure on monthly budgets from increased cost of utilities, health, and education (urban markets) have contributed to significant down trading in FMCG sector in India in recent times. The key challenges for global marketers lie in understanding the factors that can help them to consolidate their position. Marketers worldwide as well as in India must identify the key challenges faced by them and address those on a long-term basis to achieve sustainable competitive advantage and growth.

Many top global brands are suffering from a variety of problems that include little or no innovation, ineffective or little competitive action, quality problems, overtaking by competitors in key markets, customers' lack of trust because of past problems, delay in entering in key consumer segments, etc. The leading global brands like Coca Cola, Marlboro, Gillette, and other leading brands are also facing similar situation. In India also, Cadbury faced the problem of insect infestation in their chocolates. This may possibly be argued in light of the fact that many of these hi-tech companies benefit from undifferentiated marketing strategy across the globe since undifferentiated marketing strategy suits hi-tech companies (Kotabe and Helsen 2004). One point that needs special mention in this context is that it is possible for a product brand to have higher brand value compared to its parent (Nescafe at No.23 vs parent Nestle at No.62).

CHALLENGES FACED BY TOP GLOBAL BRAND MARKETERS

Kotler and de Bes (2003) has listed that the evolution of markets and the dynamics of competition is affected by several key factors (Figure 1.1). In this section key strategic marketing challenges facing global FMCG brand marketers internationally and in the Indian market have been identified for which they need to proactively formulate plans to be able to compete successfully.

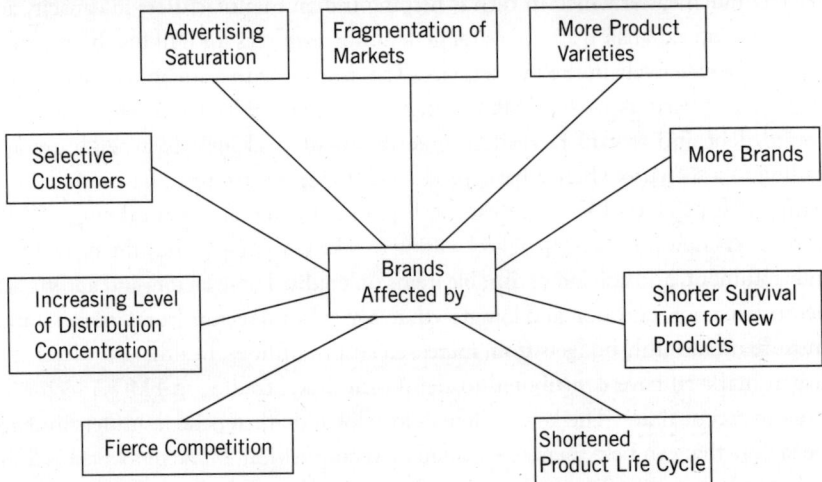

Figure 1.1   Visualization of Market Dynamics (Key Factors)

SOURCE: Kotler and de Bes (2003).

KEY CHALLENGES

The key challenges of the business environment now are:

- Increasingly inconsistent environment
- Competitors, partners, suppliers, customers (increasingly unpredictable)

Organizations have to carefully consider the environment which will have a significant impact on its performance. These environmental factors greatly influence the organization's strategic direction.

Post liberalization, entrepreneurs and investors have freedom to enter any industry, trade, or business. The government controls and licensing have been either removed or made much easier. Foreign direct investment (FDI) has been made easier in many industry categories. Indian market is gradually being integrated with the global economy. In many cases automatic approval is granted for FDI. For example, in processed food sector, barring those reserved for small scale industries, automatic approval and even 100 percent FDI is now allowed. These have resulted into increased competition and also a new set of challenges. The implications are thus:

- With growing competition, product differentiation and positioning will become more important.
- Class marketing/niche marketing will grow in importance and there will be a decline in the relative importance of mass marketing barring a few exceptions.
- The growing competition will also increase the importance of augmented product.

Purpose of strategic brand management, therefore, is to build a successful brand marketing plan in a growing and fiercely competitive business environment.

Marketers Trying New Categories for Growth

In a highly competitive and matured market, organic growth becomes extremely difficult and a slow process. Organic growth then has to come by taking away market share of competition. And in that scenario one company's gain is another company's loss. The fight in the marketplace is fought with resources. Market leader in the category in that scenario has an upper hand having higher resources and marketing muscle in command. ITC Agro, for example, is delivering growth through the exploitation of opportunity organically because ITC has enormous resource at their command and also good distribution infrastructure on the ground in place.

Businesses in a matured market have to protect their market share in a fiercely competitive market.

The other way of growth is through acquisition. Acquisition offers several advantages in the sense that it gives faster growth and also at the same time eliminates a competition from the market. Getting critical mass in the business becomes much easier through acquisition. Large companies thus go for acquisition as a route to deliver growth. Multinational corporations (MNCs) are seen to opt for acquisition when they enter a new market and acquiring a business in an alien country always helps in knowing how businesses are conducted in that country and an instant entry into the trade and distribution system which otherwise takes long time to build. Acquisition also helps to get into new categories of business. HUL has built its entire food business through acquisition route. Their series of acquisition of corporations like Lipton, Brooke Bond, Kwality, etc., gave them a dominant position in the food industry. MNCs prefer acquisition to enter into a third country for the first time. That is why we see that Coke acquired Parle, Dr Oetker acquired Fun Foods, Nutricia acquired HUL's dairy business, Heinz acquired Glaxo's food business, Kraft acquired Cadbury's, and many more. But acquisition requires huge resources and also the ability to manage the whole post-acquisition process. These days businesses are changing hands by paying over eight to ten times (or even higher) their annual sales value. Good brands are being sold at multiples of their price earnings ratio. But acquirers still make sense out of this high price acquisition because of the other synergies and benefits that it offers.

The other way of delivering growth is through diversification. All businesses try their hands in diversifying the portfolio in the related categories but only a few succeed. Diversifying into nonrelated categories seldom succeed. If we look at Indian processed food business; in each category there is a market leader holding very dominant position. For example, in biscuits, Parle and Britannia; in dairy, Amul and HUL; in soft beverages, Pepsi and Coke; in health beverages, SmithKline Beecham (SKB) and Cadbury (now Kraft Foods); in fruit and vegetable (F&V) products, HUL and Nestle, etc. These companies have earlier tried launching new products in related categories but have failed. For example, Nestle tried introducing pickles which did not work, Britannia tried fresh long-life milk in tetra pack but failed, SKB consumer products (maker of Horlicks) tried introducing powder beverages but failed, coke introduced powder beverages but did not work, Amul tried to enter pizza in popular segment but also failed. The examples can be many but the underlying statement is that most of the diversification in new categories has failed and under those circumstances corporations were reporting growth organically and protecting their market position. That was possible as market was growing for the categories that they represent. And most significantly competition was less and weak. But in the post-liberalization era, the scenario is fast changing. There are new entrants, some of them global players, each trying to get a foothold. Market also in some categories is saturated, but others are growing due to intense marketing activities of the players. Corporations are now trying to get into new categories again. We are, therefore, seeing new product introduction from all the big players.

Parle Products introduced potato chips. Despite a highly competitive market both Parle as well ITC have found scope for introduction of potato chips and that too successfully. ITC, HUL, and SKB have introduced instant noodles which were earlier represented only by Maggi of Nestle. Britannia got into dairy products and ITC into biscuits after establishing themselves in staples and branded grocery items. SKB was for years and decades selling only Horlicks, but has now also introduced instant noodles and also supports biscuits in the niche segment. Players are examining the possibilities of growth in newer segments seeing the potential of yet other new entrants. Competition in many categories is now amongst equals.

Earlier, players have failed in creating success stories in new categories. But now we have to see how it works. Category leaders this time may not be able to protect their stronghold and maintain the market share as well as leadership position. This has happened in many FMCG categories. For example, HUL had at one point of time enjoyed 90 percent market share in fairness cream category with their Fair & Lovely being almost generic to the category. Sustained efforts of other players like CavinKare and Godrej, etc., have reduced the market share of Fair & Lovely to almost 50 percent. Similar situation is likely to be witnessed in processed foods. ITC has already gained over 16 percent market share in biscuits in stiff competition from Britannia and Parle Products and that too in mass segment like glucose where success story is not that easy to create. The big food marketers in India include HUL, Amul, Britannia, Parle Products, Nestle and SKB who have diverse portfolios now and it is expected that these players will enter all growth categories in food. Coke and Pepsi are amongst big players, but they are predominantly in carbonated beverages and they are so big that together they represent the entire industry. We thought possibly no one will dare to enter this segment risking inevitable failures. But players like Red Bull, etc., have successfully entered energy drink segment which either Pepsi or Coke should have dominated. Also RC Cola has introduced product in select metro markets now. Pepsi has significant presence in natural fruit-based beverages, but that is arising out of acquisition of brand Tropicana from Seagram and Coke's presence in this segment is through the acquisition of Maaza, a Parle brand. But in this segment Parle Agro's Frooti and Dabur's Real juice are doing better.

The main reason of this new trend in launching new products by almost all the players in the market in competition with the market leaders is twofold. One is to capture and to be a player in the relatively high-growth categories in processed food. And second, their own leadership is being challenged by other players in their home ground and, therefore, delivering growth from their lead category is no longer that easy. On top of that, big players should not be seen being left behind in diversification of portfolios when opportunity exists. Consumers are going to benefit by this competition. Supply chain efficiency is likely to improve because of collective investment and innovations in the entire value chain.

New to Enter a Category Can Threaten Established Players

ITC seems to be emerging as a big challenger to other well-known players in the processed food market. They have created some degree of success in categories including biscuits and branded grocery items. In biscuits we only know about Britannia and Parle—both age-old players. Sunfeast has captured almost 16 percent market share in the glucose segment. ITC has created ₹2,500 crore (USD 500 million) food business with their three major brands, namely, Bingo for finger snacks (like potato chips), Aashirvaad for staples, and Sunfeast for packaged foods. They have a strong supply chain efficiency starting at farmers' level giving them a cost and quality advantage. Most of their products are produced through contract manufacturing route giving them an advantage for easy exit route if the launch did not work for them well enough. Also, money is not blocked in capital investment, giving them more flexibility to try out many opportunities without blocking money in large manufacturing facilities. Their distribution infrastructure penetrates into interior rural areas and most importantly they have staying power being part of large and profitable tobacco business. They cannot put money for expansion in their core business because of legal and cultural constraints and restrictions in marketing and promotional activities. Food is thus a natural extension for them and they are making the best out of this effort. The core supply chain efficiency advantage that ITC possess has helped them get into the top league as one amongst other major players in less than a decade. They also made major offensive against Frito-Lay of Pepsi with their Bingo brand. In biscuits, ITC is the third largest player only next to Britannia and Parle. We have seen many success stories at regional level, such as, Priya Foods, etc., but it is ITC which has made a major success story at the national scene. They are seen to be very aggressive in the marketing and promotional approach. And extensive distribution and supply chain advantages have come as an added support in their effort.

The latest marketing war that they have initiated is in the area of two-minute noodles with the entry of Sunfeast Yippee. This category was created by Maggi of Nestle, holding 85 percent of the market. Players, such as Indo-Nissin's Top Ramen, Capital Food's Ching's Secret and Smith Jones and CG Foods' Wai Wai have tried for many years to make a dent, but failed to take away more than 10 percent of the market share. The category over the years has become ₹1,300 crores

(USD 260 million), not big enough considering the number of years ago the product was launched. But of late the category has shown a growth rate of 20 percent drawing the attention of other food marketers. The three new entrants have thrown their hats into the ring in the last one year. They are: Hindustan Lever (HUL), GlaxoSmithKline (GSK) and of course, ITC with Knorr Soupy Noodles, Horlicks Foodles and Sunfeast Yipee, respectively. HUL has been trying to extend its Knorr soup franchise, the brand that they acquired from Best Foods International. There is some synergy also between soup and noodles. GSK, on the other hand, is trying to differentiate the products bringing in the health connotation of Horlicks and has made an aggressive entry with their multigrain Horlicks Foodles in the instant noodle segment.

The one-brand category of instant noodles, Maggi, is now all of a sudden seeing a big challenge in the marketplace with three large players fighting to take the market share in a fiercely competitive market. It has been reported that within three months of the launch in south India itself, about 4 percent market share has been cornered by these giants. You will find a significant shelf presence in all leading stores of these brands alongside Maggi which itself will be an indication that new entrants are gaining attention and consumer franchise. ITC is doing extensive sampling of the product in all large format retail outlets such as Big Bazaar. It was reported that 30 to 40 percent of those who tried the product have also bought the product from the store. Nestle, over the years, have positioned the product in the kids segment and introduced only a few flavor variants. Marketers are now questioning and extending the segment into the older age group as well. This will extend the market and will catalyze faster growth. One will recollect the irrelevant Bingo advertisement talking about mad triangle which is not only funny but immediately makes viewers think what it is talking about and thus becomes a memorable advertisement. Bingo's is a success story and Sunfeast Yippee is seriously making inroads into the Maggi share. Both Horlicks and Sunfeast have excellent brand recall and, therefore, are likely get trade support in terms of stocking the products and display in the retail shelf.

Hindustan Lever, on the other hand, is trying to bank upon its Knorr soup category and thinking that noodle is a natural extension which will help in the growth of soup category as well. Well, soup sells in the winter months but instant noodles sell throughout the year and, therefore, their approach might restrict the natural potential of the new category. HUL is also not seen as aggressive as the other two, i.e., GSK and ITC. For GSK, it is a one-product category company and as such they desperately need another success story in food. Their attempt to create success in powder beverage has failed. They also made attempts to get into biscuits and Horlicks biscuit is still available in the market, which can be considered as a mere presence in the segment for long years without a success story to talk about. This time, however, Horlicks seems to be very determined to create a success. The packaging is also very important in the instant food category and all of them made a very colorful attractive packaging design which draws the attention of the consumers and is working well for them. The pack size is 60 g to 100 g. The price ranges from ₹10 for maida (wheat flour) noodles to ₹12 to 15 for atta noodles and multigrain noodles for the lead players whereas Top Ramen sells at ₹9. Knorr Soupy Noodles sell at ₹12. HUL is said to have already reached over two lakhs (two hundred thousand) outlets in terms of distribution reach; it has a market share of less than 1 percent. As per A. C. Nielsen's report, Knorr Soupy had a market share of 3.35 percent in south India in September 2010 while for Horlicks Foodles the share was 4.5 percent. HUL covers 6.5 million retail outlets and, therefore, can quickly extend the reach if the proposition works for them while Nestle reaches only three million outlets. ITC is said to be targeting to reach 0.5 million outlets and their current reach is said to be 2.5 million outlets.

Average urban household consumption is said to be 24 packs on noodles and all are eyeing to get a part of it. It appears that because of intense marketing activities the market will also grow much faster than before. But it looks like Nestle cannot keep their dominant hold on the market which they were able to keep for such a long time. Of course, it will not be correct to say that Nestle is sitting idle and only witnessing a major onslaught on the instant noodles category which they created as first mover. Nestle had launched number of flavor variants of noodles in the year 2010 to intimately involve the customers with the product and the brand. If the new brands are able to meet customer satisfaction, there is likelihood that new history will be created in this category itself which was hitherto only known as Maggi's two-minute noodles for the kids. Competition is always healthy and good for the consumers. But for the brand marketer it is always a challenge.

Organized Retailing: A New Challenge for Brand Marketers

The retail universe in India is highly scattered and already a challenge for the marketers in terms of distribution reach. It is a mammoth task to make products available in all potential retail outlets. Total number of retailers in India is estimated to be about 13 million and large numbers are, of course, the mom and pop family owned retail stores. Even the leading FMCG companies cover only up to about 1.5 million outlets and depend on the wholesalers to cover the rest through secondary distribution. Creating an efficient distribution system is considered as the biggest advantage for the brand marketers. Many acquisitions take place only to acquire the distribution system of an established player as creating a new distribution infrastructure itself will be a herculean task for the new entrant. For example, Coke acquired Parle brands and business by paying a huge sum only to get an access to the Parle's distribution infrastructure. The retail industry is undergoing significant change with the emergence of organized retailers like Big Bazaar, More, Reliance, and Tata. With the opening up of FDI, the scenario is going to change significantly, posing new challenges to brand marketers. The new challenge will come from store label or private brands which all these foreign retailers will aggressively promote to improve their financial performance. With the opening up of a new format—value store as well as supermarkets and hypermarkets by the global retailers—the store brands or private label brands will take away a significant chunk of the market share from the existing national brands. This phenomenon has been witnessed in other countries and is likely to happen in India as well. National brands will now face competition from both the regional and local brands as well as the store brands.

India allows up to 100 percent FDI in single brand retailing today and also in the cash and carry format. In single brand retailing we have Marks & Spencer, Debenhams, etc., and in cash and carry business we have Metro, Booker, Tesco, Walmart, etc. While Metro and Booker are cash and carry operators, Tesco and Walmart are actually retailers waiting for the FDI to open up for multibrand retailing which has now happened. From 1991 to 2004 consumer electronics brands have arrived from developed countries and almost knocked the Indian brands out of the market now. Living in a truly liberalized environment with easy access to worldwide media, western marketing skills, tactics, and resources have proliferated here, making Indians more brand conscious. In a recent dipstick study it was found that zappers below 30 years of age now believe in international brands to remain trendy and fashionable with designs of better quality styling. The 31–45 years compromise generation sees wider options in international brands and is ready to spend for their economy products. The 45-plus retro generation prefers to buy Indian brands, but for better quality can shift to international brands (*The Economic Times*, August 13, 2011, Mumbai Edition).

Retail stores are multiplying like mushrooms in India but they need to localize the fashion products fitting into the local culture and competence. French Galeries Lafayette opened a store in New York's Trump Tower with 8 million USD annual rent in 1991. They failed to localize according to American customers and had to close shops within three years. With FDI opening up to 100 percent, global life-style brands with huge brand pull enter Indian market to indoctrinate the retailing system in India and if they are allowed to source freely, they will offer multiple international brands at aggressive, multilayer price points. They can also crash the price very low as they know that volumes will be very high in India. It is certainly possible for the local brands to compete and still sustain as is evident when China allowed up to 100 percent FDI in retail. Chinese brand Li-Ning managed to dislodge all international brands in sportswear in 2004 and stood second only to Nike (16.7 percent market share). Li-Ning's 14.2 percent market share came from leveraging subtle nuances of Chinese heritage to build the brand globally.

Fashion marketing is very different from FMCG marketing which is more technical, with price playing an important role and requiring rational and functional superiority. Fashion is advertising driven by visual art. Mass fashion started in the West since 1980s while following the impact and doctrine of haute couture. The latest retail marketing innovation is the total departure made by H&M which, while being monobrand retail, is co-branding H&M with reputed designer brands like Lanvin and Versace among others to give consumers a multibrand experience. Even Walmart's private label Metro induces fashion intangibles. The more fashion associates with the visual art, the more intangible it becomes, and can accordingly command its price. With retail sector opening up for multibrand retailing, the marketers will find the ball game totally different. Competing with globally established brands will require different skills, tactics, and resources. New strategic initiatives, thinking, planning, and execution will be the key imperatives of business.

CHAPTER SUMMARY

This chapter discusses the key challenges that brand marketers are facing these days in a fiercely competitive market with too many players having access to resources and fighting to take a portion of the total market opportunity in an increasingly unpredictable and ever changing business environment where old rules and familiar goal posts seem to be no longer guiding the business decisions. On top of it, technological advancement is reducing the product life cycle and product and services are required to be constantly upgraded to remain current and contemporary in tune with technological changes and advancement taking place around the industry category. Product differentiation is increasingly becoming difficult. The once popular and well-known brand can no longer claim patronage, support, and loyalty of the old customers. Too much clutter in the media is making advertising money less effective; trade channels are demanding and customers also are more discerning. In this environment, traditional brand marketing plan is not delivering the result; brand marketers have to be innovative and think strategic. In this chapter we discussed the key reasons of brand failures, new challenges that brand marketers have to face citing many cases and examples to show how brand performance is changing with the change in business environment requiring radical new thinking and actions.

Retail sector has now been thrown open for FDI in multibrand retailing which will bring many global brands as well as private label brands into the Indian market. Single-brand retailing is already open for 100 percent FDI and so are cash and carry stores. This is changing the retail environment significantly. Both store label brands as well as foreign brands will be retailed through these stores posing new challenges to our brand marketers. The chapter discusses the likely competition that these international brands will create and how local brands will be impacted in various product categories, particularly in fashion goods and in designer products. Already monobrand retailers have captured the market in consumer durable category and local brands are losing market share fast.

CHAPTER 2

Brand, its Meaning, Value, and Power

BRAND CHALLENGE

Till early 1980s the worth or the value of the corporation was measured in terms of its physical assets of all forms including land and buildings and other forms of tangible assets like the manufacturing facilities with its plant and equipments and technology. It is only in the recent past that we have realized that the real value of the business lies outside the business itself. The real value of the business, in fact, lies in the minds of the potential and target consumers and customers of the goods, merchandises and services that company offers to sell. In the early part of 1980s marketers started realizing the real value of the brand and that was the turning point in the understanding of the concept of the brand. Management came to realize and accept that the most valuable asset of the company was in fact its brand name in the portfolio of the company's business which is delivering company's performance and creating shareholders' wealth. Numerous articles, particularly in the research journal, press, and business magazines have dealt with the new concept of 'brand equity' or the financial value of the brand. In the subsequent years we have witnessed the wave of mergers and acquisitions of brands all over the world. Businesses from that time onwards started focusing on their key brands in terms of resource allocation and support to build business for the future and thus a new role of brand manager emerged. Astronomical prices were paid for mega acquisitions to buy the intangible assets contained in the brand value which is a function of the consumers' perception of the brand derived from constant exposure to the various forms of media that marketer exploits to reach out to the target customers as well as from the quality of experience they get out of using and experiencing the product. These brands then start becoming a part of their lifestyle. Sometimes astronomical prices have been paid to acquire an important brand which is capable of giving a significant boost to the existing business of the corporation. For example, in Europe the multinational food giant Nestle bought Rowntree for almost three times its stock market value and twenty-six times its earnings. In India in the recent times Reckitt Benckiser acquired Paras Pharmaceuticals for ₹3,260 crores (USD 726 million) to get control over the brands like Moov pain relief ointment, Krack heel care lotion, D'Cold cold remedy, Set Wet hair gel, and Dermi Cool prickly heat powder whose combined sales value was only ₹401.4 crores (USD 80 million). This means that approximately eight times the value of the sales was the price paid for this acquisition. Prior to 1980 companies wanted to buy a manufacturing operations of say chocolate or fruit juices and primary consideration was the manufacturing facility, quality, and make of the plants and equipments as well as the level of technology employed and post-1980 they wanted to buy brands like Tropicana, a powerful fruit juice brand of Seagram but later on acquired by Pepsi. This difference is very important in the sense that prior to 1980 businesses have changed hands and the price of acquisition was worked out on the basis of the production capacity, technology, and a business volume that comes along with the acquisition and in the later years they wanted to buy a strong brand which has a very strong and established consumer franchise.

In India we have seen many such mega acquisitions after the 1990s, in the post-liberalization era. In 1980s we had the major acquisitions of Shaw Wallace and Dunlop by late Manu Chabbria of Jumbo Electronics, Dubai. When MNCs started entering into the Indian market, one of the preferred entry route options was through acquisition of brand and business that helped them get a quick start in a highly complex market structure that India has. There were many acquisitions in the post-liberalization years, but notable amongst those are the acquisition of Parle brands by Coca Cola for an undisclosed amount and Hindustan Lever acquiring Lipton and Brooke Bond. In both these cases market leaders in the category were acquired primarily for their brand value. The other attraction for the acquirer was to gain a quick access to the local market utilizing the existing and established distribution network and system of the acquired company. Lipton and Brooke Bond brands, of course, were the results of global acquisitions taking place overseas, but in India the benefits accrued to Hindustan Lever, now known as Hindustan Unilever Limited (HUL). HUL, although a highly respected company in India, its ventures into new product launches, particularly in processed food products which is a major business of Unilever, were not successful. HUL got its foothold in food business in India through a series of acquisitions only, starting with Lipton and Brooke Bond and later on other brands including Kwality ice cream and also Dollop ice cream brands from Cadbury.

Legally speaking a brand is simply a symbol which distinguishes a company's products and services from others in the same category and certifies its place of origin depicted through its unique style, pattern, design, color scheme, and graphics which help one brand to be identified from other competing brands and its value through registration and conformity. In the financial world, however, the concept of a brand has a much broader meaning. The value of a brand comes from its ability to gain an exclusive, positive, and prominent position in the minds of a large number of consumers. For example, when a customer buys a Charagh Din,

Provogue, or John Players shirt it is not simply the Charagh Din, Provogue, or John Players logo sewn onto a shirt, it is all the different things that consumer thinks when he or she sees a symbol of Charagh Din, Provogue, or John Players. These refer to the tangible attributes of the product as well as all the other intangibles associated with it, which may be either psychological or social which the marketer creates. Brands can help consumers upgrade their social status. The tangible and intangible benefits which are derived from the consumption or use of a product of the brand are the determinants of the strength of the brand. These associations have been acquired over time through continued investment on the brand-building exercise by the company—in production in order to maintain the higher quality standard; in new product research which has been adapted to changes in the consumers' preference and taste in line with technology and competitive environment; in distribution channels; in sales force; in communication as well as in legal defense against counterfeits, etc. Brand-building exercise, therefore, is a company-wide effort to give superior experience to its identified set of customers.

BRAND MANAGEMENT IN A DYNAMIC BUSINESS ENVIRONMENT

Marketers believe that brands are very important because they shape customer's decisions and ultimately create economic value for the business, the corporation, and for the shareholders. A study conducted by McKinsey (Court et al. 1996) on twenty-seven product categories based on 5,000 customer interviews in US, Europe, and Asia revealed that brand was a key factor behind all decisions to purchase. This research suggests that brands have the real power to persuade customers to purchase one product in preference to other alternatives and options available in a similar product set. The brand becomes the major differentiator for customers' selection of products when choice has to be exercised amongst many equals in the market. Brands become all the more a powerful differentiator when a meaningful product and service level differentiation become increasingly difficult amongst the product categories produced through similar technology. In such a situation, the brand has to differentiate exploiting the intangible assets to establish its dominance over other brands. Strong brands have another measurable advantage that they can command significant price premiums. On an average, prices of the strongest brands were 19 percent higher than those of the weakest brands as revealed in the same study.

In India, Dettol, which has been the number 1 brand for many years as reported in the several surveys conducted by A&M magazine, was always priced 15 percent higher than its nearest competitor. The same authors (Court et al. 1999) have studied the performance of 130 consumer companies to conclude that total returns to the shareholders of companies with stronger brands are 1.9 percent higher than the industry average returns in a scenario where the total shareholders return of companies with weaker brands are 3.1 percent lower than the industry average return.

Why brands work for the customers? The reasons are familiar and these include: they simplify everyday choices. A customer who buys Colgate each time does not have to make decisions on the choice over a toothpaste every time he or she has to make purchase decisions on products. It reduces the inconvenience and the associated risk of complicated buying decisions. Consumers prefer to make safer choice by deciding to buy established and reputed brands. The buying decision of costlier products such as consumer durables or even fashionable goods and personal care products are more complex and involve more risk and thus customers prefer to go for an established and reputed brand which reduces the risk considerably. The same is the case for the technology products. For example, IBM mainframe or Compaq PCs are safer choices. Brands also provide emotional benefits to its customers (McDonald's) and offer a sense of community (Apple users group or Opel club). Creating strong brands, therefore, offers greatest challenge to marketers and requires sustained efforts. Other benefits associated with brands are social status, prestige, image, and confidence that the brand can offer in addition to its stated functional benefits and assured quality.

Marketing philosophy is changing with the change in market dynamics. The whole concept of brand marketing has evolved over the years from an era when it was synonymous with selling to the present era when it means everything to the business. As Peter Drucker (1954: 33–44) observed, there are only two revenue streams in business and these are—marketing and innovation, and rest are all costs. The brand or the product manager now, therefore, has an all-pervasive role to play to deliver the performance expected of him or her. Marketers' role now is more strategic. This can be summarized in Table 2.1.

Table 2.1 Changing Marketing Concept

Criteria	Old (1960–1990)	Strategic (1990 onwards)
Main focus	Initially only on product and then on customer	Strategic. The way of doing business
End objective	Profit and value creation	Building relationship
Marketing function	Selling and brand building	Organization-wide effort means everything

SOURCE: Adapted from McKenna (1991).

The key concepts of marketing thus have undergone significant change from what was understood earlier to what is practiced today as is summarized in Table 2.2.

Table 2.2   Key Marketing Concepts That Changed

Earlier	Now
Selling of goods	Customer support and customer relationship management
Acquisition of customers	Retention of customers
Profit from each transaction	Profit from customer satisfaction
Advertising in media and sales communication and promotion	Integrated marketing
Focus on sales-related data	Key focus on customer database
Cost plus pricing decision	Pricing based on perceived value and business strategy
Key decisions based on sales data analysis	Decisions are based on marketing analytics and market modeling

SOURCE: Philip Kotler (1997).

WHAT BRAND COMMUNICATES

Brand is not simply an identity whereas a name is simply an identity. It takes long years for a name or an identity to become a brand. A name has to be systematically nurtured to create a valuable brand. The brand manager's key function is to build successful brands by effectively managing all key attributes so that the brand stands out in a clutter. Simplistically speaking, brand is a combination of a term encompassing name, symbol, design, color scheme, styling, housing, and logo conveying the following:

- Attributes
- Benefits
- Values
- Culture
- Personality
- User

A brand's distinctive signs will include name, logo, symbol, colors, endorsing characters, and even its slogans.

BRAND NAME

Manufacturers produce products but customers buy brands. Pharmaceutical companies produce complex chemical compounds and drug molecules but doctors prescribe brands. Brand names thus take a very important role which can either restrict or enlarge the possibility for future exploitation of the brand. There are several approaches for deciding on a brand name. Theoretically speaking, anything or any name can be used to create a brand out of these names, as marketers through sustained creative executions create a brand out of a simple name and hence brand names can be anything. However, some discipline or method can be followed to decide on a brand name as we follow to give a name to a newborn. The brand name decisions can thus be taken based on various approaches including the following:

- Individual brand names (given for products and each one has the potential to grow)
- Separate family names (given separate names according product category or product group)
- Blanket family names (given to reinforce family's track record in business like Tata or Birla)
- Company trade names (given when a trade name is well established like Kingfisher)

Choosing a name of the brand is thus very important and choosing a name will depend on the destiny that is assigned to the brand. For example, if the brand has to go global, can the name be Chyawanprash or Pudin Hara (well-known and established brands in domestic market from Dabur India)? The names must serve extra meaning to convey the spirit of the brand. Choosing a descriptive name also amounts to missing out on all the potential of global communication.

Products do not live forever but brands can live forever if managed properly. Some products have been seen to be surviving a very long time—these could be either generic products which are essential in nature or the products may have undergone change and constantly adjusted with time to remain relevant and contemporary to its target segment(s). Otherwise, products only follow a life cycle and then finally decline and altogether disappear. Marketers can help extend the life of a product but after a certain stage the product has to die. However, brands don't have to die if managed properly. Hence brands should not get mixed solely with the product characteristics.

Many companies think that they have a brand when what they really have is just a name recognition. It might be the recognition of the name that hangs over the company door, the name on the product, or the name that describes a service. Just having recognition of the name does not create a valuable brand. It takes years of painstaking efforts on the part of the marketers to create a brand out of a name. You drive down every day to your office and you encounter Orchid food store. As you travel down the street so often you will become aware of Orchid store sell food items. It may even advertise locally and run promotions but Orchid has still not become a brand. It merely has a name that consumers associate with its contents.

A name becomes a brand when consumers associate it with a set of tangible or intangible benefits that they obtain from the product or service. As this association grows stronger, consumers' loyalty and willingness to pay price premium increase. And therefore, there is equity in the brand name. A brand without equity thus is not a brand.

To build brand equity, the marketer has to first distinguish its products and services from others in the marketplace and align what it says about its brand in advertising and marketing communication with what it actually delivers. A relationship then develops between the brand and the customers arising out of the customer's entire experience of the brand. As this relationship or the alignment grows stronger, so does the brand.

Pampers, disposable diapers with incremental and new consumer benefits were introduced by Procter & Gamble (P&G) in 1960s and positioned as diapers that were more comfortable for babies supported by the advertisement campaign that clearly communicated its superior value proposition which has helped creation of substantial brand equity for P&G over the years that followed and even now.

Nike, Coca-Cola, BMW, Levi's, Mercedes, Pepsi, and Sony are some of the best-known brands. How do these brands distinguish themselves from others in the same competitive set? What is that these brands have that other brands don't have? The answer lies in their distinctive product, consistent delivery, alignment between communications and delivery plus personality and presence. These brands succeeded in creating sustainable competitive advantage by consistently delivering the superior customer value which has made them enjoy consumer franchise all these years. These brands have provided positive experience by keeping consumers involved in all phases of development and also when changes were made to keep the product contemporary and relevant in customers' mind. All these brands are, therefore, power brands. A power brand thus must have these qualities and attributes.

Many brands have purely functional relationship with their customers. They are valued for their consistent delivery of a product or service that reliably performs certain functions. Power brands, however, create a more emotional bond that grows out of their personality. There was a time when sneakers were just sneakers—cheap, all-purpose canvas shoes. The only big decision a buyer had to make was whether to go for high tops or low tops. Then came manufacturers like Adidas, Nike, Puma, and Reebok who started making shoes mainly for running and followed them with the whole range single-purpose sneakers such as sneakers for basketball, for tennis, and so on. The trend caught on with the consumers, who began buying different pairs for different occasions. But Nike raced ahead of the rest by exploiting its brand power to move from athletic footwear into athletic clothing, projecting itself as a symbol of fitness and well-being. Nike further upgraded itself to position itself as athletic lifestyle company and roped in celebrities like basketball star Michael Jordan and the golfer Tiger Woods to endorse its goods. At the same time Nike has leveraged its brand by investing in retailing and sports and with such steps, the company was getting closer to its customers while maintaining its market share and premium pricing. As a result, it has built a market presence to deliver superior financial performance. Nike thus created what we call a power brand.

Whether it is Coca-Cola, seen as an icon of American culture, or Porsche, coveted for the macho driving experience it promises, power brands generate relationships with customers that are measurably stronger than those achieved by ordinary brands. Power brands generate enormous profits. They also open up future strategic opportunities.

Dettol is a powerful brand in the Indian context. In several surveys it was identified as number one brand in the country although the size of the brand in terms of sales is not that big. The pioneering status of Dettol in terms of much higher brand equity has opened up many more strategic options for exploitation by its owner Reckitt & Colman of India Limited (now known as Reckitt Benckiser India Limited). Till mid-1980s Dettol was only an antiseptic liquid, but in later years the brand was extended to create a soap which in due course of time has become even bigger than the parent brand. So powerful was the equity of the Dettol brand that in subsequent years Dettol shaving cream and Dettol talcum powder were also launched. Dettol soap has been further developed by introducing many variants like liquid hand wash in a pump pack and later on Dettol fresh with the claim of the same hardworking soap with good fragrance.

A name thus gradually grows to become a brand and ultimately a power brand. Not all brands have that possibility and also all brands do not get to the level of a power brand even if they have the possibility. The characteristics of name, brand, and power brand are very distinctive and can be summarized as in Table 2.3.

Power brand seems to be present in every turn and every corner, reinforcing its distinctiveness and uniqueness over other competing brands. It seems to be growing with you and ultimately becomes a part of your existence and your lifestyle. Such presence is derived from its national and international scale of operation exploiting multiple channels and in multiple product and presentation forms covering the entire category it represents. Power brands will thus be seen in all occasions,

Table 2.3 Names, Brands, and Power Brands

Criteria	Name	Brand	Power Brand
Incremental Matrix	Only Awareness	• Distinctive Value Proposition • Consistent Delivery	• Personality Presence • Communication Aligned with Delivery
Incremental Benefits	Purchase Traffic	Loyalty and Premium Prices	Increased Leverage Opportunities

SOURCE: Court et al. (1997).

all channels of communications, all places worthy of its existence and will touch everyone's life and style.

The Walt Disney Company epitomizes what a combination of personality and presence can do. Disney's theme parks offer genuinely distinctive experience built around universally recognized animated characters. The brand is supported by the execution of flawless delivery in every element of the business, coupled with integrated marketing communications focused on the theme that Disney represents worldwide: "childhood at any age." Customers have very powerful associations with the brand that often go generations back. People are seen to put a great deal of effort into planning a vacation in Disneyland and once there, buy lots of merchandise that is brought back home as memory of their visit. Others spend many hours watching Disney movies and television shows.

As a result Disney enjoys five main benefits of power brand (Court et al. 1997). These are:

- Substantial, dominant, and sustained market share and position: Disney occupies dominant market position in animated features and theme parks and is a leading producer of feature films.
- Premium prices and incremental value: Disney theme parks, hotels, and merchandise command significantly higher prices than the similar offerings from competitors.
- A track record of extending the brand to new brands, potential for brand extension: The Disney brand was launched in 1923 with the first Mickey Mouse cartoons and has since been extended to films, network, cable television programs and studios, theme parks, hotels, merchandise, and National Hockey League team, the Mighty Ducks.
- Extension to new markets and reaching out to other market segments: From the original focus on children, the brand has been extended to full range of demographic groups covering the age group from 8 to 80.

- Extension to new geographic areas and potential to go global: Disney's films and products are distributed worldwide. Theme parks are opened in the United States, Europe, and Asia.

These benefits ideally represent not what a brand can do for the company today, but the strategic options that it can create for the company tomorrow—which is ultimately the true power of a power brand.

Few power brands are in existence for centuries as unchallenged brands and the present management has just inherited those. But if a power brand is required to be created from the present state of a brand's performance, the first task is to make the brand strong and sound and then build from there. The process of moving from a name to brand and then from a brand to power brand would be similar in most situations but specific challenges would be different which are inherent to the industry types, product categories, types of competition, and also the company itself.

ROLE OF BRAND MANAGER

The job of the brand manager is to identify the specific need of the target customers and consumers, translate that need into a product concept, develop a product that satisfies that need, prepare the plan to market the product to deliver the profitability of the business by managing the brand effectively.

As the product progresses through its life cycle from the time it is introduced in the market, the marketing characteristics change, brand manager needs to have the clear understanding of those changes for effective management of the brand based on the typical characteristics synonymous with the stage of the product life cycle. Table 2.4 summarizes this aspect of the brand.

Brand manager has to ensure that the brands he or she manages are profitable over an extended period of the product life cycle. As can be seen, brand delivers maximum profit during growth and maturity period; it is, therefore, the task of the brand manager to extend these periods by taking appropriate marketing actions and arrest the decline as long as possible. This is, of course, possible by constantly upgrading and reinventing the brand to keep it alive and contemporary in the minds of the target consumer sets. With change in technology and culture arising out of free and easy communications across geographical territories and withdrawal of all trade barriers where consumers are exposed to the benefits of the development in the category elsewhere in the world, the brand manager has to be the live wire between the organization and the customers to gauge the ever changing expectations and incorporate those in the product or the brand offering to ensure the longer lasting relationship between the brand and the customers.

Table 2.4 Marketing Characteristics of Product at Different Stages

Stages of Development	Introduction	Growth	Maturity	Decline
Business support direction	Market development	Market penetration	Defending market share	Withdrawing and milking the brand
Business environment	Limited marketing activities	Intense marketing activities	Large players in the game	Few players and limited marketing activity
Target customer base	New users	New segment and selective users	Fixed identified customers	Very loyal and matured customer base
Profit margin	Low profit	Growing profit	Margins under pressure	Profit high but total profit low
Marketing expenditure	Very high	High	Stabilized	Very low
Sales volume	Low	Fast growth	Slow growth	Decline

SOURCE: Adapted from Buell (1985).

A brand manager has to have the ability to diagnose the early signals through the analysis of the brand's performance and customers' feedback received through organized research as well as from the regular market research undertaken on the brand's health and performance or otherwise to understand course of actions that are necessary at various stages of brand evolution. For example, if a medicine brand has been found to be prescribed by only older generation of doctors the signal should be picked up by the brand manager that the product life cycle will soon be in a declining phase and, therefore, will get shortened. This situation will surely demand an immediate corrective action either by developing a substitution for focusing on the younger doctors provided the medicine still holds a lot of promise.

In technology products the product's life cycle is short and more so in the present day context when technology development cycle is very short. In that scenario the brand manger has to play a key role in identifying and understanding the course of technology development process as well as kind of investment that is being made by others in competition to create future generation products in the same category. In order to remain ahead of the race, the better performing brands have to be seen by the customers as innovators and natural owners of the category.

Pharmaceutical companies spend fortunes in research and development (R&D) for creating new drug molecules and it takes years and huge resources to strike a potential winner after the product passes through all kinds of scrutiny, clinical trials and legal permissions before the new drug can be marketed. Even after going through so many tests and procedures before a potential product can be launched the marketers always have to expect that there could be better formulations coming from competitive research which can destroy the product prospects overnight. There were instances when a product had to be withdrawn after launch or even after years of successful marketing because someone found out some side effects arising out of the continued use of the drug. Very recently a popular drug, Nimesulide, an analgesic, had to be withdrawn by Dr Reddy's laboratory because of similar reasons. Nimesulide is a nonsteroidal, anti-inflammatory analgesic and anti-pyretic drug (NSAID). A section of doctors at leading hospitals like Apollo, etc.; have started recommending paracetamol in place of nimesulide while others prescribe nimesulide only in some specific cases. Leading nimesulide brand Nise belongs to Dr Reddy's Laboratory which has currently stopped manufacturing the four nimesulide fixed dosage combinations. Ranbaxy and Panacea Pharmaceuticals have a major share in the nimesulide market. Alembic and Blue Cross Laboratories have discontinued manufacturing nimesulide drops. In fact, some MNCs started campaigning against this drug to protect their own brand and formulation. Both government and nimesulide manufacturers were under tremendous pressure ever since nimesulide was banned in countries such as Spain and Finland in 2001 on reports of its hepatotoxicity. The pressure increased even more after a public interest litigation (PIL) was filed in the Delhi High Court by a few challenging the continued marketing of nimesulide in the country. The ongoing controversy on the side effects of nimesulide is helping other alternatives like aspirin and paracetamol to make inroads into the ₹2,500 million (USD 50 million) nimesulide market and thereby help the other drugs to recover some of its lost market share. The market share of paracetamol had shrunk since the government gave approval for nimesulide way back in 1994.

Brand manager plays a vital role in ensuring smooth transition to new environment without causing any significant damage to the company's future business opportunities. Brand manager thus performs an all-pervasive role in the organization to ensure that not only new, vibrant, and profitable brands are created but existing brands are managed for their longer term prospects.

UNDERSTANDING THE POTENTIAL OF A BRAND

At birth a brand has all possibilities and thus has immense potential. Like a newborn it has all the possibilities; it can grow to any heights and it can go places. It can be given any meaning, any identity and it can be developed in any way possible. But as time elapses, the flexibility reduces considerably and, therefore, it loses some of its freedom. However, reality is that all brands cannot have the same potential. The potential of the brand is also dependent on the product category it belongs to, uses, possibility of further development into many variants and options, competition, and most importantly the resources that can be committed behind the promotion, marketing, and development of the brand.

Brand identity is derived from various attributes including brand objectives, the product itself including the specific characteristics and unique features, and its symbols. Product in its entirety and its presentation and delivery mode are, therefore, the first source of brand identity. Brand embodies the delivery of customers' expectations and thus has a direct bearing on its identity. For example, the brand Benetton is directly identified with the spectrum of color that they can be made available in line with the change in fashion. Unlike competitors, Benetton innovated the technique of dyeing pullovers after they are made and not before which distinguishes themselves from others. Benetton thus is prepared to be with the whims of fashion to do last minute changes as required and demanded by the customers.

A brand has both latent and patent associations. Brand manger has thus an opportunity to exploit both the patent and latent associations depending on the possibilities in a typical market environment that exists. Brand also has several positive attributes or assets which can be exploited and several negative attributes which are its limitations or liabilities. The brand potential is, therefore, the sum total of all these patent and latent, positive or negative associations. It is the responsibility of the brand manager to decide which of these apparently opposite attributes give the maximum potential for the brand and all marketing program has to be planned taking into the market opportunity as can be seen from the customer analysis and the product characteristics that support the need.

Patent brand associations have attributes which are visible and, therefore, tangible. Latent brand associations are intangibles attributes that can be exploited depending on the market opportunities. Positive features of the product are actually a set of assets that are to be exploited whereas the negative features are those which can be considered as liabilities. Together it will determine the total potential of the brand. The cross combination of these two opposite dimensions, namely, patent and latent, assets and liabilities serves to represent the brand's potential.

The total brand value proposition has to be designed and delivered in such a way that right value is perceived by the customers. Selecting the right value proposition, therefore, is the key to successful management of the brand.

VALUE

Value is what the customer perceives against a price charged for the brand. The value equation can thus be represented by:

$$V = B/P$$
Where V = Perceived value
B = Perceived benefits
P = Price charged

Value thus is enhanced by increasing the numerator or benefits derived from the use of brand or reducing the denominator or the price charged for the product or even both. It is the task of the brand marketers to work, plan, and promote the brand continuously in a manner so that brand value increases over time as compared with its own competitive set. Constant and regular monitoring of brand health will help in identifying the kind of tasks required to restore brand health.

The Value Brand Delivers

Key task of the marketer is delivering superior value in relation to its own competitive set.

Choosing the Right Value

To deliver the right value, the brand manager has to choose the value by appropriate customer segmentation, focusing on the selected market by having appropriate value proposition.

Providing the Value

To provide the chosen value the product has to be designed and developed to be in line with the chosen value proposition. Other factors such as service delivery and service level, pricing, distribution, etc., also have to be in conformity to the chosen value. Decisions related to whether the product has to be made or outsourced also have relevance to the chosen value. If higher value can be captured by getting the product manufactured by a third party without compromising other issues including quality, manageability, etc., the marketer should opt for outsourcing.

Communicate the Value

The advertisement and communication exercise, designing the sales force structure, and sales promotion, etc., are the three important elements of communication to the customers.

From a thorough understanding of the customers' expectations and needs, the brand manger has to identify and choose the right value proposition. In this respect all products have to have the core which the product has to deliver (core benefits) and around which enhancement and true extra are designed and delivered as shown in Figure 2.1.

Figure 2.1   Providing the Value of the Brand

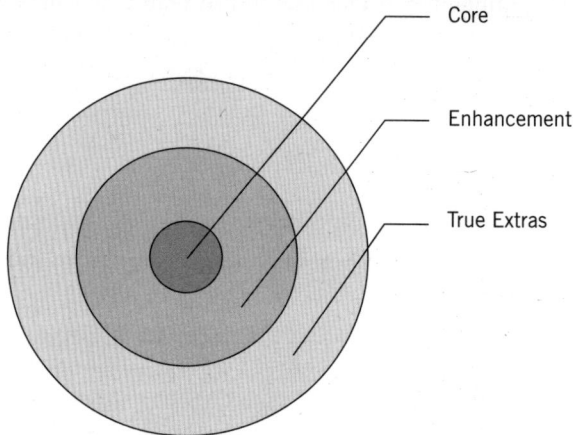

- Core
- Enhancement
- True Extras

SOURCE: Kapferer (1994).

The key task of the brand manger is to significantly increase the value of the brand he or she handles. Customers would be willing to pay the price which is lower than the perceived value of the product irrespective of the cost of the product. Two products having similar benefits thus can sell at different prices only when the perceived value is different which branding can help to make. Only the brand value can create a difference in the perceived value of two products having identical uses, quality, reliability, and functional benefits. The objective of managing the brand would, therefore, be to significantly increase the value of the brand by constantly trying to remain in the minds of the targeted customers by delivering the customer expectations and more often by exceeding the expectation. To achieve this, the brand manager has to have market orientation and the organization has to have a long-term strategic vision.

TOP GLOBAL BRANDS

A. C. Nielsen Study (2001)

A number of consumer product companies such as Nestle, P&G, Unilever, Coca-Cola, and PepsiCo have successfully developed global brands. However, exactly which brands can qualify as global brands is a matter of debate. According to a study conducted by A. C. Nielsen (2001) covering 200 brands across 30 countries in North America, Europe, Middle East, Africa, Asia Pacific and Latin America, only 43 consumer product brands have reached the status of global brands (over 200 brands researched for this study). The study has only considered those brands as global brands which have a sale of over USD 1 billion, have at least 5 percent of their sales outside their home region and a geographic presence in all major regions of the world. The categories with maximum number of global brands have been beverages and tobacco, a distant second (Table 2.5). Overall, most of the brands have a high concentration of sales in either North America or Europe (62 percent on average). For three brands, both North America and Europe have equal predominance (Gillette, Pedigree, and Always). Of the 43 brands that have made to the list, none originated in the Asia-Pacific region. However, the issue for some concern is that in terms of sales growth, the annual average growth rate across the 43 brands is less than 10 percent.

The other key issue as highlighted in the study is the manufacturers', predominance. Though there are 23 manufacturers in these 43 billion-dollar brands, eight of the 23 companies have more than one brand on the list (Table 2.6). Nearly three-quarters of these sales (USD 125 billion from these 43 brands) have been attributable to the eight manufacturers with multiple brands on the list.

Table 2.5	Strongest Branded Consumer Packaged Products Worldwide	
Categories	*No. of Brands*	*Key Brands*
Beverages	13	Coke, Diet Coke, Pepsi, and Diet Pepsi
Tobacco	4	Marlboro, Benson & Hedges, Camel, and L&M
Snack foods	3	Pringles, Lay's, and Doritos
Pet foods	3	Pedigree, Whiskas, and Friskies

SOURCE: A. C. Nielson Survey (2001).

STRATEGIC VISION OF BRAND MANAGEMENT

Strategic vision involves long-term goals and farsightedness by the top management of the company regarding where to compete, how to compete, and when to compete. It might even be necessary to take a decision not to compete under certain business

Table 2.6 Top Global Brands for Leading Marketers	
Company	*No. of Brands*
PepsiCo	6
Philip Morris (incl. Kraft)	5
P&G	5
Coca-Cola	4
Kimberly-Clark	2
Gillette Company	2
Mars	2
Nestle	2

SOURCE: A. C. Nielsen Survey (2001).

environment. Such decisions are to be taken with full knowledge of the market needs and trends, the existing competition, and the strength and/or weaknesses of the organization. Rapidly changing markets and competitive threats require high degree of skills on the part of the executive in charting the course of the organization through a rapidly changing business environment. Top management must anticipate the future direction of the business and competitive environment and deal proactively with future threats and opportunities. It must select the product and market areas where it can compete the best and develop market-driven strategies to gain competitive advantage.

Under certain market environment, businesses are required to compete with some select players and at the same time cooperate with other players in order to manage the business to deliver the expected and desired result. Such approach is now called "co-optation" meaning both competition and cooperation at the same time. It can also be pointed out here that it is necessary for the brand manager to identify and select the competitor with which the brand has to lock in for a fight in the marketplace. With the same strategy one cannot possibly fight with everyone in the market and, therefore, identifying the competitor is critical to the prospect of success.

DERIVING COMPETITIVE ADVANTAGE

Corporations derive competitive advantage by offering superior value to the customer through:

- lower prices than competitors for equivalent benefits and or
- offering unique benefits that more than offset a higher price.

Several considerations are to be taken into account for achieving customer satisfaction and for gaining competitive advantage such as:

- Analysis of customer requirements should look at the group of buyers with similar preferences.
- Opportunities are generally created by finding the buyers' requirements which are not being satisfied by the current offering from competition.
- Customer satisfaction analysis should aim at finding the best opportunities for the organization to create superior value.

The entire process, therefore, has to be customer-focused. The lower middle and lower income group households were using washing soap cake (bar soap) for washing their clothes and that process was quite laborious and time-consuming for housewives. Hindustan Lever's Surf was too costly for them and it was unaffordable. It was Nirma who could capture that opportunity to introduce cheaper washing powder and thus helped to satisfy a basic need of the customer and upgraded the washing process to bucket wash for a large section of the population in the country around which a huge business opportunity was created. In subsequent years Nirma became a big threat to the giant like HUL. Seeing Nirma's success in later years many new brands were created from similar principles of competitive advantage. The process of superior value creation has to be continuous in order to remain relevant to the customers. Although several factors contribute to the success of an organization, competitive advantage is a core requirement. In later years Nirma could not hold onto its superior value proposition and other smaller players caught on with Nirma and subsequently even overtook Nirma. As an answer to Nirma's value proposition, HUL introduced Wheel and then Wheel Active. And there were many smaller regional brands which came up, such as, Fena and Ghadi in north India, Safed in East India and so on. Today Ghadi is the number one brand in detergents, having registered a sale of approximately ₹2,400 crores (USD 480 million) and Nirma has been pushed to number three position having sales close to ₹1,000 crores (USD 200 million). Ghadi's sustained television advertisement campaign—"Pahele Istemal Kare, Phir Viswas Kare" (use it first and then believe it) really worked as a powerful campaign for them.

"It is always better to be first than it is better to be better," said Al Ries and Jack Trout, the leading marketing strategists (Ries and Trout 1994). If you want to occupy the leadership position in any category, you will have to innovate or create that category and enter the category first.

There are marketing pundits who think that it is risky to venture into creating a new category and hence it is better that someone else does it. And, when a segment is created it is easier to enter it with a better but me-too product to take away a market share from the first mover. But that is not always true. The task of the second entrant to establish a brand or category can never be easier. It is definitely going to be more difficult because experience tells us that those who entered the category first have really remained invincible market leaders for long time to come proving the hypothesis that "there is always a first mover advantage" or as they say, "the early bird catches the worm."

This principle applies to any product, any brand, or any category. This is particularly true when the consumer's mind is always being bombarded with all kinds of information, including information on new products, through the use of multiple media. In this age of information explosion, the first person, first product, or first name that enters the consumer's mind will leave the strongest impression and have the highest recall value. The second, even if it is better or superior, cannot even remain alongside the first one in the prospect's mind, not to speak of easily replacing the first one. Nobody remembers the second player. And the third player has very bleak chances of creating a success story, as observed by Al Ries and Jack Trout (1994). The same authors have given numerous examples from the international market to prove the point.

If the first product becomes a remarkable success, it often becomes synonymous with the category which means it becomes generic to the category. For example, Hindustan Lever's Dalda which is a brand name for hydrogenated vegetable oil (HVO). People might be buying any brand or even loose HVO but when asked will say that the food is cooked in Dalda. The Dalda was generic to the category and was also the market leader. It is a different matter that HUL subsequently divested the brand to world leader in edible oil business—Bungee group of South America as HUL found the brand and the business as nonstrategic to their core business and thus decided to exit the category. Bungee in due course of time even launched edible oil under the same brand Dalda. One reason why the first brand tends to maintain its leadership is that the name often becomes generic. Xerox, the first plain-paper copier became the name for all plain-paper copiers.

Rasna, on the other hand, has a great success story. The brand was first launched in western India during early 1970s as a cheap substitute of squashes, cordials, juices, and carbonated beverages—with very limited marketing support.

The new concept that Khambatta introduced was the Rasna concentrate, and can best be described as "one minus concept" which means that the product has all the ingredients excepting one which the consumer has to add. Most often, this ingredient which is not added in the product is a costly and bulky ingredient which increases the cost of the product significantly but consumers add that item conveniently without realizing what it costs to them. Rasna was, therefore, developed as a composite of flavor pack acid-preservative and color pack, and consumers have to add sugar for taste.

After seeing Rasna's success, many players including multinationals attempted to enter that category but none succeeded in establishing another brand in "one minus concept" of soft drink concentrate which Khambatta created from nowhere.

During the late 1970s and early 1980s, brands such as Trinka from Corn Products (now known as Best Foods International and acquired by Unilever), Ju-C from Kothari General Foods, Hasras from Kissan and and Dipysip from Dipys from UB Group have tried to enter that category but all have failed. General Foods which is now known as Kraft Foods and belonging to USD 65 billion Philip Morris Group also made an attempt to introduce their global brand of powder beverage Tang. They did set up a manufacturing facility in Hyderabad for Tang and initially attempted to distribute the product through their own distribution infrastructure and later on through Dabur's distribution set up but both of their attempts failed and such a powerful brand which has global presence did not succeed in Indian market against Rasna.

Whoever has attempted to introduce a new product idea, or a new concept has much higher probability of success in creating a segment for themselves. The second player in the game with a me-too product to offer has relatively lower rate of success. The second player still has a chance provided he can differentiate and carve out a niche for himself in the consumer's mind. There is very little possibility for the third player.

Not all products succeed if introduced first, but then either the idea is bad or the product is well ahead of its time or too late. If the idea is well ahead of time, it only takes longer time to get established and one should have the ability, resources, and tenacity to continue.

Leading brands in any category are almost always the first brands that enter into the prospect's mind. Examples are Bisleri in packaged water, Kingfisher in Beer from United Breweries in alcoholic beverages, Nirma in cheaper detergent segment, and Ujala in dye-based fabric blue.

The question often raised is that if you are second in the prospects' mind, are you then doomed to languish forever like many other unsuccessful second brands? But it is always not necessarily so because there are many other guiding principles also at work which determine the success or failure of a new concept (Ries and Trout 1994).

In the United States and in other developed economics, it is often seen that a corporation loses market share to its nearest competitors in a short span of time. This phenomenon is not generally witnessed in India where industry leaders are seen to maintain their dominant position over the years.

We have seen case histories like Nirma dominating the detergent segment and giving Hindustan Lever a run for their money. But Nirma is in a different segment; its consumer profile is not same as that of Surf. Nirma's dominance in cheaper price detergent segment forced Hindustan Lever to launch Wheel.

After the exit of Coke in 1977, Parle was able to gain market leadership, controlling about 60 percent of the country's carbonated beverage industry from about 20 percent when Coke was in India. But when a powerful multinational like Pepsi came and opened shop in India, Parle was initially seen to be quite scared about losing market share and offered a lot of resistance to Pepsi's entry. But they could withstand the onslaught of Pepsi and maintain their leadership position till they "gave in" to Coke. The reason being when Coke reappeared in the Indian market, most of the erstwhile Coke bottlers who had shifted and taken Parle franchise started talking to Coke again for rejoining which weakened the position of Parle in the market. This has prompted Parle to sell their brands and business to Coke. But even after selling brands to Coke, Thums Up still sells more than Coke in India.

In India brand loyalty is quite high and it takes a long time for consumers to switch brands. But with increased level of awareness and more media pressure, this trend may reverse now. So far we have seen competition in different price and consumer segments with various players trying to carve out a niche in the marketplace. With increased competition and more and more MNCs coming in, we will see the real fight for brand share. The mere fear of that fight has prompted many Indian business houses, particularly in the consumer products segment to either go in for strategic alliances or sell out.

Whenever there is competition, it is the leader who is very vulnerable because smaller players have their own local pockets of strength and often go unnoticed. In order to fight a leader, it is essential to study its market behavior and its strengths and weaknesses. It is the weaknesses of the leader that the competitor exploits.

Most common weaknesses of a market leader could be (i) high cost structure, (ii) age-old technology, (iii) inefficient and outdated production facility, (iv) built-in bureaucracy and complacency resulting in slow reaction time, (v) inflexibility, and (vi) compulsion of delivering shareholders' expectation and maintaining share price at stock market, etc. If these are coupled with other problems like pressure of shareholders to produce desired financial performance, which restricts the market leader's ability to spend and do innovations to fight competition, then the task of the competitor to gain market share from the leader becomes much simpler.

One of the easiest routes to attack the market leader is by offering quality at a lower price. It is generally seen that a leader can never fight on the price front because it has already taken a premium and dominant position in the marketplace with much higher volume of business.

It should be remembered that quality should not be perceived as lower in relation to lower price. The quality should be as good or perceived to be even better than the leader and fight should be on price–quality equation. If the competitor can manage this communication exercise very efficiently, the possibility of success is very high.

Initially this exercise may not be sustainable, as the bottom line will come under serious pressure. But if the competitor can maintain a low cost structure through innovation, thereby ensuring a good margin even at lower price, it will increase his ability to fight the leader. This task is easier if the leader depends heavily on the performance of the brand for its bottom line. In that case, the leader cannot afford to continue such price war indefinitely—for every rupee spent by the competitor, the leader has to spend much more. But the MNCs have enormous financial muscle and staying power and can outlast the local leaders in a brand fight.

Another way to fight a leader is to launch a tactical war by launching schemes and activities in localized geographical market, forcing the leader to spend and react for protecting their share in the whole country and thereby spending many times more.

In both these exercises, the competitor must clearly understand the market structure, behavior of leader in that structure and how the leader was able to maintain its position in relation to its financial performance. One more important factor is that without having a real advantage in cost leadership, it would be counterproductive to launch a price war with the leader. Look at Pepsi, the company has so far not made any profit and possibly if all its accumulated loss is taken into account, they are unlikely to make profit soon. Realizing this, their partners Punjab Agro and Voltas have already dissociated with Pepsi. In spite of having multinational advantages, Pepsi could not create any significant dent in Parle's position because structurally Pepsi was an unviable proposition. It has realized this and is now trying to get out of those unviable investments. Besides, Pepsi did not have any cost leadership over Parle. In fact, Parle had the cost advantage.

In Western countries companies are seen to lose brand share and leadership position in a very short time—a trend not seen in the Indian market because market here is highly segmented and competition is much less. With liberalization, situation here also would be very much similar and as we can see, competition has already increased manifold. The value perception between two brands changes with education, exposure to media, and product awareness. And consumer societies and activists are exactly trying to do the same—helping to increase consumer awareness. When consumers become increasingly aware of the product constituents, performance, benefits, and hence the value, the difference between the two brands reduces as long as quality is comparable. The premium of a brand is thus the value consumers attach to unknown benefits and quality attributes. When this unknown becomes known, the premium reduces.

The global premium brands were created by large corporations through strategic marketing and after spending huge advertisement and promotional funds. They are now being challenged by smaller companies which can deliver identical products through identical technologies at much competitive prices.

Today consumers are very discerning and are not willing to pay for organizational inefficiencies. Organizations are, therefore, busy understanding the value of the brand and how much premium it can fetch to decide about the future course.

Philip Morris cut the price of Marlboro cigarettes in the U.S., followed by P&G which reduced the price of its Pampers diapers. Large corporations are realizing that promotional money only helps to push the trade stock but not consumer offtake. Under the circumstances, it is always better to reduce price and pass on the benefit to consumers to establish new price value–benefit equation.

Restructuring might mean reducing the hierarchy and number of people, disposal of nonstrategic business, resources reallocations, etc., to derive cost economy. In restructuring, very profitable businesses also are sometimes hived off if the organization in its own assessment considers itself not the "natural owner" of the business. Corporations can be considered as "natural owners" provided they are significant players in that category, have key core competencies in the business over competition, and set the consumer trend by providing leadership in the category. It was clearly established by various studies that profit is not the sole criterion for running a business unit if the business is not naturally yours because in the long run such profit cannot be sustained in a highly competitive environment. Better growth is obtained if such resources are diverted to support the business which is naturally and strategically yours.

The other way of gaining market share is to get into product variants or such segment which the market leader is not satisfying. When all attempts of Parle failed to establish a cola brand against Coke in India they launched Limca—a lemon–lime drink—in the early 1970s which was able to keep the entire organization going. When Nestle decided to get into the tomato ketchup market and "Kissan" was the market leader, they expanded the market by introducing variants like sweet-n-sour ketchup. Once the competitor is seen to be innovative in a particular market segment, the leader obviously will be seen in poor light. This makes the competitor's task easier.

In the liberalized market environment, local leaders will have to prepare themselves for the transition not only by making the organization lean and mean and by incorporating cost-effective technology and superior marketing skill but also by realigning themselves with the changes in market structure. Otherwise, they are likely to lose out to global brands.

PRODUCT INNOVATION

In a competitive business environment only those will survive who can be more innovative to outperform the competition in terms of product performance and services. Although human talent is the first requirement, getting innovative output and winning products needs efficient innovation management. In retrospect, success always seems simple but making an innovation work is not that simple particularly when nine out of every ten products launched in the market have failed. The innovation can be a result of hard, organized, and purposeful work if the need for it is identified. But innovation could also be either the result of an accident or the "the wild imagination of the genius mind" which of course cannot be taught (de Bono 1992).

The latter type, described as an extraordinary incident, is definitely a rare affair and it is the first type which contributes to over 90 percent of all innovations that have ever happened in this world. The innovation that is a result of organized and purposeful work can be practiced.

As is generally said, "Necessity is the mother of invention"; the need gets the innovative mind working. Many breakthrough innovations were made under pressure. Thus when survival itself is threatened, organizations look for great innovations to happen which can sail them through the difficult days.

One of the essential conditions of innovation to happen is, therefore, identifying the need for it. The second most important aspect of innovation management is to identify the person or group of people who are capable of finding a solution to the problem. That person may or may not be within the organization but once the team or the individual is identified the task is to provide resources, support, and encouragement for the result.

An innovative product is the result of a bright idea that comes from the assessment of a particular need.

Sony's development of the Walkman is a brilliant example of how existing technological capabilities can be utilized to create an entirely new product to meet the need.

The changes in the market structure of a particular industry offer significant opportunity for innovation. For example, as a fallout of liberalization, Indian car manufacturers suddenly faced global competition and to keep their own product(s) acceptable in the marketplace, local models are undergoing changes in design, performance, quality, fuel economy, cost, aesthetics, and finally safety aspects including environmental safety. These factors influence changes in customers' expectations. These external changes have the most predictable consequences. Service industry, health care industry, and consumer goods industry can make realistic predictions about the future needs from these external changes and direct their innovative practices to exploit the opportunities these changes will offer.

Finally, the most important source of innovation is new knowledge derived from technological breakthrough. Knowledge-based innovation differs from all other forms of innovation in its basic characteristics such as time span, predictability, failure rate, and the management challenges. This is particularly true for the kind of innovation that we currently see taking place in the areas of information and communication technology and biotechnology including medical biotechnology and genetic engineering. When technology is fast changing, the product life cycle becomes shorter and hence the question of making innovation faster than the competition for exploitation of the opportunity. Otherwise, entire effort can become non-remunerative for the follower with a much lesser and residual market opportunity. Exploitation of knowledge-based opportunity not only can provide new market opportunity but also can be a source of fame for an organization. But the risk associated with it is also high either on account of technological failure or technological redundancy.

The uncertainty associated with innovation justifies the high failure rate of the innovative firms. It is only a part of the story that the vast majority of attempts at innovation fail. The real reasons lie in the apparent inability to anticipate the future impact of successful innovation even after establishing its technical feasibility. Often, there is no recognized way of knowing which new discoveries may turn out to be relevant or what realm of human activity eventually they may apply to. But private organizations will naturally allocate their R&D resources to projects that they hope will turn out to be relevant and the organizations are expected to be capable of making their own assessment and judgment which will differentiate successful and innovative companies from the rest (de Bono 1992). One success story can easily justify nine failures and hence it is worth taking risk of uncertainty in the search for any radical innovations to happen.

MARKET ORIENTATION

To create success stories an organization has to be totally oriented toward the market; that makes the customer the focal point of a company's entire business operation. A business can be said to be market-oriented when its culture is so designed and managed which enables it to continuously create superior customer value. As such becoming market-oriented involves obtaining information about customers, market, and competition and then viewing that information from a complete business perspective and deciding how to deliver superior customer value and finally taking actions to provide those values to the customers.

The classical marketing concept advocates starting with the customer needs or wants, deciding which needs to meet and then involving everyone in the process to satisfy that identified customer need. However, in fact, one can find two different kinds of approaches in product management, namely, company-oriented approach and customer-oriented approach. The first approach attempts to push the company's needs and objectives for the customers to accept. This is like going against the current and, therefore, mostly fails. The market-oriented organization, on the other hand is more than a philosophy in the sense that it provides a process for delivering the customer value. Becoming market-oriented, therefore, requires finding out what value buyers want to help them meet their purchasing objectives as buyers' buying decisions are guided by the key attributes and features of the brand that offers best value for them in their actual use situation. Therefore, buyer's actual experience in using the brand is compared to expectations to know or determine the customer satisfaction.

MANAGING A BRAND IN THE 21ST CENTURY

Market structures globally are fast changing. As trade barriers are being withdrawn the global market is gradually emerging as an opportunity for all businesses and products. In this process products and services are freely moving from one part of the world to another. Products and services are thus required to be globally competitive. Also organizations are required to have the ability to design, develop, and market the products and services in a dynamic global business environment which requires different skill sets and culture. The market thus has become highly competitive. With the gradual withdrawal of trade barriers as per the guidelines of World Trade Organization (WTO) international brands are easily making their entry into local markets. The mode of the entry of the multinationals is also different. Some of them are even entering through trading route by appointing distributors which is a low-risk entry option which many large multinationals are exploring to test the ground. Large retail stores are stocking those products and consumers are not only getting many options to choose from but also comparing the products' quality and delivery mode available from multiple sources. Products and services have to be designed for their ability to exploit the global opportunity. The products, therefore, have to meet not only the quality criteria but also the statutory and regulatory issues governing the trade and commerce for the product categories.

With the Internet revolution the consumers are having easy access to all kinds of information. Sitting at home, customers can collect all they want to know about a product—its features, price, quality, and also about the companies producing those products. Customers, therefore, can do their own research before they decide to buy a particular product. Through these channels, prospective customers are made more knowledgeable by feeding them with product and other related information which in traditional marketing model is not possible.

Today's brand manger has to deal with more informed and knowledgeable customers. Internet also has opened up direct online marketing opportunity for the marketer. All companies are increasingly realizing the power of Internet and, therefore, provide all details on the net for the customers who would like to shop online avoiding the trouble of physically visiting the stores. Customers are now having more buying power than before.

The retail trade has been undergoing dramatic change. Organized retailing is catching up in India in large measure. Customers would like to shop in an appropriate environment. Shopping itself has become more pleasurable then before. Customers would like to take decisions themselves after seeing and comparing all kinds of product offerings on the retail shelf. They would like to take more informed decisions. Products and services are thus required to make much more disclosures and communication exercise is a much bigger challenge for the marketers. Customers are increasingly becoming conscious about their rights and privileges and if the products are not delivering the stated promises, marketers may lend themselves into a difficult situation at the cost of losing the image and the market.

Consumer protection laws have become more stringent in all countries providing the rights and privileges of the customers. The legal system for redressal of consumer complaints has been made easier and faster. There are voluntary consumer forums who offer services for dealing with any such consumer complaints. These organizations also act like a watchdog on the marketers offering their goods and merchandise. They also spread consumer education and even give training. Businesses have to deal with the more enlightened consumers these days. In India we have Center for Science and Environment (CSE) in Delhi started by late Anil Agarwal which keeps manufacturers on their toes. They constantly analyze the products of the brand marketers and publish their findings in newspapers and in their own journal *Down to Earth*. Their finding of pesticide residues in all leading beverage brands, which forced government to form a joint parliamentary committee to investigate, is a case in point. There are many such issues that they regularly raise in public interest for which brand marketers will have to be very alert always.

Intellectual Property Right (IPR) Act has become a very important issue to be managed effectively in order to protect the brands and all proprietary rights associated with the products. Care has to be exercised about any possible and even unintentional violation of the IPR Act. Soon product patents will be a reality in India which will change the market opportunity for many product categories. Our domestic pharmaceutical companies made fortune taking the advantage of process patent by producing many drug molecules through slightly different process routes and competing effectively against the product inventor in the international market. The product patent regime will stop such opportunity altogether. Businesses, therefore, have to be more innovative in such scenario.

Markets in various parts of the world are increasingly seen to join together in order to have collective bargaining power. Following liberalization, it has emerged that the creation of a common market having common laws in respect of free flow of goods, services, people, and knowledge across the country is a crucial determining factor for building global competitiveness and thereby achieving economic prosperity.

Recognizing the tremendous economic advantages conferred by borderless trade, the European Union (EU) in 1992 opened up sovereign boundaries to create a common market, an effort which was progressively followed up with the introduction of a single currency. This single historical act has served as a catalyst in the strategy for economic expansion within Europe. The EU has since emerged as the largest economy in the world producing better quality products at lower cost. As a result, its intra-regional trade has increased manifold.

Although in terms of consumer preferences, tastes, their culture, and demographic and psychographic profile India is not a homogeneous market, marketers normally attempt to market the same proposition for pan-India market. Products liked and preferred in south may not find acceptance in north or east and as a result many marketers view the Indian market as different in different regions and brand marketing approach including the product offering differently. Many marketers thus think four regions (north, south, east, and west) are like four different countries as far as consumer behavior is concerned. But efforts are being made by the government and trade associations to unify the taxation system, etc., for easier accounting and free flow of goods and services. With the new management information system and the implementation of e-governance, the check posts and entry barriers and multiple taxation systems will be removed facilitating faster and cheaper movement of goods. According to a study conducted by the Federation of Indian Chambers of Commerce and Industry (FICCI) in India there is an estimated loss of ₹20,000 million (USD 4,000 million) due to holdup of transport vehicles at various check posts. The introduction of a unified value added tax (VAT) system which is now going to be superseded by goods and services tax (GST) regime will make things easier for the marketer in India, which was earlier considered a very complex market.

HOW BUSINESSES ARE CHANGING

From the foregoing we can say with some degree of confidence that the marketplace now is not what it used to be. There are radical changes as a result of major societal forces such as major technological innovations and advances, globalization, deregulation, and most importantly competition. These forces have made it imperative for the businesses to change their approaches.

- Customers increasingly demand better quality. As they are more knowledgeable now they can perceive the product differences and, therefore, they are not that loyal anymore. They shop more intelligently now than before. They take more judicious purchase decisions. Their loyalty cannot be taken for granted.

- Brand marketers are facing increased competition from domestic players including small regional players who have their protected niches and also from foreign brands which have forced them to spend more on advertisement and promotion and thus profit margins are shrinking. Also the money spent on advertisement and sales promotion is not that effective because of too much cluttered media.
- There are increased number of methods and channels available to reach the customer such as direct marketing to consumers, multi-level marketing, direct to home sales, Internet marketing. Social networking sites are being used to promote products by marketers now. There is, therefore, the emergence of new marketing models. Traditional retailers have lost some of their business and as a result retailers would like to only stock powerful national brands to compensate for the costly and limited shelf space that they have.

With the change in business environment, organizations are also trying to change and adjust in many ways. They are constantly trying to evolve better methods to reduce cost and improve efficiency. These can be summarized as:

- Reengineering business processes to eliminate the non value-adding activities from business operations.
- Outsourcing the noncore activities so that businesses can only concentrate on key functions and activities to improve efficiency.
- E-commerce: Business-to-business purchasing is growing fast on the Internet. Customers can collect all pertinent information that they require on the net and click to order and pay. Organizations are thus gearing up and having portals to facilitate such transactions.
- Forming alliance: Instead of fighting alone in the battlefield many new alliances are seen to be forming to exploit the collective synergy in the marketplace.
- Partnering with the suppliers: Suppliers are considered as partners in the business and a new set of alliances and relationships are emerging to fight the common goals and objectives.
- Benchmarking: Organizations are benchmarking themselves with the market leader in the category as well as with best practices to help them imbibe the best practices and processes to proactively react faster to the ever changing market environment.
- Market-oriented: Instead of only organizing the product to satisfy an identified need more focus now is to organize the entire market segment.
- Global outlook: Think global and act local. This is what is being termed as both global and local or "glocal."

- Decentralized operation: Instead of being managed from top down more emphasis is on the decentralized environment and empowerment of employees to act local. Entrepreneurship and what we call "intrepreneurship" at the local level is encouraged (Philip Kotler 1997: 28).

To adjust to the new environment marketers are rethinking their concepts, philosophies, and tools. Some of this new thinking in the new economy is summed up as below:

- Customer relationship marketing (CRM): Instead of focusing on transactions focus is on building long-term, profitable customer relationships. Companies now focus on their most profitable customers, products, markets, and channels.
- Customer life time value: From managing or making profit on each sales focus is on managing life time sales. Companies are offering to their regular customers a special package and value to retain them for life.
- Customer share: Instead of focusing only on market share some companies now focus on customer share. They offer more variety of products to the same set of customers whom they have identified as attractive and profitable and, therefore, also most valuable. They train their sales staff and other employees in cross-selling and up-selling. Similarly, a bank can focus on the share of their existing customer's wallet rather than only trying to get more customers.
- Target marketing: Instead of selling to everyone some companies are focusing on the specific target market. Availability of focused media such as specialized newspapers, journals, magazines, and local TV channels is helping in such efforts.
- Customer database: Instead of collecting the sales data, building rich data warehouse of customers makes companies more informed about the customer buying behavior, preferences, demographics, and even profitability by customers. They can design special packages for the customers to keep the customers permanently hooked to the company's products and services. P&G is said to have a database of over 3 million customers and all decisions that the company takes are in close consultation with their valued customers. Even new products are developed with involvement and input from this customer base.
- Customization: Instead of selling the same product in a similar fashion to all customers as is done in mass production, focus is on the customization for individual customers as per their requirement. In automobile industry it is

practiced by offering special features and arrangements and many auxiliaries and options.

- Channel members as partners: Considering the channel members as part of the business itself and as partners to deliver better value to final or end customers. Earlier approach was considering channel intermediaries as customers.
- Integrated marketing communications: Instead of relying heavily on one mode of communication, for example, only on TV channels, blending several or multiple options to deliver a consistent brand image to target customers at the point of sales or every opportunity of brand contact.
- Everybody in the organization is a marketer: A change in thinking that marketing is done only by the marketing department, sales department, customer support system, and personnel involved in such functions there is recognition of the fact that every employee must be customer-focused. A recent report in the newspaper that a Coca-Cola truck driver was fired because he was seen consuming the competition product, Pepsi, is a pointer to that kind of new thinking.
- Model-based decision making: A change in the organization's decision making process—from data-based decisions or even on intuition and gut feeling based on limited information to fact-based model for taking prudent business decisions (Philip Kotler 1997: 28).

Brand manager will have to play new role taking into consideration new rules of the game as unleashed by the forces of liberalization and globalization which has been described in this chapter. Throughout this book we will attempt to help brand marketers sail safely through this rough yet very promising business environment ahead. As has been said, successful companies will be those who will change with the change in their own market environment by constantly evolving themselves with the forces of change and with the challenges unleashed by new set of competition.

CHAPTER SUMMARY

In this chapter we discussed what a brand name is and what it communicates, what are its values, and how a name graduates to a brand and ultimately a power brand. Also what it takes for a name to graduate to a brand and a brand to become a power brand and what are the advantages and incremental values that a power brand delivers to the business and its shareholders in terms of significantly higher financial performance and returns. The chapter also deals with understanding the potential of a brand, value of a brand, and how the right value is chosen and delivered. The chapter deals with some of the well-known global brands to discuss their importance and value to the business and how those brands are being managed in challenging environments and how the role of brand managers is increasingly becoming different and more demanding and also how the brand manager's role and responsibility have changed over a period of time as business environment has changed as well as with the various stages of product life cycle. We have then discussed how to build a long-term strategic vision for the brand which a marketer has to manage and then set objectives and tasks to create competitive advantages for the brand to overcome the challenges of new business environment and competition through product innovation and market orientation. There are many examples discussed from real-life market to show how the life of a product and brand gets shortened with new findings and technological changes posing serious threats and new challenges to brand marketers. The chapter also discusses the approaches to become more innovative and market-oriented in order to ensure the survival and growth of the brand and also to ensure the health of the brand in a competitive market environment. Finally, we discussed what it means in terms of managing a brand in the 21st century.

The chapter includes numerous examples and caselets to show how brand managers are now delivering growth in new business environment and how established and well-known brands are facing challenges and losing market share due to the onslaught of new entrants with access to resources.

CHAPTER 3

Building Brand Identity in Challenging Times

Not all brands have a distinctive identity. It needs to be systematically developed and built with conscious marketing efforts over the longer term of the useful life of the brand. As we have said earlier, products do not live forever as they have a specific life span but brands can remain forever if managed properly. Brands, therefore, need to be managed to create a distinctive identity. A few brands, however, are known for their identity—what they are, what they stand for, and what makes them so unique. Advertising campaigns launched to position the brand distinctively in the target consumers' mind may vary from campaign to campaign. But the core value proposition which the brand promises remains the same as long as that chosen position is meaningful, relevant, commercially significant, and delivering the company's objective. However, very few brands have the character which distinguishes itself from the rest with respect to what brands stand for over the longer term. For managing the brand over the longer term it is necessary to give the brand a definite character and identity. In order to understand the basic concept for creating a distinctive brand identity we need to explain what the general term "identity" means in different contexts.

CORE CONCEPT OF BRAND IDENTITY

The concept of identity in relation to brand management can be compared to the many forms of identity that even an individual citizen requires to receive the benefits and services including social securities and other public services to live in this world (Kapferer 1994).

We need to carry our personal identity card which carries the individual's photograph and address and also indicates who he is and what he is along with other personal identification marks which distinguish an individual from the rest. This is something similar to our Voter Identity Card or even Unique Identification Device (UID) or even Smart Card. Brands also need to have specific features which are unique to the brand that separate it from others in the same category (Kapferer

1994). As and when these criteria of identification of an individual change, a new identity emerges. But there is something core to one's identity which makes him distinct which never changes, like his family history, date of birth, finger print, etc., as captured in biometric identification tools (Kapferer 1994). There is, therefore, some core property of an individual which never changes. For managing the brand for longer term thus there will be some core value proposition which will remain the same as long as the brand exists. Brand managers will be required to keep these core characteristics which are intrinsic to the brand intact while deciding specific branding, communication, and promotional as well as marketing strategies and plan for the useful life of the brand and avoid any contradiction to arise in the consumers' minds and toward this end creative execution and brand strategy development has to be carefully selected. For example, Dettol is positioned as an antiseptic and, therefore, its marketer (Reckitt) avoids claiming or describing it as a disinfectant. The difference between antiseptic (protection against harmful germs) and disinfectant (kills germs) is very clear. One protects against infection (antiseptic) and the other kills germs once infected (disinfectant). Dettol thus is distinctively positioned as an antiseptic liquid which protects. The picture of a sword on the Dettol logo is symbolic of protection and in all communication you will find the reassuring statements: "Dettol Protects" and "Be 100 percent sure." Even in television advertisements we can see these assurances which constantly remind consumers about the unique identity of the Dettol brand.

IMPORTANCE OF BRAND IDENTITY

The concept of identity in brand management has become increasingly important in terms of designing and formulating the communication strategies and exercises in a society saturated and bombarded constantly with communications of all kinds. Everybody who has something to offer to their target customers wants to communicate these days in some form or other. Without effective communication a product will not succeed in the marketplace. Before implementing any brand communication plan we need to understand the whole purpose of it and, therefore, should raise the questions: What do we communicate? What is the communication objective? What purpose our communication should serve? Purpose of these communications is basically to create an identity of the brand. Therefore, brand marketers must clearly know what identity they want to create for their brands well before preparing the blueprint of their communication strategy, plan, and actions. Competition has increased manyfold over the years, advertisement budget has also increased to compensate for the increased cost of media and also to cut through the clutter in communication. While marketers are trying with alternative forms of communication, alternative media options, and even alternative marketing channels, it has increasingly become too difficult to survive in the complex and competitive marketing and business environment. Creating differentiated identity for the brand to occupy a unique position in the consumer's mind and hence a unique identity has thus assumed more importance. Creative communication thus is a very important task for the brand managers.

The other reason why brand identity is assuming increasing importance is the constant pressure that is put on brands for similar competitive products appearing in the market with me-too proposition. When brand innovates it sets and creates new standards, other brands then have to catch up if they want to stay in the race.

Besides, technology is responsible for similar products produced through similar technology hitting the market creating identity crisis. Automobile cars are produced with near equal technical performance. Many automobile manufacturers even source critical components like gear box, steering wheel, brake system, or even the engine, etc., from the same source of supply and vendors either for cost or productivity reasons. The products are thus technically same and also similar in performance. In that case intangibles and aesthetic features are required to be exploited for unique position in the customers' minds.

Last, diversification and product line extension also create confusion in customers' minds. Products extending to new geographical areas and penetrating into new customer segments diffuse certain image and influence image and identity distortion. We still can put together bits and pieces and will have difficulty in understanding the global coherent identity of the brand.

KEY QUESTIONS FOR BUILDING BRAND IDENTITY

For giving the brand a distinctive identity we need to get clarity on several issues which include the following:

- The vision and mission, objective, and aim of the brand
- The identified need(s) that the brand can fulfill
- What makes the brand different (differentiated identity or existence)
- The core value(s) that the brand stands for
- Key design features and characteristics that make the brand recognizable and distinguishable
- The permanent character of the brand

These questions constitute the basic character of the brand. Brand marketers normally create an official and approved documentation answering these basic parameters which helps the organizations in addressing all communication issues and thus in better brand management as there must be specific guidelines to ensure that there is indeed one brand forming a solid and coherent identity in the prospects' mind. The official document provides the approved guidelines to brand managers defining his scope and limitations in deciding on new campaigns and promotions as some of these parameters are permanent features of the brand and in some we have the flexibility without compromising the basic character of the brand. Brand identity, therefore, defines clearly what must stay as permanent features and what can be changed.

We cannot overemphasize the fact that we are now living in an over-communicated society or in a society becoming saturated in communications. Everybody wants to communicate today and there are multiple options for communication available. Internet has opened up new avenues of communication and everybody wants to say something to the rest of the world. The availability of products and services is manyfold; more than ever before. Advertisement budgets have increased significantly. There is, therefore, a communication explosion. Communicating these days is no longer just a technique but it is a feat by itself. Creating a brand identity in clutter is, therefore, a big challenge to the brand marketers.

BRAND IDENTITY AND BRAND IMAGE

Identity is what the marketer wants to create and image is what the customer ultimately perceives. Customers may or may not always get the intended perception that brand marketers want to create. Brand marketer wants to specify the brand's meaning, aim, and self-image through various creative executions and communications but the customers may or may not receive or perceive exactly the same image that the marketers want to create. Competitive activities and other extraneous factors and also the effectiveness of implementation are responsible for creating an often distorted image of the brand and the marketer's responsibility is to see to it that the impact of the extraneous factors is minimized, if not totally eliminated. The extraneous factors often come from various situations, for example, when companies don't have a clear idea about what their own brand identity is and then try to imitate competitor's marketing communications. Other reasons include when companies want to create an image which appeals to all segments of the customers and end up creating a diffused image or when companies resort to creating a fantasized identity of the brand as one would like to see it, not as it actually is. These apparent sources of noise only create dissonance in the minds of the consumers. Such communications do not help consumers to remember the brand in its right form and identity because they are remotely connected or drastically disconnected with the core properties and components of brand identity. These extraneous factors should be avoided. Therefore, before consumers receive the various signals we must know what to send and how to send it. Competition in the marketplace is also trying to create hurdles and distortion in whatever brand marketers are attempting to establish and thus dilute or distort the identity that brand marketers want to create. Communication strategies and their creative execution should be powerful enough to cut through these hurdles to establish the intended identity.

Figure 3.1 shows that an ultimate brand image is a synthesis made by the customers of all the various forms of communication that they receive, including brand signals such as brand name, visual symbols including logo, design and styling, color scheme, etc., physical products, advertisements, sponsoring, patronage, promotion, etc. Image is the result of interpretation and decoding various messages and communication, extracting its core meaning and interpreting signs.

Core assets and characteristics of the brand are used to create an identity through creative communication exercises to ultimately form an image in the consumer's mind. Efforts have to be made to create an image in line with the intended brand identity. Schematically it is shown in Figure 3.1.

Figure 3.1 Brand Identity and Image

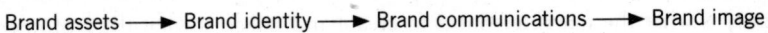

Brand assets ⟶ Brand identity ⟶ Brand communications ⟶ Brand image

MANY FACETS OF BRAND IDENTITY

When competition was relatively lesser and products were few in the marketplace, product's unique selling proposition (USP) was the key concept. But in the current context of global competitive environment, marketers need newer concepts and tools for tackling the new market situation. In order to become strong in the marketplace, a brand must be true to its identity. Identity concept is crucial for reasons like if a brand has to be durable, it should send coherent signs and signals and also has to be realistic. It is the key responsibility of the brand managers to manage this aspect of the brand effectively throughout the useful life of the brand and avoid having any distortion in the identity and the resultant image.

SIX DIMENSIONS OF BRAND IDENTITY

The various facets of brand identity include physique and personality which marketers try to create, reflection and self-image which customers receive as they perceive the marketer's communication and culture and relationship which is the result of usage and experience of the product.

Brand physique and personality are normally conceptualized, created, and communicated by the brand marketer after taking a reasoned decision on the product positioning, target customer, and what brand should stand for in its own competitive set. Marketers have a picture of physique and personality which they communicate but consumers get a reflection and image of the brand depending on the meaning they derive from brand communication. Marketers may even fail to create the intended image corresponding to the identity of the brand.

- **Physique:** Physique is both the brand's backbone and its tangible value and is generally made of the brand's salient objective feature and, therefore, it relies on certain key product and brand attributes. Dettol always has light brown color and is in a glass bottle. Several researches have suggested that consumers have strong association with these basic physical attributes. Whenever an attempt was made to upgrade and modernize Dettol, consumers rejected it. A brand thus needs to remind customers of its roots.
- **Personality:** A brand has a personality of its own. Through constant and creative communication it builds up its true character. The way brand speaks of its products and services shows what kind of person it would be if it were a human being. The easiest way to create instant brand personality is to give the brand a spokesperson, whether real or symbolic. This explains why a famous character or personality representing the brand has become so widespread and well-accepted approach of the brand marketers to establish the brand character. Selection of the personality has to gel with the core value proposition that the brand stands for.
- **Culture:** The brand has its own culture. The product is not only a concrete representation of this culture but also a means of communication. Coca-Cola and Pepsi-Cola are the products of typical American or western culture, whereas Rooh Afza is a product of typical Indian culture. These products when extended to new geographical territory have to transit to become relevant to a new culture. Sometimes brand positioning decision has to take into consideration these issues. Mercedes embodies German values. Even at 260 km per hour, a Mercedes has perfect drive, stability, and handling. Even the surrounding landscape may be whizzing by, but the Mercedes remains stable and unperturbed. The brand symbol of Mercedes further epitomizes this spirit. Other well-known and established global automobile brands also stand for some unique culture of their own. For example, Renault has a cultural tendency to favor human values over others, such as the urge to constantly challenge one's limit (Porsche) or always compete and perform

(BMW). When brand and company bear the same name, corporation's culture gets transferred to the brand it launches. For example, Tata's (an Indian group which has now emerged as global player through acquisition of Tetley, Corus, Jaguar, etc.) culture is what links to the brand of the firm. Brand culture plays essential role in the launch of new products as can be seen from the launch of Bacardi Rum which is white rum with Caribbean cultural setting.

- **Relationship:** A brand establishes a close relationship with its consumers in due course of time. This is more particularly true in case of service sectors such as banking or insurance. In fact service by definition is relationship. Customers on long usage and experience build a relationship with the brand which gradually becomes part of his or her personality. Marketers have to support such relationship and help building it stronger so that a loyal customer base emerges in due course of time. In competitive environment brand marketers find it increasingly difficult to get hard-core loyal customers. Demanding and more knowledgeable customers constantly oscillate among the closely competing brands delivering near equal values.
- **Reflection:** A brand always reflects its customers' image. People always relate brands to the kind of users that they have in mind, which is a reflection of the brand. Thus we have certain brands that are for young people and certain brands that are meant for older people, even for the same product category such as cars, watches, pens, or cosmetics.
- **Self-image:** Brands do speak about our self-image. Through our attitudes toward certain brands we indeed develop certain types of inner relationship with ourselves. In promoting a brand one pledges allegiance, demonstrating both a community of thought and of self-image which facilitates or even stimulates communication.

LEVELS OF BRAND IDENTITY

In order to understand brand identity levels in their proper perspective one needs to closely examine the various facets and dimensions of the brand. A close examination of the brands in the market around us will reveal that a brand has an inner core and an outer cover or envelope that together decide the brand identity in totality. A basic understanding about what the brand stands for, why it has been introduced or produced, what benefits it delivers to its customers, how it is used and what is its core value proposition are, therefore, essential to get clarity as well as a clear understanding of the brand identity.

The brand identity can be more clearly understood if we take an example, say, of LG as shown in Figure 3.2.

Figure 3.2 Brand Identity for LG

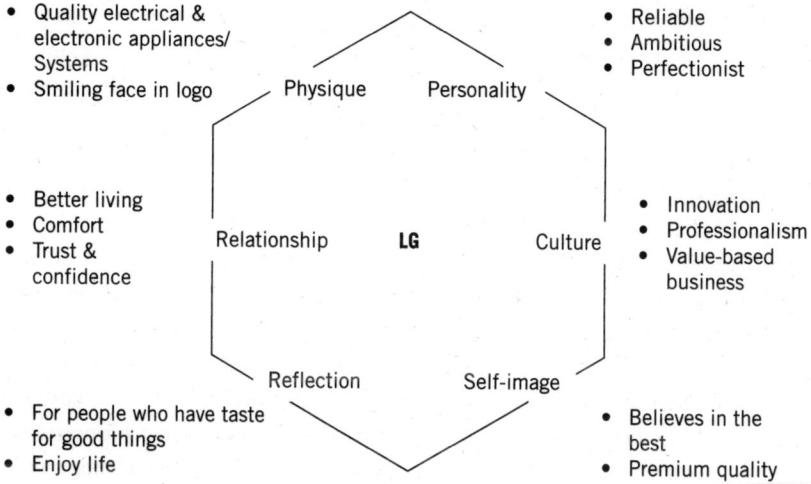

- Quality electrical & electronic appliances/ Systems
- Smiling face in logo

Physique

Personality

- Reliable
- Ambitious
- Perfectionist

- Better living
- Comfort
- Trust & confidence

Relationship

LG

Culture

- Innovation
- Professionalism
- Value-based business

Reflection

Self-image

- For people who have taste for good things
- Enjoy life

- Believes in the best
- Premium quality

SOURCE: Adapted from Kapferer (1994).

MANY LAYERS OF THE BRAND

Inner Core

This represents the central or essential core of the brand and thus can also be called the central theme or identity. The inner core is normally covered or enveloped by many layers of peripheral brand identity elements. It, therefore, indicates the essence of the brand. The core or the central identity will provide the reasons why the brand has been created first of all. In order to have a sustainable brand identity, an analysis of customers' behavior, customers' profile, competition and a critical self-analysis including the company's strengths and weaknesses are, therefore, essential.

What is central to the brand identity can be deciphered by asking the simple question: what does the brand stands for? The immediate answer that comes as top-of-the-mind response may suggest the brand's core. This can be explained by taking a few examples from the commonly known or well-known and established brands of long standing.

- Dettol: An antiseptic and stands for total protection
- Lux: A bathing soap for young and beautiful women
- 3M: Innovation product that improves the quality of life
- Pepsi: A soft beverage that provides fun and excitement
- Nirma: A detergent that provides value for money

The core, central, or inner identity of the brand does not easily change. For successful brands it is all the more essential to protect the central core identity as any diffusion or dilution of the identity will greatly harm the performance of the brand and jeopardize its long-term potential. The physical manifestation and programs supporting the brand may sometimes change but the core is not changed every now and then as it reflects a brand's philosophical angle that deals with the fundamentals of the brand's core value proposition. It should be noted here that a brand's success depends to a great extent on its inner core and central identity. The core identity provides justification as to why the brand was born and has reasons to exist. The questions that need to be answered thus include: What is the essence of the brand? What are its beliefs and basic values? What missions it seeks to accomplish? What is its spirit? Who is behind the brand? What are the organizational values? What are the strengths and capabilities of the organization that intends to promote the brand?

The core identity thus captures the value proposition of the brand? For example, the slogan, "Let's make things better" clarifies the core value proposition of Philips. The driving spirit is just not to make better products but to improve the quality of life of the customer itself. Similarly *General Electric* (GE)'s lighting division captures the brand's core identity through its sign-off caption: "We bring good things to life." This is indicative of saying that GE just don't make lighting bulb and lighting products—these are only the physical manifestation of what the brand stands for and also intends to do. The brand intends to infuse life itself. Cola-Cola for many years ran the campaign saying, "Things go better with Coke." They don't say that they make fizzy soft cola beverages that will quench your thirst and that is only the physical manifestation. The slogan communicates that Coke is for all occasions and not only when you are thirsty, which really extends the horizon and helps the brand grow. Through a brand rejuvenating exercise Britannia coined the new slogan: "Eat healthy, Think better." That Britannia makes healthy products is a physical manifestation of the brand's inner value and core identity. But Britannia brand intends making better thinking people through healthy eating habits. These slogans capture a brand's essence and, therefore, make strong selling propositions and resolve the difficult question: What is the brand intended to be? This has far reaching implications for people behind the brand who are supposed to manage the brand for success.

Cinthol was a successful brand from the house of Godrej. It was positioned initially as a brand giving confidence and the key to it was that Cinthol had deodorants—the source of confidence. The brand was subsequently positioned as a male and masculine soap and popular film stars and other sport personalities like Imran Khan were hired to endorse the brand. Earlier it had a niche position for itself and later on it directly entangled with the successful Liril brand from HUL which was positioned as freshness communicated through its lime associations.

Cinthol then changed its position and started showing new commercial clearly positioning itself as an alternative of Liril showing a slice of lime and waterfalls which were communicated by Liril for years. Cinthol further saw many extensions such as Cinthol cologne, Cinthol lime, Cinthol international, etc. The focus thus shifted from brand's core values to basic ingredients and attributes and the inevitable happened as the brand suffered from the absence of core proposition which guides the consumer to take buying decisions. The brand managers actually did not do their job correctly and their actions made the once good and powerful brand Cinthol very weak and vulnerable.

Outer Core of the Brand

The brand manifests itself as stated earlier through its basic identity elements. These elements include the product itself, the symbol, personality, slogan, endorsers, brand character, users' profile, and packaging. All these parameters together decide and characterize the brand identity. The outer core of the brand, therefore, provides the basic picture of the brand and helps to give it a meaning. The outer core, therefore, suggests what the brand stands for. It is thus the reflection of the inner core. Managing the brand thus requires careful decisions in relation to the basic elements of the brand so that together they depict the cohesive whole of the brand as intended by the inner core. The inner core identity sometimes is too qualitative, philosophical, or even abstract, which may pose difficulty in decoding the brand's intention. And thus it is for these tactical reasons that the outer identity may be used to provide direction and meaning to the brand.

This can possibly be explained by taking an example. The core value proposition of, say, McDonald's is quality, service, consistency, and value. Throughout the world McDonald's restaurants are built to reflect that core value proposition. McDonald's will never compromise in deciding about the outer core elements which will be either in conflict or that might create confusion. The outer elements are designed in terms of products, décor, ambience, style, packaging, service, look, and other basic elements to ensure that they are consistent. Therefore, a brand's outer core dictates what is legitimate and what is not. Only then a complete, comprehensive, and consistent brand is created by organizing these elements in the desired fashion. McDonald's outer core incorporates product scope (the type of products that are offered at the restaurant), personality (family-oriented, middle class, convenience seekers, and fun loving), character (Ronald McDonald), sub-brands (McBurger, McNugget, McDonald Happy Meal). Some of the elements of the outer core of the brand are adapted to suit local market conditions to ensure greater level of acceptability to local customers and their culture but central core is never tampered with. It, therefore, serves as a guide to the efforts for building the brand globally recognizable.

Inner core and outer core together determine the brand value proposition as shown in Figure 3.3.

Figure 3.3   Brand's Inner and Outer Core

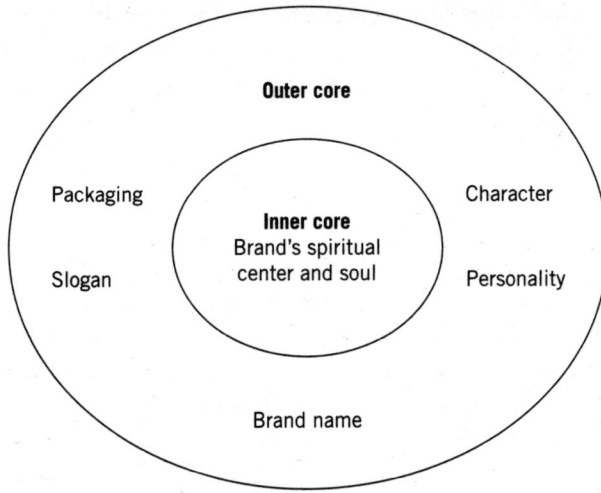

Outer core

Packaging

Character

Inner core
Brand's spiritual
center and soul

Slogan

Personality

Brand name

SOURCE: Adapted from Kapferer (1994).

BRAND POSITIONING

Positioning basically starts with a product, be it a physical product, service, merchandise, a person, organization, or institution. Positioning is what you do with respect to the mind of the prospect.

Al Ries and Jack Trout in their book (1982) on positioning said: "To be successful today, you must touch base with reality. And the only reality that counts is what's already in the prospect's mind. To create something that does not already exist in the mind, is becoming more and more difficult, if not impossible."

The basic approach of positioning is not to create something new and different, but to manipulate what's already up there in the mind, to retie the connections that already exist. But it would be also wrong to assume that marketers cannot try to put something radically different thought, belief or facts which either don't exist in the prospects' mind now or challenges the existing thought and belief. But that exercise is more difficult than to just manipulate what is already up there in the target customers' mind. But whatever we try do, the task of positioning starts with the understanding of the customers' mind with respect to why prospects will buy your products or services in the first place.

Today's marketplace is no longer responsive to the strategies that worked in the past. There are just too many products, too many companies, and too much marketing noise. The changes that are normally made to product formulations, packaging, design, etc., are in real sense to redesign the outer core of the brand to make it suitable to occupy an acceptable position in the prospects' mind.

Positioning has become now a buzzword among advertising, sales, and marketing people. Positioning has changed the way the advertisement game is being played today. In our over-communicated society the impact of advertisement is really very low and many times the message that is communicated gets drowned in many other modes of communication the customers are bombarded with. This is because as Al Ries and Jack Trout (1982) observed, "advertisement is not a sledgehammer. It is more like a light fog, a very light fog that envelopes your prospects." Millions of dollars have been spent trying to change minds with advertisements and once the mind is made up it is impossible to change it again and certainly not simply with advertising only. The average person will still listen to something which he or she has never heard before. And in an over-communicated society a person can absorb only that much communication which can be retained by the mind. When the mind is supersaturated any additional input can find place only when something else leaves the mind, that is, at the expense of what is already there. Thus marketers will have to understand the current beliefs and perceptions of the target customers with respect to a product category or even competing brand(s) and the reason why.

The best way to communicate to an over-communicated society is through over-simplified message. In communication, as we say, less is more. In politics, says John Lindsay, "the perception is the reality." Same is true in case of advertising, in business, and also in life. When customer is always right. And we have no other choice. It thus makes ample sense to focus not on products but on the prospects' mind. And that is the key task of brand marketers today.

The importance of positioning as a powerful concept was realized by the marketers in the 1970s when market started becoming crowded with increased brand proliferation. And the customers realized that there have to be valid reasons for patronizing a particular brand in a product category. It is against this background that a distinctive need has been felt to occupy a unique position in the customers' mind which was later recognized as a powerful tool.

And thus emerged the biggest challenge for the marketer—to identify successful positioning platform for the brand that they were asked to manage, which has significant commercial potential.

The concept of position has its roots in military warfare. B. H. Liddell Hart, a leading military writer and analyst had done analyses of battles that were fought on earth as old as Greek wars and as new as the World War I. From his analyses of 280 attacks which were mounted directly from the front, only six were successful

(Liddell Hart 1967: 67) which means a success rate of only 2.14 percent. The lesson that we can learn is that never position yourself against the strengths of the defender. On the contrary, by positioning against the apparent and identified weaknesses of the leader otherwise, the defender would ensure much higher degree of success. Therefore, as a rule, position must provide relative superiority. Even a superior force will be decimated in no time if they choose to wage an attack from the wrong position. The position analyses is a key to determining the military strategies. Position in battle field refers to the physical space or position that forces occupy relative to their enemy with an objective to ensure success. Whereas in marketing the position is relating to the space in the customers or prospects mind where all players in the game are constantly bombarding and it is a war-like situation there in the marketplace.

Wars begin with the conflict of interest and that could be land, property or from the defense force or even trade interest and conflict political priority, interest, control and compulsions. But in case of marketing the conflict arises out of the race among marketers to win the customers and increase the brand share. Customers normally do not respond to the products or services the way the physical products are offered. On the contrary, they respond to the products, merchandise or services from their own perception about the total product offering. And the positioning is all about ensuring the right perception that marketers want the customers should have. For brand positioning, therefore, one has to use all the inner and the outer elements of the brand that constitute the brand's identity to create the right positioning platform. All these elements, therefore, need to communicate the chosen position through the integrated communication strategies, designs, plans, actions that will be implemented by the brand marketers.

Positioning a brand thus means creating and emphasizing the distinctive characteristics that make it different from its identified competitors and appealing to the public for whom the brand was created. It is very common to distinguish brands according to their positioning. Positioning is a very crucial concept. A product offering will be considered by the customer if it falls into the identified selection process of the potential buyers.

Positioning thus will have to deal with two essential issues:

- In which category the brand belongs
- In what way the new brand is different from other brands available in the same category

Identification of the desired and available positioning platform will result from a careful analysis of the following questions as depicted in Figure 3.4.

Figure 3.4   Positioning a Brand

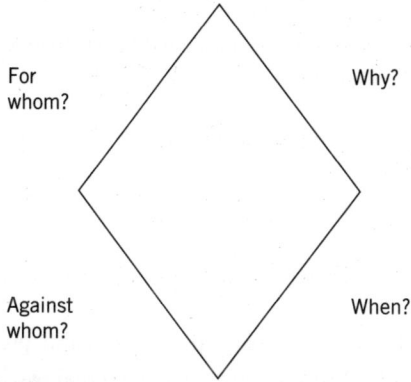

SOURCE: Ries and Trout (1982).

Brand marketer thus has to answer these four key questions—why, for whom, when, and against whom. For answering these questions brand marketers will have to carry out research to understand the consumers mind with respect to the decision criteria corresponding to their identified need for a product category and why one brand in that category is preferred over the others.

Why does brand exist? This is first question that we need to answer and that comes from the basic promise and benefits the brand offers to the consumer. For example, Cadbury's Perk satisfies hunger in between meals.

For whom the brand exists? This refers to the target segment of the consumers to whom the brand is positioned. For example, Coke is targeted for everybody from all walks of life on all occasions. All products cannot have such universal acceptance and, therefore, a target segment needs to be identified based on the product benefits offered.

When is this brand to be used? This refers to the occasion when the product will be consumed. For example, Cadbury's Perk is positioned to be consumed anytime, anywhere whereas Cadbury's Dairy Milk is to celebrate anything, any occasion of happiness, or to start anything new or even new relationships as is revealed in their advertisement message.

Against whom the brand will be compared? In competitive market this refers to the other similar products against whom the brand is positioned or with whom the brand is competing or even intended to compete. Sometimes, marketers through differentiation try to occupy a unique position in the prospects mind but consumers may still compare the brand with other alternative available while making a buying decision.

EVALUATE AND CHOOSE A BRAND POSITIONING PLATFORM

The underlying issues that need to be addressed for evaluating and choosing a positioning platform are the following:

- Is the chosen positioning platform credible? Does our product support the chosen platform?
- Does it capitalize on the competitor's shortcomings and weaknesses including latent weaknesses?
- Is the chosen positioning distinctive, specific and unique? And also is it sustainable?
- Is the identified positioning platform a sustainable proposition that cannot be imitated easily? It is also to be remembered that two brands cannot occupy the same position.
- Does the physical appearance, look, product benefits, pricing compatible with this positioning.
- How strong will be the consumer's motivation for this positioning?
- Is the market size attractive for the chosen positioning?
- Is the positioning platform chosen offer significant economic opportunity for the company?

Let us take the example of a few successful brands to identify the basic tenets of positioning (Figure 3.5).

Many brands fail in the marketplace and are often repositioned if the product is considered to have basic promise. While identifying the brand positioning this aspect should be kept in mind that current positioning will leave any possibility of any alternative positioning in case the current position fails. This exercise is normally referred to as repositioning the brand.

In the marketplace, some brands have a very distinctive and unique position and some have diffused positioning. Obviously, those have diffused positioning will not perform and will not deliver the expected results. Some of the brands which are positioned well are listed as follow:

Dettol	:	Antiseptic
Fair & Lovely	:	Fairness
Close Up	:	Freshness, Confidence
Bisleri	:	Safe
Captain Cook	:	Free-flowing salt
Dispirin	:	Soluble aspirin for faster relief
Aspro	:	Microfine aspirin for faster relief

Figure 3.5 W's of Brand Positioning

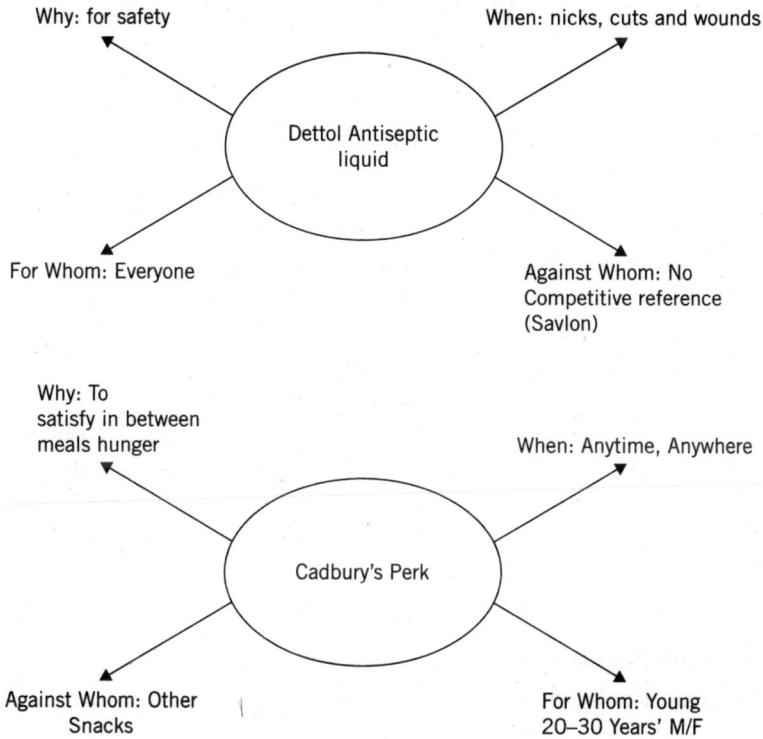

Why: for safety

When: nicks, cuts and wounds

Dettol Antiseptic liquid

For Whom: Everyone

Against Whom: No Competitive reference (Savlon)

Why: To satisfy in between meals hunger

When: Anytime, Anywhere

Cadbury's Perk

Against Whom: Other Snacks

For Whom: Young 20–30 Years' M/F

For identifying a positioning platform several options need to be addressed before taking the decision as all options available will not necessarily deliver the similar performance and results and will not be equally powerful. A biscuit can be either positioned for providing nutrition or even on fun platform or even as a snack item. Which options will be attractive will depend on competitive business environment as well as on significant commercial opportunity of the chosen position.

While core value proposition is never compromised, often brand requires local adaptation to be successful. Because the local cultural issues if in conflict with the total value proposition the brand can run into problem. The following example will illustrate this point how global brands were forced to go for local adaptation in specific market environment in order to be successful. P&G has a range of shampoo in many fragrances and in attractive colors. When P&G introduced their shampoo in Thailand the product did not do well and company was totally confused not really knowing what is the reason until they conducted a research which confirmed the local belief that anything for hair has to be black in color. Local belief is that any color other than black is not good for their hair. It can be noted here that normally hair remains black even in old age for the people in this region and their belief is very strong.

Those who have created a success story definitely were the first to enter the category. They displayed ability to think ahead of others. They innovated and had taken the risk to put the money behind their dream. Success comes to those who dare and dream and act, it seldom favors a timid. To create successful business also one has to be visionary with abilities to foresee what would be the scenario that is likely to emerge in the days to come. Brand managers of today need to have those qualities to create brand that would be sustainable. Only enterprising people can thus become successful brand manager in challenging times.

Let us now take a case to understand how marketers decide to position themselves in the marketplace and as the market environment changes why it is necessary to adjust to the need of changed customers' requirement and also because of the new rules of the game unleashed by the new set of competition. Nirula's is the face of India's first modern fast food restaurant chain successfully operated for over three decades. McDonald, KFC, Domino's, Pizza Hut, etc., came much later and redefined the category. In that scenario how Nirula's reacted can be seen from the following case study.

Case Study: Nirula's Branding Strategies and Product Positioning Background

Established in 1934, Nirula's today are a diversified group having a chain of Elegant Business Hotels, Waiter Service Restaurants, Family-style Restaurants, Ice Cream Parlors, Pastry Shops and Food Processing Plants in India. The chain caters to over 45,000 guests every day.

A modern netizen-friendly Cyberbar with multiple Internet terminal posts and a well-stocked bar serving premium liquors, wines, beer and cocktails, it is a true business-with-pleasure place which is open on all days (except dry days) between 11:00 am to midnight.

Nirula's today is a well-known name in the hospitality industry. Nirula's family was the first to offer western style fast food in India. They came to Delhi in 1928. They realized the paucity of good eating places in and around New Delhi, began 'Hotel India' in 1934 with 12 rooms and a restaurant with a bar license. They also specialized in catering to parties and soon, Nirula's catering became famous.

The Brand's Journey from Early Days

It 1939, while the Second World war had started, Nirula's rented more space in Connaught Circus (what is currently the ground floor of Nirula's, in L-block) and opened a Restaurant with music and dancing, serving a six course dinner for only ₹1 (only 2 cents). The restaurant proved to be popular with both Indian and foreign guests. It also started serving Indian food and introduced ballroom dancing.

Before 1947, Nirula's had also opened the first fruit preservation unit in Delhi. The jams and squash and other preserves were marketed under the name of Nirula's and had an all-India distribution. With the partition of India in 1947, the supply of raw material was disrupted and this unit was closed.

In 1950, Nirula's started the 'Chinese Room' which was the first restaurant of its kind in India. Nirula's created history by being the first Indians of non-Chinese origin to have a Chinese food restaurant in India.

In 1954, Nirula's were the first ones to introduce espresso coffee in India. Georgia, the inceptors of espresso coffee machines gave Nirula's sole distribution rights for their machines and Nirula's have sold these to the luxury hotels and first-class restaurants. Nirula's store was opened in the 1950s with a section for cold meat and delicatessen products and a separate section for bakery and confectionery produce.

Nirula's Hotel was started in 1958 and was the first modern 3-star hotel in India. In 1960 two specialty restaurants were opened. La Bohame was a modern restaurant where tea, coffee, snacks and meals were very popular. It was the most popular restaurant of its time in India. Gufa was an Indian restaurant with Indian-style seating and an all-silver Thali service in a romantic atmosphere.

The Pastry shop was independently introduced in 1972 and did extremely well. The quick-service food business was again ventured into by the opening of the Snack bar in 1972 and Hot Shoppe in 1977, which was instant success. The first Ice Cream Parlor in India was started in 1978. Potpourri restaurant with the first salad bar in India and the Pegasus Bar were started in 1979. All of these exist till today.

Brand Elements

Nirula's brand element consists of the following:

- Logo and Symbol: Nirula's uses the red/white color sequence (having its full name) along with the peculiar font-face that Nirula's has been using for its outlets right from the beginning. This has helped in building Brand Recognition.
- Slogan: *Why CHICKEN out, when you can CHICK-INdian at Nirula's?*: Suggests the Indian non-vegetarian consumer to prefer Nirula's over similar non-Indian non-vegetarian food joints like KFC.
- Tagline: Snacky full-meals...Indian style: Indicates that the meal is Indian, wholesome and can be consumed quickly like a snack.

Brand Identity Prism

The brand identity prism defining the brand values of Nirula's on the basis of some of the parameters can be visualized. It is very crucial for any brand because it gives the brand some factors on which it can relate to its customers' needs plus check on to its performance, i.e., whether the brand is able to deliver what it had promised to its customers. The key factors considered are Physique, Personality, Culture, Self-image, Reflection, and Relationship.

Nirula's Brand Identity Prism can be visualized as shown in Figure 3.6.

Figure 3.6   Brand Nirula's

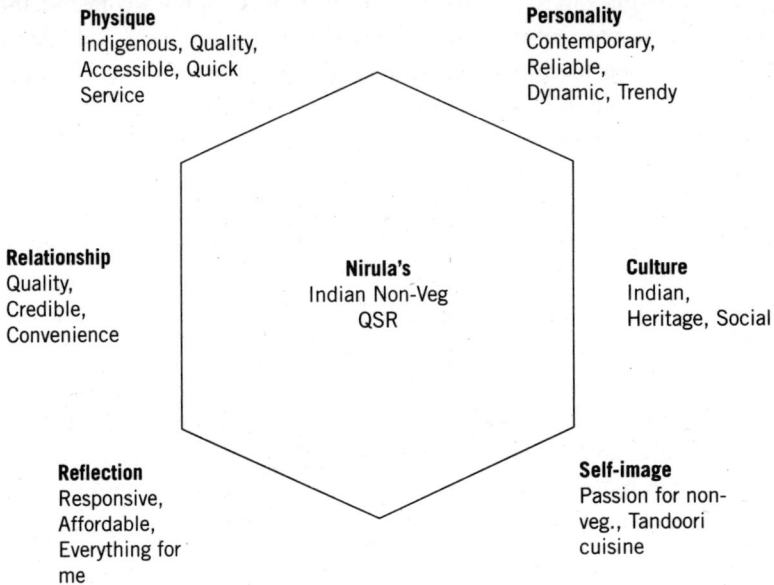

Physique
Indigenous, Quality,
Accessible, Quick
Service

Personality
Contemporary,
Reliable,
Dynamic, Trendy

Relationship
Quality,
Credible,
Convenience

Nirula's
Indian Non-Veg
QSR

Culture
Indian,
Heritage, Social

Reflection
Responsive,
Affordable,
Everything for
me

Self-image
Passion for non-
veg., Tandoori
cuisine

The Expansion of Fast Food Restaurant Business

It was only by early 1980s that Nirula's decided to expand itself. It's first restaurant outside Connaught Place opened at Vasant Vihar in 1980 and soon followed by Chanakya Puri (1981) and Defence Colony (1986).

In 1985 the Central Kitchen, comprising of the first section bulk kitchen, Ice Cream section and the bakery section was opened at Okhla, thus enabling Nirula's to expand faster. Also in 1985, Nirula's opened their first restaurant outside India in Kathmandu, Nepal. Production facilities were also set up. Another followed this in Kathmandu in 1986 and one in Pokhra, in June 1993. Meanwhile Nirula's also took over the management of restaurants at Tej's (in November 1985), Karol Bagh (in March 1986), New Friends Colony (in April 1988), Bungalow Road (in October 1990), East of Kailash (in August 1994), Gurgaon (in January 1998) and Faridabad (in February 1998). Nirula's also set up a unit in Noida, a suburb of Delhi. This unit started with a restaurant in January 1987 and was soon extended to also include a Hotel (March 1991), the first of its kind in India offering the most modern and attractive facilities at very reasonable prices. It also started catering services for the Railways in July 1993 by providing food on the August Kranti Express from Delhi to Bombay. In 1994, a Food Delivery Service was started at L-block, Chanakya and Defence Colony and was soon extended to all the units. Nirula's was the first to introduce in the country services on such a large scale.

In January 1996, a restaurant complex with a large family-style restaurant, Pastry Shop and a Potpourri restaurant was commissioned in Preet Vihar. An "express" Restaurant, where the thrust was on take-away and delivery service, was opened for the first time at Vasant Kunj in March 1996. Another outlet at Bawa Potterries Complex at Vasant Kunj opened in August 1996. Second express restaurant was opened at Rajindra Place in 1997. Two restaurants were opened in Haryana in quick succession—in Gurgaon and Faridabad in 1998. Negotiations are in progress for opening more Hotels and restaurants in and around Delhi and in major metro cities in Northern India. The companies even plan on opening its outlets in Singapore and in South East Asia.

Besides opening new outlets to cater to the ever-expanding market, Nirula's have always believed in expansion and improvement of its existing facilities. It has always welcomed other restaurants stating that the new entrants assist in developing the overall business. Even though a number of new restaurants have started, Nirula's is still the most popular chain of restaurants with highest sales per square foot. They continue to experiment, introduce new items and continue to give the citizens of Delhi and tourists what they desire—excellent quality food at a reasonable and affordable price in pleasant surroundings and such a variety that everyone in the family feels catered to—'Fun Foods for the Whole Family'. Nirula's stands for Quality, Service, Cleanliness and Value for Money.

Competition with Global Brands

The situation changed with the emergence of some of the global brands which have redefined the rules of the game and whole category.

The major competition of Nirula's is with some of the top brand names in the market like McDonald's, Pizza Hut, Dominoe's, Baskin Robbins, KFC, etc. Nirula's is trying hard to sustain itself in this competitive market. But it seems that on several parameters Nirula's is lacking now as compared to its competitors which have positioned themselves as Fast Food Restaurants.

We have conducted a survey with the customers to understand Nirula's position when compared with its competitors on many parameters. The question Nirula's is now facing with respect to its position in the customers mind is: Is Nirula's able to tell its customers that it is associated with fast food?

The key finding from the survey was an eye opener. Customers no longer preferred Nirula's over specialty fast food, western restaurants, thereby indicating the lost ground for Nirula's in the recent years (Table 3.1). Thus, from the result it is clear that Nirula's is lacking its positioning as a specialty fast food restaurants. Its competitors have gone far ahead in the race. Nirula's is a clear fourth choice after McDonald, Domino's and Pizza Hut as fast food joints. The competitions thus are able to push Nirula's product positioning from most favored to almost last in the chain. When new generation fast food restaurants appear as competitions Nirula's was not able to upgrade its typical traditional family restaurants to modern fast foods joints. The décor, ambience, service, and offerings fell short of customers' expectation when they started comparing those coming from Specialty Fast Food Chains like Domino's and Pizza Hut.

Table 3.1   Preferred Place for Fast Foods

Preferred Place to Visit for Fast Food (Rankings 1- Most Preferred 7 - Least Preferred)							
	Barista	McDonald's	Pizza Hut	Domino's	Nirula's	Café Coffee Day	Baskin Robbins
Mean	4.93	2.27	3.2	3.37	4.37	4.1	5.77
Mode	6	1	3	2	4	3	7

SOURCE: Independent academic research by author.

As ice creams have emerged as a fast-growing category with all formats of restaurants pitching for them, it was pertinent to find the level of association of Nirula's within this category. The findings show that Nirula's enjoys second position after Baskin Robbins indicating that as compared to Fast Food, Nirula's has made its customer aware about its association with ice creams (Table 3.2). As in ice cream category Nirula's is still a dominant player it should focus on this category offering and create new innovations and differentiations.

In order to evaluate the synchronization between Nirula's brand image with the services provided by them, respondents were asked to associate the food categories with Nirula's (Figure 3.7). Respondents associated Nirula's with ice creams, Indian snacks and Indian full meals. Burgers, Pizzas are laggards, losers. So, Nirula's should

Table 3.2 Customers' Preference of Place for Ice Cream

Preferred Place to Visit for Ice Creams (Rankings 1- Most Preferred 7 - Least Preferred)		
	Mean	*Median*
Baskin Robbins	1.87	1
Nirula's	3.14	3
Café Coffee Day	3.55	4
McDonald's	4	3.5
Barista	4.45	4
Domino's	5.5	6
Pizza Hut	5.52	6

SOURCE: Independent academic research by author.

Table 3.3 Delivery Attributes Customers Value Most for Their Preferred Fast Food Brand

	Mean	*Mode*
Food Taste	2.43	1
Hygiene	3.25	1
Variety	4.00	1
Price	4.04	2
Service Speed	4.22	6
Ambience	4.54	7
Seating Space	5.32	7

SOURCE: Independent academic research by author.

avoid keeping burgers, pizzas as an option in the menu and should concentrate on adding new varieties in those options which customers look for in Nirula's. This will increase customers' interest in coming to the restaurant as they will get lots of varieties in their favorite food items which they will not get in other restaurants.

Brand Performance and Image

Though Nirula's seems to have failed to establish itself as brand name in the restaurant business, as compared to its new global competitors, it has not

Figure 3.7   What Nirula's Means to Customers

Percentage of People among surveyed who find Nirula's Completely or Mostly Associated

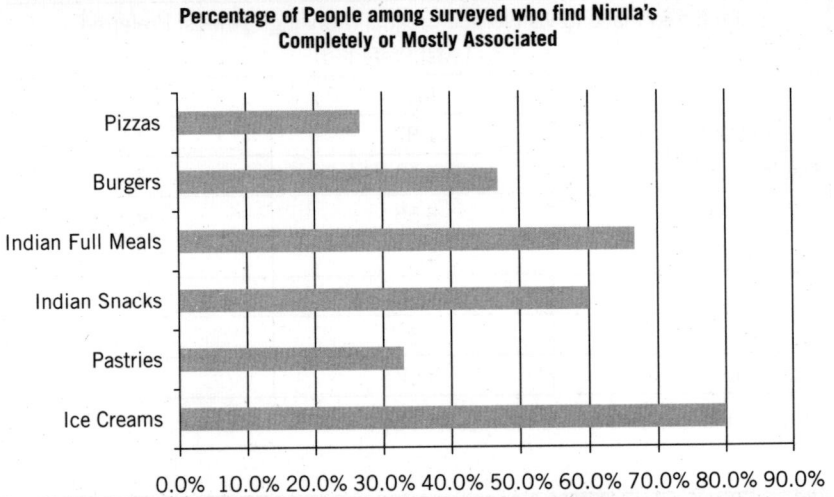

0.0% 10.0% 20.0% 30.0% 40.0% 50.0% 60.0% 70.0% 80.0% 90.0%

SOURCE: Independent academic research by author.

Figure 3.8   Respondents Evoke Strong Imagery

Percentage of Respondents who evoke strong imagery

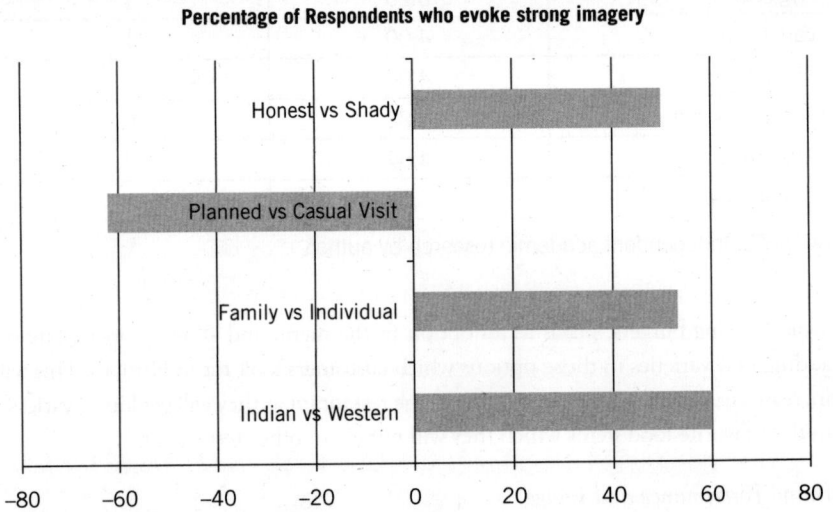

−80   −60   −40   −20   0   20   40   60   80

SOURCE: Independent academic research by author.

compromised on any aspect of performance, be it food taste, hygiene, variety, service speed and quality, ambience, or seating space. This was further validated by the response of the customers toward Nirula's ability to perform on the ground (Table 3.3). It was clear that Nirula's has never compromised with hygiene aspect and also given importance to the varieties keeping in view the competitive market and customers' needs. But the factor at which it loses some of its point is that customer perceived the brand as costly or high-priced brand as compared to the other brands.

In order to gauge the brand image, i.e., what image do people have in their mind when they think of Nirula's, respondents were asked whether they see Nirula's as a family or individual restaurant, Indian or western, casual or planned, etc. This survey brought out the brand image of Nirula's among its customer as being Indian, family oriented, honest and meant for casual visits (Figure 3.8).

However, its efforts to modernize have proved to be unsuccessful. So, according to the survey Nirula's should focus more on being Indian family restaurant, rather than going for fast food restaurant image.

Key Observations

After observing the results of all the above-mentioned survey we can conclude about the current position of Nirula's as a brand as follows:

- Nirula's brand salience enjoys last position among competitors in its category.
- Nirula's brand recall is weak in categories other than ice creams.
- Half of the products on Menu do not generate recall from customers.
- Its brand imagery is not communicated.
- Consumers no longer find Nirula's offering unique nor find its offering relevant.
- Nirula's hardly evokes emotional bonds with its consumers.

New Positioning

The failures on the part of Nirula's in establishing itself as a fast food specialty restaurant forced them to reposition themselves as "Indian Non-Veg Quick Service Restaurant." This strategy of giving the brand a new position was a good step taken by the management, because it was clearly seen through the survey conducted that Nirula's was seen as a family restaurant and is also known for its service quality and speed, so it was a step in the right direction.

The restaurant has all the basic facilities of a restaurant, i.e., the points of parity are: Quality, Hygiene, Quick Service, Consistency, Limited Menu, Limited Table Service.

However, the points of differentiation which could keep them ahead of their competitors were: Authentic Indian Non-vegetarian Food, Home Delivery, and Pickup.

Marketing Mix for New Positioning of the Brand

In terms of marketing mix Nirula's should make necessary changes as suggested below to justify the new positioning platform that they have chosen to occupy. These are:

- Product: Their strategy should be to provide authentic, tasty and quality Indian non-vegetarian food. Small servings, quick service, affordable and consistent taste were some of the other basic points which they will focus on. Also menu needs to be standardized to bring in operational synergies and to focus on items that customers associate Nirula's with as revealed in the survey. Convenience in terms of home delivery and take-aways would support their differentiating elements, for example, dry chicken preparations, mutton boneless dishes, etc.
- Place: They should go for franchise and company-owned food courts in malls, metro stations, airport, offices and marketplaces. Their priority locations should be high-density residential areas in order to increase the number of footfalls.
- Promotion: Aggressive BTL activities like organizing non-vegetarian fiestas, for example, Eid celebrations should be carried out. Print ads in city newspapers. Advertisements in local radio stations, OOH advertisements in metro stations and high-traffic junctions will create brand reinforcement. Value meals, combo offers and coupons should be offered to promote trial, repurchase (retrials) and attract groups on a regular basis. A centralized home delivery system to capture customer data and service them better should also be implemented.
- Pricing: Aggressive pricing will reinforce their claim as affordable family restaurant. This will generate new trials.

It should also take care of the facts and issues where there is a gap between delivery and customers' expectations. This is essential for them, because if they do not identify the gaps and conduct a gap analysis, they would be wasting their resources in a wrong direction and at the end never achieve a successful position in the market and eventually fail to create the required brand image in the mind of the target customers.

Geographical Expansion Strategy for Future

Nirula's should focus on Tier II cities. It should start from Tier II South Indian cities (65 percent non-veg.) and subsequently move upwards Launch Indian non-veg. QSR first for creating category associations and penetrating new markets supported with promotional activities. It should somehow try to focus more on ice creams, etc., because customers related Nirula's with ice creams.

CHAPTER SUMMARY

In this chapter we discussed the core concept of the brand identity and the importance of the brand identity and then went on to understand the key questions that we need to raise with specific brand in order to decide what image we need to create for the brand exploiting the many facets and dimensions and key attributes of the brand identity. The image that consumers get is the ultimate perception on the brand based on the marketers' creative execution of the integrated communication exercise exploiting the core identity elements of the brand. It is thus not the identity that we create but image that consumers perceive or get based on what brand marketers do and what competitors do to nullify what brand marketers wanted to create. Brand has inner core and outer core and there are several levels of the brand identity which we discussed. Brand identity has several dimensions which have been explained by taking numerous examples from the well-known brands in the marketplace.

The chapter then takes up the core concept of brand positioning and its importance in brand marketing. The core elements of brand identity will help us to understand what are the many possible positioning platforms that brand can decide or choose to occupy depending on the opportunities available, competitive positioning platforms and the brands core value proposition. The chapter discusses how positioning options are identified, evaluated for market opportunity and finally decided based on which entire brand marketing plan is designed and executed.

The chapter then discusses a real life case study based on the survey conducted on the case to explain some of these core concepts. The example discussed will help readers know how brand positioning platform can become irrelevant when new competition arrives and in that situation what actions brand marketers should take. The chapter has cited numerous examples to drive the core concept of brand identity, brand image, brand positioning, and their relationships.

CHAPTER 4

Building Brand Equity in Fiercely Competitive Environment

THE BASIC CONCEPT

Brand marketers and advertising agencies have been arguing for quite some time now to convince others that brand should be considered as the most valuable asset for a company. Businesses have realized that when product differentiation amongst various options is narrow, it is the brand that becomes the most influential for switching the buying decision. As the competition increased the concept and importance of brand became increasingly clearer. The better and stronger brand can, therefore, improve the financial prospect of the business. Brand value can be leveraged to enhance the financial performance of the business. This realization is a recent phenomenon. It is as late as early 1990s that it became clearer that the brand is much more than just an identity and product differentiator. Brand is really an asset. It is this financial angle of the brand that led to the new concept of brand equity.

Brand equity is the financial value of the brand. The core issue on the brand equity debate is: how brand can deliver much superior value to its owner as well as to its customer and also how this equity can be protected and enhanced as this would be perhaps the most valuable asset for any business over longer period of time. In the earlier phase of the evolution of the brand management concept in the 1970s and in the early part of 1980s businesses were valued based on sales and profits. Firms making small profit were worth very little. All this has changed during the later part of 1980s when there was a big wave of takeovers, mergers, and acquisitions in the international business arena. In the Indian context that wave came much later and we saw major acquisitions and mergers only during post liberalization in the 1990s. During 1980s in India the major acquisitions were Dunlop (an automobile tyre manufacturing brand in India), Shaw Wallace (in alcoholic beverages and in FMCG business) by Manu Chabbria of Jumbo Electronics, Dubai, and Vijay Mallya of United Breweries (UB) group, respectively. UB group acquired many breweries and distilleries during that period. In the post-liberalization period the number of such acquisitions increased dramatically. Even most of the multinationals which entered Indian market during that time preferred acquisition of the Indian businesses and brands. In 1970s and 1980s businesses were acquired for their physical assets like plant and equipment. But in 1990s businesses were acquired mostly for their brand value. When businesses were acquired primarily for their brand value, there was an increase in multiples of price earnings ratio when the target company had well-known brands. The realization then dawned on many CEOs and finance directors of businesses that the value of a brand is a distinctively different concept from the net income of the business.

Since then the buzzword has been brand equity. That followed the work of many agencies to report brand awareness, perceived value of the brand, and top-of-the-mind awareness of the brands, etc., for scores of domestic and international brands. Although accounting standards are yet to be framed for valuing brands, the acquirers followed their own methods for ascertaining the value of the brands as it is seen that some of the brands changed hands at unbelievable prices. Brook Bond acquired Kissan brand from UB group and then Hindustan Lever acquired Brook Bond. Hindustan Lever also acquired Dollops ice cream brand from Cadbury and Lipton brands during 1990s paying huge price for those brands. In fact the entire growth of Hindustan Unilever (HUL) was the result of those series of acquisitions. HUL did not succeed earlier in their attempt to create success stories in food business which is Unilever's major business category globally. Through a series of acquisitions of food businesses HUL has now a significant presence in food category. Brook Bond and Lipton are, of course, the results of international acquisitions.

Brand equity as we understand today is thus the financial value of the brand. Marketer's task is to improve upon the brand equity by converting brand assets to brand equity. Brand assets are the combination of brand awareness, brand image, perceived quality, evocations, familiarity, liking, and their association and impression in their customer segment, etc. These assets finally result into the delivery of the added value to its customers as perceived by them from the use of the brand. And to create that added value perception there is a cost involved which can be termed as cost of branding including the cost of the invested capital that has gone behind brand-building exercise which when subtracted from the added value perception attributable to the brand alone, we get the brand equity. This can be represented by the following equations:

Brand Equity = Brand Asset − (cost of branding + cost of invested capital)

Brand Asset = Brand awareness + Brand image + Brand's perceived quality + Evocations + Familiarity, Liking, Emotional Bonding, etc.

Brand asset is the added value that is perceived by the consumers. Brand's financial value (brand equity) will thus be brand asset minus cost of branding and cost of invested capital.

Brand equity thus would be measured by various parameters including the price that the brand can fetch in the marketplace in competition against other brands positioned against it which can be attributed to the brand itself. Added attraction and customer loyalty the brand has, are other measures of its equity. Studies have shown that brand value can be leveraged to improve the financial performance of the brand. However, to what extent brand image or assets can be leveraged depends upon the business and economic environment in which the brand operates. It has been seen that as competition increases and as there is increased level of consumer education, the ability of the brand to demand more premium decreases. Therefore, in the 1990s we have seen that better and superior brands could demand much higher price premium but the scenario is not the same in later years. This is depicted in Figure 4.1.

Figure 4.1 Leveraging Brand Equity

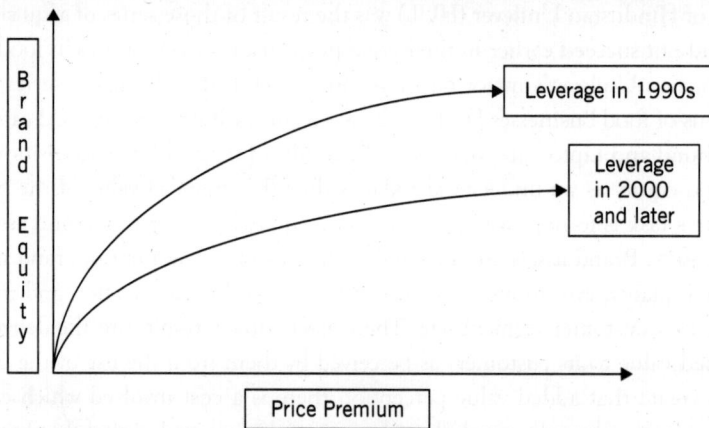

SOURCE: Kapferer (1994).

In a fiercely competitive market, brands, and even established brands, are under pressure. As consumers are becoming more and more knowledgeable and as they have many choices from offerings from equals, getting price premium is becoming extremely difficult and, therefore, possibility of leveraging the brand equity has become significantly reduced in later years than in the early part of 1990s during the post-liberalization era when fierce competition had just started.

To build brand equity in the competitive environment has thus become a big challenge for the marketers in view of the fact that building strong brands has been shown to provide numerous financial rewards to the corporations and thus has become a top priority for many organizations.

To understand the total set of values inherent in the brand and how they are delivered from the customer's perspective, we need to collect and collate various data related to brand imagery, brand performance, and brand communication.

Brand is the source of significant value that the product can fetch in the marketplace. Brand equity is thus directly linked with the quantum value the brand adds to the product. Marketers are increasingly recognizing the importance of brand equity and leading marketers have expressed various kinds of opinion on the subject, some of which are listed below which will help to clarify the basic concepts on the subject:

"Brand equity can be measured by incremental cash flow from associating the brand with the product" (Farquhar 1989).

"Broadly stated, brand equity refers to the residual assets resulting from the effects of the past marketing activities associated with the brand" (Rangaswamy et al. 1990).

"Brand equity is a set of brand assets and liabilities linked to a brand, its name and symbol, that add to or subtract from the value provided by a product or service to a firm and or to that firm's customers" (Aaker 1991).

"Brand equity is the added value that is attributable to the brand name itself which is not captured by the brand's performance on functional attributes" (Sikri 1992).

"Brand equity can be thought of as the additional cash flow achieved by associating brand with the underlying product or service" (Biel 1992).

"Brand equity consists of differential attributes underpinning a brand which gives increased value to the firm's balance sheet" (Chernatony and McDonald).

"Brand equity is defined in terms of marketing effects uniquely attributable to the brands—for example, when certain outcomes result from the marketing of a product or service because of its brand name that would not occur if the same product or service did not have the name" (Keller 1993).

"The brand 'equity'—The total accumulated value or worth of a brand; the tangible and intangible assets that the brand contributes to its corporate parent, both financially and in terms of selling leverage" (Upshaw 1995).

"Brand equity as the totality of the brand's perception, including the relative quality of products and services, financial performance, customer loyalty, satisfaction and over all esteem towards the brand. It is all about how consumers, customers, employees and all stakeholders feel about the brand" (Konapp 2000).

In essence, all these authors have been saying that brand equity is that added value which the customer attaches to the brand. Brand equity can thus be broken down into several components of the brand as shown below:

Brand Equity = Brand Awareness (perceptual esteem + knowledge + stature) + Brand Association (differentiation + relevance which is brand strength) + Brand Premium Price.

Brand Awareness: It is the perception or image about the brand. It relates to how liked the brand is (esteem) and how well the brand is known (knowledge). For example, the brand, International Business Machines Corporation (IBM) might communicate such images as "high quality," "high priced," "latest technology," "largest company," "highly reliable," etc., depending on the market segment. The sum of these associations is called brand image.

Brand Association: Does the customer feel that the brand offers something unique? (differentiation). Or does the customer think that the company is capable of giving him/her what he/she needs? (relevance).

Brand Premium: How much more does the customer think the brand is worth than other competing products and brands in the same segment with similar technical specifications and features? For example, Kleenex has very high awareness but no perceived differentiation; that is why the customer never insists that he must use only Kleenex branded tissue, although he might refer to any tissue as a Kleenex.

Brands which have very high differentiation factors are typically growing brands. Also when esteem is greater than knowledge then the brand is healthy and growing. For example, all MP3 players have a high relevance factor but iPods occupy a differentiated position in terms of perception of uniqueness in the customer's mind. This reflects in Apple's superior financial performance in the portable MP3 player category.

The qualitative attributes which affect brand equity can thus be shown as in Figure 4.2.

Only certain parts of the overall image actually increase or reduce demand for the company and its products. Those are really brand equity elements, the subset of brand image that everything being equal, positively or negatively shifts demand. Positive equity elements allow a company to charge higher prices or win more sales at the same price than a competitor with a similar product and a weaker brand.

If the same bottled carbonated beverage is shown to customers in the unbranded form, with a local brand name and then as Coke (Coca-Cola) and consumers are asked to indicate what they are willing to pay for the product, the price indication when it is Coke will be significantly higher even though product is same. This incremental value is totally attributable to the brand itself.

Figure 4.2   Qualitative Attributes Which Affect Brand Equity

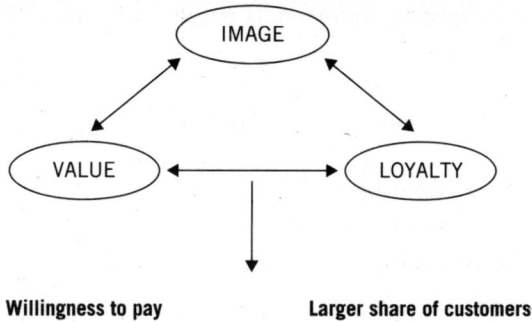

Willingness to pay   Larger share of customers

SOURCE: Aaker (1991).

BRAND IMAGE

The image attributes are:

- Aspirational value
- Publicity—PR and word of mouth
- Familiarity and recognition
- Association
- Fun
- Popularity
- Current user's profile

The perception is at both the company (corporate) brand level and at the product brand level. Some corporate (company) brand-related attributes are:

- Trust and ethical issues
- Reputation and integrity
- Corporate social responsibility
- Company's products and technology

These image attributes are ranked to get an "Image" score. The image score will help marketers to understand the leverage potential of the brand.

BRAND LOYALTY

It takes a long time for the company to create a loyal set of customers and consumer franchise which is a result of sustained marketing effort supported by the quality product offering with unique features and benefits and customer service to create unique experience at each touch point.

Ability to retain existing customers is largely experiential. These attributes include:

- Level of satisfaction after using the product
- Loyalty
- Commitment to repurchase
- Recommendation and advocacy
- The quantity consumed

Loyal customers tend to use the product more than casual customers. The loyalty or attributes to retain customers are again ranked to get "Loyalty" score. The degree of loyalty offers the leveraging potential.

BRAND VALUE

How much more are you willing to pay because of the brand name? The relevant attributes that will determine include:

- Quality
- Originality and uniqueness of the product
- Accessibility
- Convenience
- Courtesy (in product/service delivery)
- Creativity
- Brand personality

One method of measuring value is the brand/price trade-off method. In essence, this is a simple conjoint analysis. This is accomplished by setting up choice situations for respondents where, at the first level of choices, all prices are equal across brand names. The only basis for choosing among brands is the psychological association one has with a given brand name. We expect the customer's first choice to be his/her favorite brand. But as the price increases in relation to other brands, we can witness how many customers are willing to pay a premium. That is, we can quantify how "Immune" a brand might or might not be to increases in price. This allows us to scale their loyalty for the brand in the context of a reasonable range of prices and create an overall index. The loyal customers are expected to be willing to pay certain amount of premium for the chosen brand as long as price value equation is favorable in the sense that customers consider value of the brand in overall terms still higher than the price he or she is willing to pay.

Brand equity will thus depend on a set of qualitative as well as quantitative attributes some of which are mentioned below.

Other qualitative attributes which affect brand equity:

- Practicality
- Ability to evolve
- Innovativeness
- Fashion quotient or hypeness
- Communication consistency
- Relevance to social issues
- No compromise with the quality and performance
- Lifestyle choice and social status
- Benchmarking ability
- Brand image
- Brand vision
- Ethics

Quantitative attributes that contribute to brand equity:

- Market share
- Product growth rate
- Industry growth rate
- Operating profit margin
- Market capitalization
- Advertising spend
- R&D spend
- Capital employed
- Historical costs
- Stock market price trend
- Market value to book valuation
- New product launches including product variants
- Innovation made

It is the responsibility of the brand marketers to work and prepare the brand marketing plan and execute such plans so that the brand equity always and progressively improves with time. Otherwise, brand manager will fail in discharging his responsibility toward the business and the brand he is entrusted to manage.

It can be mentioned here that all these qualitative and quantitative attributes will not have similar impact on the brand equity. Some of these attributes will have much larger impact than others will have. The more important measures of the equity, therefore, lie on brand performance like market share, growth rate, operating profit, and advertising spend, etc.

Typical measures of the performance of the brand would thus be the following:

- Growth in market share
- Growth in sales in real term (volume growth as opposed to growth through price increase)
- Brand pricing (can brand fetch a premium price over its nearest competitors and still grow)
- Growth in profitability

This would normally mean brand's top line and bottom line growth keeping the marketing support in line or higher than the industry category average spend in relation to competition. The brand which has higher market share should have necessarily higher equity.

The matrix in Figure 4.3 illustrates the relationship between brand equity and market share:

Figure 4.3   Brand Equity and Market Share

BRAND EQUITY (High)	➢ High brand equity & low market share ➢ Equity under leveraged ➢ Investigate in store conditions	➢ High brand equity & strong market shares. ➢ Strong brands
BRAND EQUITY (Low)	➢ Weak brand equity & low market share ➢ Growth opportunity	➢ Weak brand equity & strong market share ➢ Valuable, build brand equity
	Low ⟵———————————————⟶ High	
	MARKET SHARE	

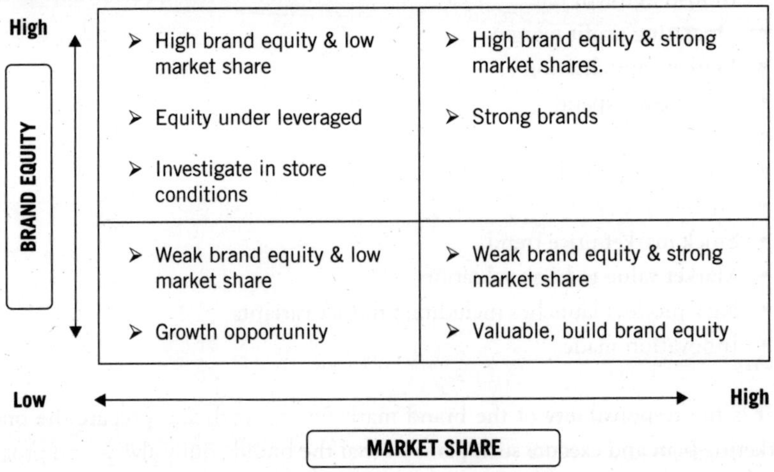

SOURCE: Adapted from Aaker (1991).

There are companies with high brand value, medium brand value as well as low brand value. Examples of companies with high brand value as a percentage of total value will include Nike, Coca-Cola, Nokia, Disney, McDonald's, and Mercedes. Examples of companies with medium brand value as a percentage of total value will include Microsoft and IBM and examples of companies with low brand value as a percentage of total value are GE, Intel, and Marlboro. In India brands with high brand value will include P&G, Unilever, Nestle, Reckitt Benckiser, and Tata; medium brand value will include Parle, Britannia, ITC, Kingfisher, and Godrej and low brand value will include Birla, Dabur, and Marico.

Strong brands with strong equity help to build profitable business in terms of increasing shareholder value. Table 4.1 will illustrate this fact.

Table 4.1 The Contribution of Brands to Shareholder Value

Company	Brand Value in $bn in 2002	Brand Contribution to Market Capitalization of Parent Company (%)	Brand Value in $bn in 2001
Coca-Cola	69.6	51	69.0
Microsoft	64.1	21	65.1
IBM	51.2	39	52.8
GE	41.3	14	42.4
Intel	30.9	22	34.7
Nokia	30.0	51	35.0
Disney	29.3	68	32.6
McDonald's	26.4	71	25.3
Marlboro	24.2	20	22.1
Mercedes-Benz	21.0	47	21.7

SOURCE: *Business Week*, Interbrand/JP Morgan league table, 2002.

There are models to show the sources of the brand equity and the outcome of the brand equity. One such relationship on the outcome of sources of brand equity is shown in Figure 4.4.

From this diagram it is evident that the sources that drive brand equity are brand awareness and other considerations and factors that are associated with it will definitely lead to a certain outcome which helps to build the shareholders' value and wealth.

Figure 4.4   Sources and Outcome of Brand Equity of Winning Brands

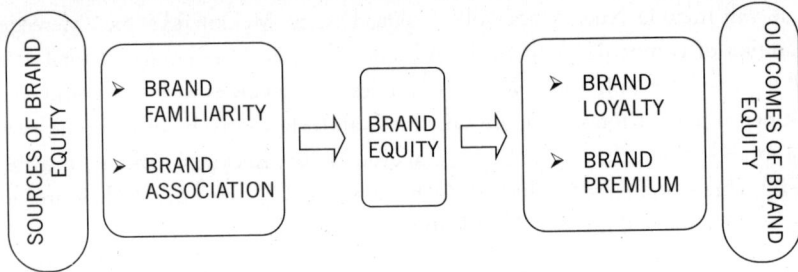

SOURCE: Nielsen (2001).

This is the methodology developed by A. C. Nielsen. In contrast to the attitudinal approach to the brand equity measurement embodied in other approaches, "Winning Brands" begin from a behavioral observation of brand equity.

Brand equity is measured in terms of a customer's frequency of purchase and the price premium paid. Once favorable behavior is observed, the methodology seeks to analyze the attitudinal characteristics of those customers. Key intangible assets of a brand can significantly change the physical performance of the brand in the marketplace. Some of these intangible assets are more important in terms of their influence of buyers' buying behavior than others.

Four broad categories of intangible assets that support the superior market performance of businesses are:

- Knowledge intangibles: These could be patents, software, recipes, specific know-how including manufacturing and operational guidelines and manuals, product research including product trials data, information databases, technology, customer database, etc.
- Business process intangibles: These include unique ways of organizing the business including innovative business models such as Dell's flexible manufacturing systems and techniques, supply chain configuration, multilevel marketing, direct marketing, etc., which provide significant advantage over competition.
- Market position intangibles: These can cover retail listing and contracts, distribution rights, licenses such as landing slots, production or import quotas, third generation telecom licenses, government permits and quotas and authorizations, certifications, etc., raw material sourcing contracts at preferential rates, exclusive rights and contracts with certain market segment, etc.
- Brand and relationship intangibles: These can include trade names, trademarks, trade symbols, domain names, design rights, trade address, packaging,

copyrights over associated colors, smells, descriptors, logotypes, advertising visuals, written copy, and other associated goodwill such as general predisposition of individuals to do business with one brand rather than another brand.

BRAND EQUITY MODELS

Lot of work has been done on the issue related to determining the equity of a given brand. We thus have several models of brand equity. There are organizations such as Young & Rubicam specialized in reporting the brand equity of select brands on a regular basis. There are even proprietary models being used for brand equity to understand the value of a brand in a given time. Essentially they capture select dimensions which determine the equity of the brand as described above. We will discuss the select brand equity models in this chapter.

EQUITY BUILDER MODEL

Equity builder explicitly addresses how brand equity translates into perceived value and price. This model essentially considers the key elements of brand assets which can be directly co-related with the perceived value of the brand and hence the price premium. These key elements can thus be called as brand asset valuator. This is illustrated in Figure 4.5.

Figure 4.5   Brand Asset Valuator from Young & Rubicam

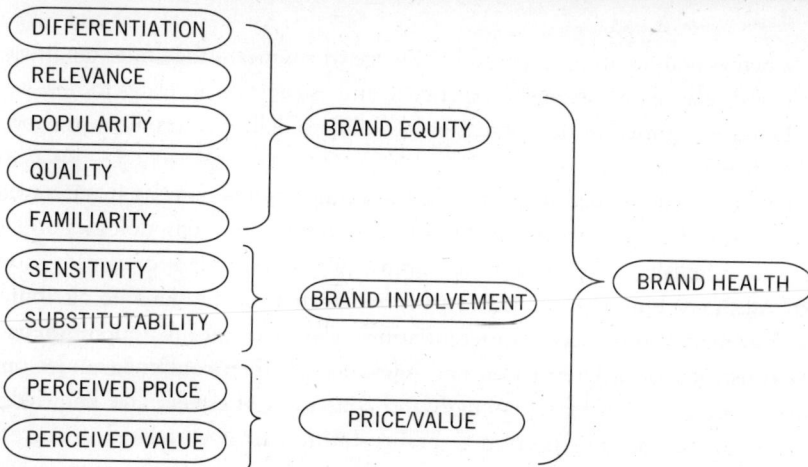

SOURCE: Equity Builder Model (based on 48 image attributes).

BRAND ASSET VALUATOR MODEL

Brand asset valuator from Young & Rubicam takes into account two broad parameters of brand asset. These are:

- Brand strength
- Brand stature

Brand strength is determined by how unique the brand is in relation to its competitive sets and also how relevant and appropriate the brand is in relation to its requirement of the users group which can be depicted in Figure 4.6.

Figure 4.6   Brand Strength

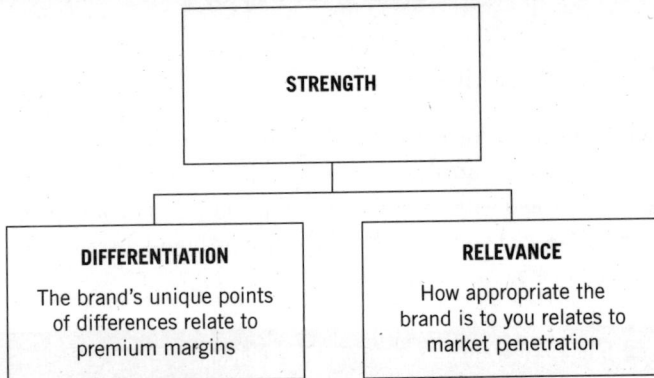

Whereas brand stature relates to knowledge which means the understanding of the brand relating to customers' experience and esteem which relates to how well the brand is regarded in the context of its ability to deliver its promises as shown in Figure 4.7.

The model developed by Young & Rubicam is noteworthy as it rejects the category-specific approach taken by other brand equity methodologies and it seeks to establish a pure measure of brand equity independent of category context. All 2,500 brands in its U.S. survey are related on the same 48 attributes and four macro constructs of differentiation, relevance, esteem, and knowledge. The constructs of differentiation and relevance are then combined under one criterion or matrix of brand strength and constructs of esteem and knowledge are combined into one criterion as brand stature that is correlated to current market share.

Figure 4.7 Brand Stature

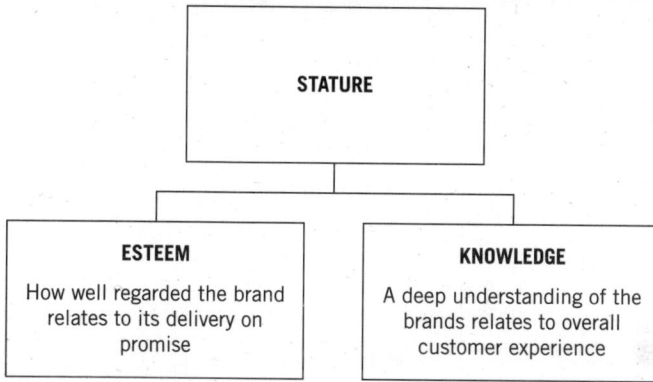

KEVIN LANE KELLER MODEL (CUSTOMER-BASED BRAND EQUITY MODEL)
==

The approach of this model considers that brand is a blend of the rational and the emotional attributes measured in terms of performance characteristics and imagery as shown in Figure 4.8. This model provides a comprehensive means of covering important branding topics as well as useful insights and guidelines to help marketers set strategic direction and also helps in taking key decisions related to brand marketing.

According to the Kevin Keller model, building a strong brand involves four steps: (i) Establishing the proper brand identity, i.e., establishing breadth and depth of brand awareness, (ii) creating appropriate brand meaning through strong, favorable, and unique brand associations, (iii) eliciting positive and accessible brand responses, and (iv) forging brand relationships with customers that are characterized by intense, active loyalty. Achieving these four steps involves establishing six brand-building blocks, namely brand salience, brand performance, brand imagery, brand judgments, brand feelings, and brand resonance. The most important brand-building block, brand resonance, occurs when all the other brand-building blocks are established. With true resonance customers express a high degree of loyalty to the brand and they thus interact with the brand and also share their experiences with others. Firms that are able to achieve brand resonance should be able to derive many benefits such as greater price premiums and more efficient and effective marketing programs.

The customer-based brand equity model of Keller provides a yardstick by which brands can assess their progress in brand-building efforts and also guides the marketers on the kind of research initiatives that they should undertake. (A set of

Figure 4.8   Customer-based Brand Equity Pyramid

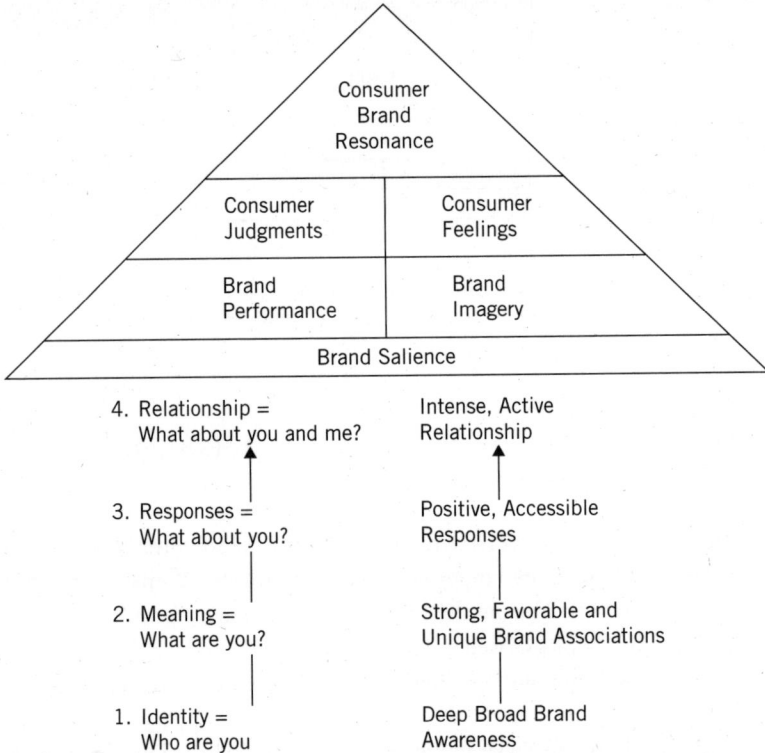

```
                    Consumer
                     Brand
                   Resonance

         Consumer              Consumer
         Judgments             Feelings

          Brand                 Brand
        Performance            Imagery

                Brand Salience
```

4. Relationship =   Intense, Active
   What about you and me?   Relationship

3. Responses =   Positive, Accessible
   What about you?   Responses

2. Meaning =   Strong, Favorable and
   What are you?   Unique Brand Associations

1. Identity =   Deep Broad Brand
   Who are you   Awareness

SOURCE: Millard Brown.

measures for the brand-building blocks as suggested by Kevin Lane Keller is given in the Appendix.)

The four basic steps that are proposed by Keller have to be accomplished in sequence, which means that each step is contingent upon the successful completion of the previous step and as such each step involves accomplishing certain objectives with the customers, both existing and potential. These four steps represent a set of fundamental questions that customers invariably ask about brands. These are:

Who are you? (brand identity)

What are you? (brand meaning)

What about you? What do I think or feel about you? (brand responses)

What about you and me? What kind of association and how much of a connection would I like to have with you (brand relationships).

As Keller said, there is a sequence in this "brand laddering" process which means that meaning cannot be established unless identity is created and responses cannot occur unless the right meaning has been developed and finally a relationship cannot be forged unless proper responses have been elicited.

BRAND-BUILDING BLOCKS

Keller has provided some structure to understand the four steps of the brand equity development process which can be considered as basic "brand-building blocks" as shown in the brand pyramid (Figure 4.8). Creating significant brand equity will thus involve reaching the pinnacle of the pyramid and will only occur when the right brand-building blocks are in place. Corresponding brand steps representing different levels of the pyramid are illustrated in Figure 4.8 while Figure 4.9 examines the various sub-dimensions of brand-building blocks.

As mentioned earlier, creating right brand identity requires creating brand salience which relates to aspects of customer awareness of the brand. To what extent has

Figure 4.9   Sub-dimensions of Brand-Building Block

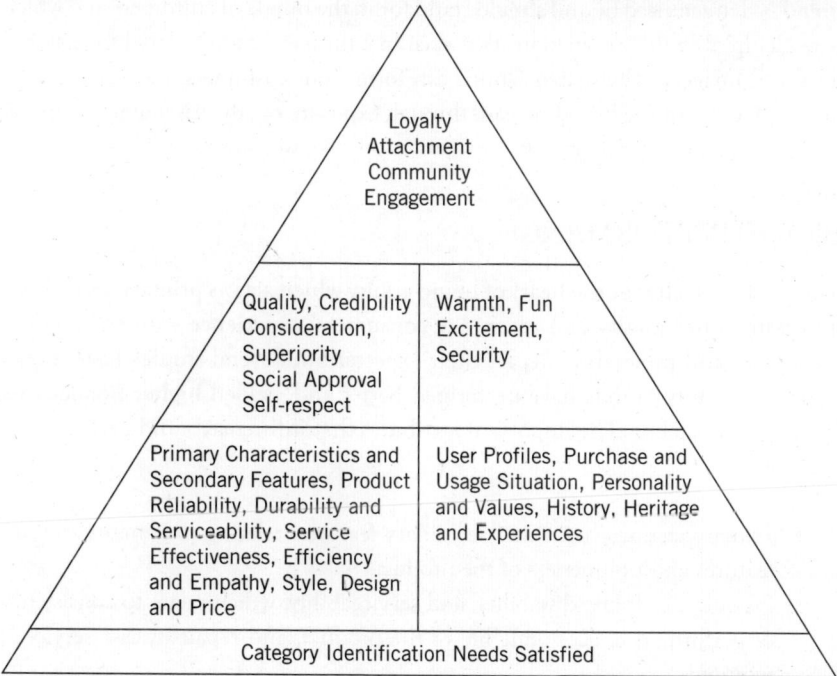

Loyalty
Attachment
Community
Engagement

Quality, Credibility Consideration, Superiority Social Approval Self-respect

Warmth, Fun Excitement, Security

Primary Characteristics and Secondary Features, Product Reliability, Durability and Serviceability, Service Effectiveness, Efficiency and Empathy, Style, Design and Price

User Profiles, Purchase and Usage Situation, Personality and Values, History, Heritage and Experiences

Category Identification Needs Satisfied

SOURCE: Kevin Lane Keller.

the brand top-of-the-mind awareness in customers' minds and how easily the brand is recognized and recalled and how pervasive is the brand awareness? Brand salience thus forms the foundational building blocks in developing brand equity and thus provides three important functions. Firstly, salience influences the formation and strength of brand associations that makes the brand image and meaning. Secondly, salience influences the likelihood of the brand being in the consideration set while making purchase decisions from a very handful and selected brands. Thirdly, for a low involvement category customers may make choices based on the brand salience alone. For example, in mosquito repellent category consumers might take decisions based on only brand salience.

Brand awareness can be distinguished in terms of two key dimensions, namely, depth and breadth. Depth means how easily customers can recall or recognize the brand and breadth refers to the range of purchase and consumption situations in which the brand comes to mind. Thus a highly salient brand is one that possesses both depth and breadth of brand awareness.

BRAND MEANING

Creating brand meaning involves establishing a brand image meaning—what the brand is characterized by and should stand for in the minds of customers and which is made up of brand associations that exist in customers' mind related to performance and imagery. These associations can form from customers' own experiences and contacts with the brand or even through exposure of advertisement communications and also other forms of communications like word of mouth.

BRAND PERFORMANCE

The product itself is at the heart of brand equity which acts as primary influencer. To create brand loyalty and resonance consumers' experience with the product must meet and preferably surpass their expectation. Several studies have shown that high quality brands have performed better and yielded higher financial returns on investment. The important attributes that influence brand performance include:

- Primary characteristics and secondary features, relating to benefits and key features and uniqueness of the products
- Product reliability, durability, and serviceability, which relate to consistency of performance, economic life of the product, and repair in case service is required

- Service effectiveness, efficiency, and empathy, which relate to complete satisfaction of the customers with the service, speed, and responsiveness. Service empathy refers to the extent to which service providers are seen trusting, caring, and having the customers' interest in mind.
- Style and design—would go beyond the functional properties including looks, feels, sounds, and smells, etc.
- Price—this is most important in the sense that price has to be commensurate with the value of the brand as perceived by the consumers and the position that brand occupies in the consumers' minds.

BRAND IMAGERY

The other types of brand meaning will involve brand imagery which normally deals with the extrinsic properties of the product or the service including the ways in which the brand attempts to meet customers' psychological and social needs. Many different types of intangibles can be linked to a brand such as:

- User profiles: Who uses the brand, their mental or demographic profile. Is the brand "popular" or a "market leader?"
- Purchase and usage situations: Where the product is available—department store, grocery store, supermarkets. When and under what circumstances product is being used or recommended to be used by customers.
- Personality and values: Five dimensions of brand personality that are identified are: sincerity (down-to-earth, honest, wholesome, cheerful, etc.), excitement (daring, spirited, up-to-date, imaginative, etc.), competence (reliable, intelligent, successful), sophistication (for example, upper class and charming) and ruggedness (tough).
- History, heritage, and experiences: Brands may take on associations and events of the past, experiences of friends and peers including personal experiences.

Brand associations that make up the brand image and meaning can be characterized and profiled into the following dimensions:

- Strength: How strongly is the brand identified with brand associations?
- Favorability: How valuable is the brand association to customers?
- Uniqueness: How distinctively is the brand identified with brand associations.

To create brand equity it is important that the brand has strong, favorable, and also unique brand associations in that order. Only uniqueness is not enough if customers do not evaluate the association favorably. It can be pointed out here that not all strong associations are favorable and not all favorable associations are unique. Creating strong, favorable, and unique associations is a real challenge to brand marketers but it is essential to create customer-based brand equity.

BRAND RESPONSES

Brand response is how customers respond to the brand which can be distinguished according to the brand judgment (rational) and brand feeling (irrational). Brand judgment will be dependent on the following:

1. Brand quality: Depends on the perceived quality of the brand.
2. Brand credibility: This refers to the extent to which the brand as a whole is seen as credible in terms of perceived expertise (competent, innovative, and market leader), trustworthiness (dependable, sensitive to the interest of the customers), and likeability (fun, interesting, and worth spending time with).
3. Brand consideration: Consideration is more than awareness of the brand and it depends on how personally relevant customers find the brand is, i.e., to the extent they find the brand appropriate and meaningful for themselves.
4. Brand superiority: This relates to the extent to which customers view the brand as unique and better than other brands in the consideration set. Do customers think that this brand offers significant advantages over the other brands available.
5. Brand feelings: It is the emotional response of the customers toward the brand. These feelings can be mild or intense, positive or negative. These feelings arise out of:

   - Warmth: refers to soothing feeling.
   - Fun: refers to amused, joyous, lighthearted, playful, cheerful, etc.
   - Excitement: relates to the extent customers feel they are energized, cool, sexy, etc.
   - Security: feeling of safety, comfort, and self-assurance (removes worries).
   - Social approval: feeling positive about the reactions of others to them.
   - Self-respect: this occurs when brand makes consumers feel better about themselves—a feeling of sense of pride, accomplishment, or even fulfillment.

As Keller observed, first three are experiential and immediate, increasing in level of intensity. The latter three are more private and enduring, increasing in level of gravity.

BRAND RELATIONSHIPS

Brand resonance refers to the nature of the relationship that the customers have with the brand and to the extent that they think that they are "in sync" with the brand. Brand resonance can be broken down into four categories, namely:

- Behavioral loyalty: Relates to how often customers purchase the brand and how much quantity? The brand must generate sufficient purchase frequencies and volumes.
- Attitudinal attachment: Only behavioral loyalty is not sufficient for resonance to occur. Some customers might buy only because of necessity as that is the only brand stocked or available. A customer with a great attitudinal attachment to a brand might even really love the brand.
- Sense of community: Identification with a brand community may reflect an important social phenomenon whereby customers feel a kinship or affiliation with other people associated with the brand.
- Active engagement: It occurs when customers are willing to invest time, energy, money, and other resources into the brand beyond the money spent on purchase or consumption of the brand. For example, customers may like to join club of the brand like say "opal users group club" or visit website of the brand and provide useful suggestions and comments to the marketers.

Brand relationship can be characterized in terms of intensity and activity. Whereas intensity refers to the strength of the attitudinal attachment and sense of community or loyalty toward the brand, activity refers to how frequently the consumer buys and uses the brand as well as engages into other activities not related to purchase and consumption or in how many other ways loyalty manifests into consumer behavior? A good example of brand resonance will be Harley-Davidson or even Apple.

It is essential to recognize that the power of the brand and its ultimate value to the firm resides with the customers. It is the knowledge about and experiences with the brand over a period of time that they end up thinking and acting in a way that allows the firm to reap the benefits of brand equity. But marketers have the responsibility to design and implement the most effective and efficient brand building and marketing programs and the success of those programs depends on how consumers will respond which in turn will depend on what impression and knowledge about the brand marketers are able to create in consumers' mind. Even strong brands must engage continuously in brand-building activities to enhance their equity.

MILLARD BROWN'S BRAND DYNAMICS MODEL

This approach characterizes the relationship that a customer has with a brand into one of the five stages: presence, relevance, performance, advantage, and bonding, Only presence would mean that customers have only a basic awareness of the brand while "bonded" customers are intensely loyal, at least in their attitudes. The underlying premise is that the lifetime value of customers increases the higher up they are in the pyramid as shown in Figure 4.10.

Figure 4.10   Customer Relationship with the Brand

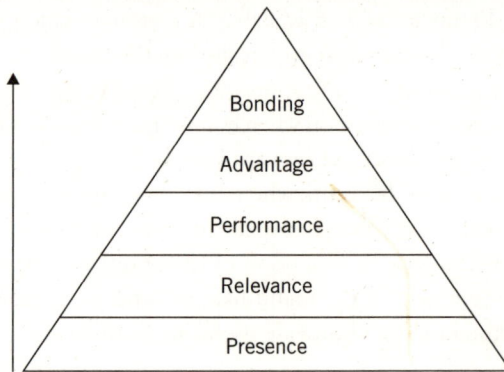

All these models and approaches suffer from the fact that they are attitudinal in nature and have yet to establish the definitive relationship between measures of attitudinal engagement and/or loyalty and observed behavior. This means do customers actually end up doing what their attitudes suggest? This may not always happen in reality. Customers sometimes react and display impulsive behavior as well. It is not appropriate to assume that customers will always display rational behavior.

Marketers have to try relentlessly to build the equity of the brand by designing and implementing the basic building blocks of brand equity. This requires long-term vision of the brand and a clear understanding of the environment in which it operates. The example of Kao Corporation of Japan discussed in this section will illustrate the point.

RELATIONSHIP BETWEEN VARIOUS MODELS

Kevin Keller customer-based brand equity model was designed to satisfy five main criteria such as comprehensive, cohesive, well-grounded, up-to-date, and actionable. But as explained and discussed here, there are several other industry models of brand equity like Young & Rubicam's Brand Asset Valuator and Millward Brown's Brand Dynamics model. However, there is a close relationship between these three industry models.

The four pillars that make up the foundation of Young & Rubicam's Brand Asset Valuator model can be directly related to the aspects of the CBBE model: (*i*) Differentiation (Superiority), (*ii*) Relevance (Consideration), (*iii*) Esteem (Credibility), and (*iv*) Knowledge (Resonance). Similarly, the five sequential stages of Millward Brown's Brand Dynamics model—Presence, Relevance, Performance, Advantage and Bonding—can be related to the four ascending steps of CBBE model, namely, Identity, Meaning, Responses, and Relationships and specific CBBE model concepts such as Salience, Consideration, Performance or Quality, Superiority, and Resonance.

Research International's comprehensive brand equity model called Equity Engine has two key factors, namely, affinity and performance with affinity composed of three dimensions and three sub-dimensions: (*i*) authority (heritage, trust, and innovativeness), (*ii*) identification (bonding, caring, and nostalgia), and (*iii*) approval (prestige, acceptability, and endorsement). As can be seen, each of these dimensions and sub-dimensions can also be directly related to the components of CBBE model of Kevin Keller and in that sense it subsumes concepts and measures from each of the three other industry models and provides additional substance and insight. It should be noted that although these models provide the blueprints for brand building, suitable editing and refinement might be required for the specific needs of the users.

EXAMPLE OF KAO CORPORATION

Kao Corporation is Japan's leading FMCG company competing with multinational corporations like P&G, Unilever, and Colgate. CEO's own vision for the company is:

"Eventually there will be a few players operating on a global scale and we should be one of them."

Motoki Ozaki, President and CEO

Vision of Kao Corporation

We aim to be a "global group of companies that is closest to the consumer/customer in each market," earning the respect and trust of all stakeholders and contributing to the sustainable development of the society.

Kao Corporation is, therefore, committed to deliver customer and consumer value. Kao executives are trained to get their fingers dirty, to learn from the real world and not to rely on research reports and sales data analyses only. Kao strongly believe that they must be confident that they really understand the market and consumer before they undertake any development of new product.

Their product development principles are:

- Each product must be useful to society
- It must use innovative technologies
- It must offer consumer incremental value
- Each product must be compatible with the trade
- Company must be confident that it really understands the market and the consumers well.

Table 4.2   The Market Share of Kao Products

Product Category	Market Share (%)
Liquid Bleach	65
Softeners	55
Body Shampoo, Facial Foams, Laundry Detergents	40
Sanitary Napkin, Kitchen detergents	35
Diapers	33
Shampoos	20
Toilet Soap	15
Toothpaste	10

Kao Corporation attempts to deliver value across business functions to unearth incremental value for the consumers. For example, Kao corporation's production is wholly automated. Like typical Japanese corporation they have large research and development staff working on product development. Twenty-five percent—2,000 out of 8,000 staff members are working in the R&D department. Also four of the top six executives are scientists. Artificial intelligence is used for management information system (MIS) which helps them to deliver orders within 24 hours to any of their 300,000 retailers across the country. Table 4.3 will give a snapshot view of the competitive comparison.

One can see that in all parameters Kao have been achieving better results in relation to its competitors.

Table 4.3 Comparative Performance of Kao Corporation in Japan

Key Indicators	Kao (%)	Colgate (%)	P&G (%)
Cost of Sales	51	57.5	62.5
Operating Income	7.2	7.7	9.5
Interest Expense	0.6	2.3	1.8
Inventory as a Percentage of Total Assets	9.5	19.6	14.3
Debt/Equity	1.3	1.8	1.6
R&D/Sales	4.3	1.5	2.9

CHAPTER SUMMARY

Here we discussed the core and basic concept of brand equity and then explained the qualitative as well as quantitative attributes of brand equity with examples. The core elements of the equity builder are covered in the chapter to understand how equity is built and nurtured. Brand equity is the real measure of brand value and, therefore, can greatly influence the performance of the brand in the marketplace. In this chapter we discussed the relationship between market share and brand equity. There are many models for determining the brand equity and some of those are even proprietary models used by well-known consultants on the subject. We discussed some of the better known brand equity models to explain the process of building brand equity. A case study explains how brand marketers are creating incremental values in business and delivering those for the benefit of its identified consumers and customers in order to ensure superior performance in a fiercely competitive environment.

CHAPTER 5

Branding Strategy and Brand Extension

World Organization for Industrial Property defines brand in legal terms: "a symbol serving to distinguish the products or the services of one company from those of another." Thus globally brand has two primary functions:

- To distinguish different products from each other
- To indicate a product's origin

But when a company starts growing, realizing both the objectives simultaneously becomes difficult. A brand's character helps us in the following:

- To identify and recognize the brand
- To guarantee the brand
- To give brand a durability
- To differentiate from the rest and also personalize

Brand-building strategy has to be carefully crafted to create brand equity in a cluttered market. Creating a new brand takes lots of resources and, therefore, a good brand with high equity offers opportunity to extend into other related products.

Brand extension is the use of an established, well-known, and high-performing brand in a new product category or even subcategories. While an established brand name can be extended to a new product which is either related or unrelated to the parent brand, some ground rules have to be followed in order to create a successful extended range of products under one established brand. Strategically it is important to extend a powerful brand to a related category of products but one can still find that a renowned and well-known brand has helped an organization to launch products in new categories successfully. For example, Nike is a well-known brand for sports shoes. And it has been extended to soccer balls, basketballs, golf equipments as well as to sunglasses. Whereas soccer balls, basketballs, and golf equipments all fall into the category of sports goods and hence a related category, sunglasses are a lifestyle product. If the rub-off benefits of the parent brand have to be derived, product extension category has to be chosen carefully. In this case Nike sunglasses also have to be positioned, marketed, and promoted as sports accessories which a stylish sportsperson will prefer to wear. However, extension to completely nonrelated categories can create many problems and even do harm to the brand image of the parent brand. If the customers of the extended categories have values and aspirations synchronizing those of the core business and if those values and aspirations are embodied in the brand, it is likely to be accepted by customers in the extended categories as well.

Sometimes businesses take decisions to extend a popular and established brand to nonrelated areas and they suffer. Kingfisher is an established beer brand and a market leader in its category, well ahead of its nearest competitors. United Breweries group under its current chairman was nurturing the ambition to get into many other businesses including technology business and thus thought it relevant to change the company logo to UB group (instead of United Breweries group which relates to brewing only) and in subsequent years extended its flagship brand, Kingfisher, to aviation industry whereas United Breweries also started UB Air earlier but failed. Started with great fanfare and positioned as premium class airlines at affordable price—"king class flying experience at affordable price"—Kingfisher Airlines did not work. Today Kingfisher Airlines is in fact in great financial difficulty. The news items that appear about Kingfisher Airlines stating that nobody wants to fund them at this stage and that the company has been forced to ground most of their aircrafts, being unable to operate them, only bring negative influence and image to such a powerful beer brand. Even if Kingfisher had succeeded in its venture of extension to airlines, the question would have still remained about the impact it would have had on Kingfisher beer brand. One can, therefore, debate whether this was a right decision and what was the compulsion to extend Kingfisher beer brand to airlines.

WHY BRAND EXTENSION

It requires huge resources to create a brand. In today's environment it is even costlier. The success rate of new products is also low. Extending an existing brand involves much less cost and, therefore, an organization can try and launch new products in their search for new success stories and grow faster. Failure rate of new brands and new launches is very high. Also, it has been observed that the rate of success of brand extensions is much higher than the new brands. Brand extension has several advantages:

- Introducing a new brand is very costly and time consuming
- Introducing a new brand will delay new product launch
- Failure rate of new brand is higher than the extended brands
- Ever rising cost of advertisement increases the cost of launching new brand
- Brand extension gives access to an accumulated image capital of the parent brand

- Trade confidence of an extended brand is higher and hence easier to get the shelf space in retail universe
- Extending the brand enables the reinforcement of the image capital of the brand and fuels its growth
- Brand extension enables the brand to break away from the mono product
- Launching cost of new brand is much more than that in case of brand extension
- Brand extension reinforces the confidence in the parent brand

Classic concept of brand is:

1 Brand = 1 Product = 1 Promise

However, for a product which has very high potential it is better to give a new brand name rather than extending an existing brand name. It is better that we extend the brand name to products which have synergies and fit in with the parent brand. Extending to nonrelated products often leads to failures. Also, it diffuses the image and position of the parent brand. Brand extension is a good strategy if there is a typical fitment and complementarity with the parent brand and product. Normally, a successful brand can become a candidate for extension as there would be a rub-off effect on the extended categories which will greatly improve its success potential. Choosing the right brand extension is thus critical to the creation of a successful category. The points that need to be taken care of are:

- The perceived quality of the brand
- The impression of transferability of know-how from the category of the parent brand to that of the extension
- The degree of perceived complementarity between the original product and the extended product
- The degree of perceived substitutability
- The perceived difficulty in manufacturing the extended product and also whether it sounds credible

Choosing the right brand extension is also important from the point of view that failure of the extended product is likely to have negative impact on the parent brand.

LIMITATIONS OF BRAND EXTENSION

Although successful brand offers significant opportunity for extension to related and synergistic product lines, it cannot be done mindlessly. Extension also has some limitations. These are:

- Too much extension may create diffused image for the parent brand
- Should not be extended to the nonrelated product
- Brand extension is not the right strategy for a high-potential product

BRAND STRATEGY DEVELOPMENT PROCESS

Depending on the type of company, strategy formulation is done. For example, for a global company the strategy has to be partly global and partly local as a global company is often required to adjust to local conditions. Whereas for a local company strategy has to deliver the local business objective.

Company's current performance also needs to be ascertained. The company could be a profit-making company or a loss-making company or even having a mix of profit- and loss-making divisions. And the strategic imperatives would be different for different levels of current performance. Division-wise branding strategy would thus be different.

Before undertaking the task of strategy formulation one needs to understand also business issues covering:

- To what extent the business can absorb shock
- How long can a loss-making business be supported. The various options could be:
  - As long as one can afford without reducing the profit objective of the core business
  - As long as the project is good and there is scope for growth
  - As long as technology is relevant

Brand strategy development process starts with a detailed portfolio analysis to understand the portfolio priority in order to create the long-term brand vision. From brand vision we derive brand objective and strategy. This is, therefore, an organizational decision and not left to the brand manager himself to decide as these decisions have long-term impact on business. Brand manager has to involve the corporate management who represents the key stakeholders in this exercise. Schematically this can be shown in Figure 5.1.

Businesses have to take critical decisions with respect to their product portfolio in terms of their long-term imperatives and priorities regarding business growth strategies to assist brand management team to build branding strategies. In that respect some of the key decision areas would be:

- Retaining and nurturing profitable businesses. Sometimes profitable businesses are also divested if they are nonstrategic

Figure 5.1 Brand Strategy Development Process

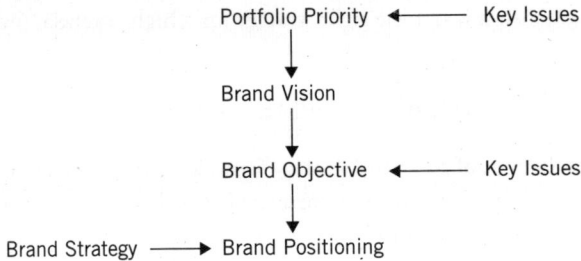

```
         Portfolio Priority  ◄──────  Key Issues
                  │
                  ▼
          Brand Vision
                  │
                  ▼
         Brand Objective  ◄──────  Key Issues
                  │
                  ▼
Brand Strategy  ──►  Brand Positioning
```

- Core business and noncore business. How long is the noncore business to be retained
- Whether the business is profitable or sick will determine what kind of strategy will work in the organization. Signs of sickness will include not healthy, skipping dividend, making losses, continuing to incur losses, eroding net worth of the business, 50 percent of the firm's net worth eroded.
- Portfolio analysis on profit, growth, technology, and competency
- Extending product life cycle of a declining product, occasionally done to generate cash to support star brands. Reckitt used to skim Robinson's Barley to generate only cash profit without any support as the business was nonstrategic
- Introducing new product and innovation. If your company is technology-based it can survive only on innovation

Brand vision is a qualitative statement which embodies the long-term aspiration of what we are striving to make the brand become. Brand positioning statement must complement the brand vision in that it should provide the rationale for the brand's existence from the consumers' perspective. It is also critical that brand positioning provides competitive superiority.

Objective must be strategic in nature affecting longer-term health of the brand. All objectives must be SMART (Specific, Measurable, Aggressive, Resourced, and Time-Scale) and brand strategy has to be developed to deliver superior value to the target consumers.

Strategic objectives of the brand have to be clearly known to identify key strategic options. Related key issues, their measurements, and key imperatives should also be clear.

Let us clarify what these terminologies mean:

- Objective: What we are seeking to achieve
- Strategy: How we can achieve that objective

- Key Issues: Which of the brand's key issues will be addressed by this strategy
- Key Tasks: Major activities which need to be undertaken
- Measurements: Targets, method of measurements and time-scale
- Implications: Known key implications of the proposed strategy

For all new strategic initiatives there will be some element of risk. One has to therefore, carry out risk assessment in terms of risk affordability, minimizing the risk, risk avoidance, and finally a risk mitigation strategy as nothing can be done in business which will not have an associated element of risk. Avoidance of risks of all forms will thus drastically reduce the scope of doing any substantial and meaningful activities within the business for growth and prosperity.

Depending on the kind of value that brands deliver, they can be classified as:

- Parity Brands: Brands that offer similar values in comparison to their own competitive set. Most of the generic products fall into this category where product innovation is difficult.
- Inferior Brands: Brands offering lesser value or even suffering from competitive disadvantages.
- Mismatch Brands: Brands that offer value not in line with the customers' need.
- Overpriced Brands: Brands that offer superior value but at a higher sacrifice.

The key brand-building elements are required to be measureable, meaningful, likeable, transferable, adaptable, and protectable and brand managers should choose the right brand-building strategy to build on these key elements.

After a careful examination of all these key elements covering business health, business priorities and issues, portfolio analysis, individual brand vision and objectives, resources available and how they can be allocated, and risk associated with it, the brand marketer comes to brand strategy decision regarding whether to go for:

- Brand extension
- Line extension
- Multibrands, or even
- New brands

POTENTIAL OF BRAND EXTENSION

There are various factors that can determine the potential of a brand which is a candidate for extension. These are:

- Define and measure the current "brand equity" for the parent brand
- Determine what images, attitudes, and associations are most critical to driving current equity
- Determine the degree to which the product's current equity is transferable to other potential categories
- Identify and sort the strong from the weak extension possibilities in terms of overall business potential

Ultimately, an "equity transference and business potential" map would be created to show which concepts are most likely to carry the core brand name well, and the overall sales potential for each. Dettol is a popular brand with very strong equity. One can plot business potential and equity transference to see how well the fitment would be for various products if those have to be launched under Dettol brand name. This has been shown in Figure 5.2.

Figure 5.2   Brand Extension Map of Dettol Antiseptic Liquid

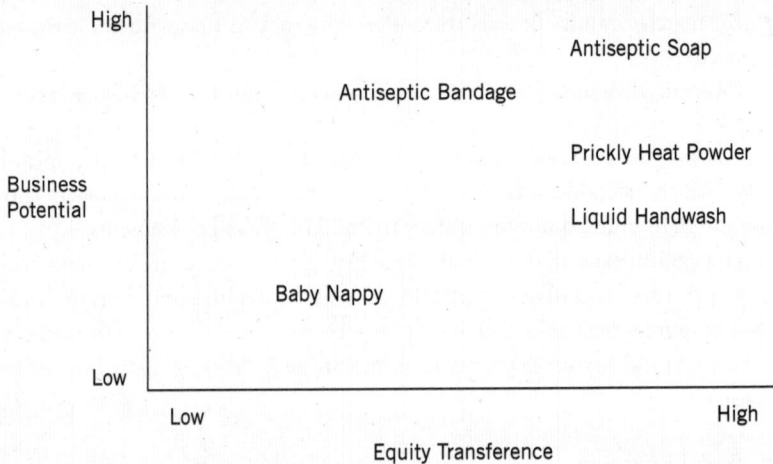

SOURCE: Adapted from Kapferer (1994).

STRATEGY DECISION AREAS FOR MARKETERS

Marketers have broadly four Ps to focus on, namely, Product, Place, Promotion, and Price (marketing mix). The different sub-elements under each of these four Ps is enumerated in Table 5.1.

Table 5.1	**Decision Areas for Strategic Action**		
Product	*Place*	*Promotion*	*Price*
Physical goods, Service, Features, Benefits, Accessories, Quality level, Installations, Instructions, Warranty, Product lines, Packaging, Branding	Objectives, Channel types, Market exposure, Kinds of middlemen, Kinds of location of stores, logistics, Recruitment of channel partners, Managing channel	Objectives, romotion blend, Sales people (kind, number, selection, training, motivation), Targets, Advertising (kinds of advertisement media types, prepared by whom), Sales promotion, Publicity, etc.	Objectives, Flexibility level over product life cycle, geographic terms, Discount, Allowances

SOURCE: Adapted from Kapferer (1994).

The success of a brand in a competitive environment will depend upon four Cs, namely, Customer, Cost, Convenience, and Communication. The decision area under four Ps will have to address four Cs in order to satisfy customers' need by providing benefits and values better than the competition.

Overall brand objective could cover a wide range of areas such as market share, growth, product line objectives including new product development and upgrades, communication objectives, distribution and financial objectives, pricing and profitability. And the strategy formulation will thus cover:

- Product strategy
- Advertisement strategy
- Promotion strategy
- Pricing strategy

BRAND BUILDING IN LOW INVOLVEMENT CATEGORY

There are many products in the market which are purchased by consumers based on only their functional attributes. It really does not matter which brand he or she has bought as long as it delivers the expected results and performance. Generic products normally fall in that category. A typical example can be household insecticides. There are many brands including multinational brands like Mortein (from Reckitt), Hit (from Godrej), All Out and Raid (from SC Johnson), Maxo (from Jyothy Laboratories) and a host of other brands competing in the market for a share of the huge market that exists. Although marketers have been trying to position their brands identifying some differentiated platform based on the intangibles but these products are basically the same, produced from similar ingredients and dosage form using similar technology. This is also a low involvement category as it does not matter which brand is used as long as it delivers the promise or the typical benefits that the product is supposed to deliver and in this case it is either driving away, killing, or destroying insects such as mosquitoes, flies, and cockroaches. Only when it fails to perform these duties that the consumers will think of a brand switch from the consideration of quality failure of the product. So even after using a mosquito repellant cream, if mosquito bites then there will be a case of product failure. But buying decisions were not taken from brand image point of view. Pricing, therefore, is very important for this type of product which is basically a low involvement category.

The crucial issue in a low involvement category is to find or identify a cognitive frame of the consumer. The other factors which will help in creation of a success story include:

- Must get the membership in acceptable set of brands. This means as long as your brand is perceived as same or as good as other acceptable brands in the same category it should work for you.
- Must seek superiority in one or two important attributes. For example, Mortein claimed to be better than other competing brands in terms of strength (power) and effectiveness.

Brand marketers are, therefore, constantly trying to find some important attributes which will help them to claim superiority amongst other brands available in the same category. Some examples will clarify the same. These are:

- Revive: Instant starch
- Cibaca: Angular toothbrush
- Kiwi: More wax
- Disprin: Soluble aspirin for fast relief from pain
- Ujala: Only four drops needed (*Chaar boondon wala*)

For making brands successful we need better brand strategy reflecting competitive situation and superior brand strategy that combines both customer and competitive angle.

Products need rejuvenation to keep consumers involved in a relationship with the product so that they always find the product contemporary, failing which there is always a chance for brand switch. Marketers, therefore, always bring in some changes in the product appearance even if it is only physical appearance like the packaging. We, therefore, can see that marketers claim that the product now is "New" or "Improved" every now and then. This is necessary to give a good feeling to the consumers that marketers are always working on their brands to make them contemporary and relevant to the times. And if there is a technological shift then it has to be incorporated into the product. Otherwise, the product will not sell. This is a key imperative for the brand leader. A leader in the category has to be seen as natural owner of the brand in the sense that if there is any new innovation possible that has to be seen to be done by the leader. Otherwise, for brand leader there will be a credibility loss for the brand. Technology shift can even throw a brand completely out of the market. And even if the current technology used for manufacture of the product is still relevant, some improvements, cosmetic changes, or some changes even in the look and appearance have to be done by the marketer to maintain current leadership as well as current market standing. For example, if there is any change in the type of packaging, it is better to switch to newer generation packaging material. This is what we call upgrading the product to the current level of expectation.

Detergent manufacturers make minor changes in every two years and make a major change in formulation every five years. And this is how Ariel keeps its qualitative leadership in the American market. It can be seen that to remain relevant, contemporary marketers need to do many innovations which have strategic implications in the business. The strategies marketers adopt include:

- Renew product
- Integrate new and emerging needs under same position (for example, Volvo stands for security)
- Constantly inform and remind consumers about superiority
- Constantly strengthen the brand reputation
- Communicate the cognitive value (combination of brand salience and perceived difference) of the brand, for example, best and cheapest

Coke follows 3A strategy ensuring Availability (through intense distribution network extending even up to rural hinterland), Affordability (keeps the price affordable or even creates affordable options for all sections of the consumers), and Awareness (through exploitation of all forms of media and promotion to keep reminding about the brand as a power brand does). This strategy typically supports coke's positioning as "a product for all occasions, for all time and for everyone in the society" which is like a universal positioning.

BRANDING STRATEGIES

To enter into a product category we need to understand the characteristics of the market in terms of the following:

- Actual and potential market size: What is the current market and to what extent it can grow to understand its potential?
- Market growth: At what rate market or industry category is growing?
- Market profitability: Is the market attractive and profitable?
- Cost structure: How are different cost elements added up in the entire value chain? What is the estimate of potential industry earning (PIE) and is it attractive? Cost structure of some industry category may even make it structurally unviable and what is the utility of entering in that category with yet another brand extension?
- Distribution system: Current distribution system. Is the trade motivated and charged yet to accept another product. What is the new innovation in distribution system? Is the distribution system changing?
- Trends and development in the category: What are the new innovations and developments including technological developments taking place in the category? In a stagnating category there is little scope for brand extension and different strategies for rejuvenating the category are required.
- Key success factor: What are the critical success factors for the category to bring in a significant change in growth parameters? How can those be influenced?

Brand assets and competencies have to compete successfully. How will these change in future? How can assets and competencies of the competitors be neutralized by strategies? These are the key questions that we need to answer to formulate appropriate branding strategies.

If we carefully examine the products and brands that are there in the market we can easily find some relationship between them. These relationships can be categorized into various classes or models of relationship. Marketers have followed various strategies to create new brands and successful products. There are six models of brand–product (or service) relationship. These can easily be characterized and thus can be clubbed under a group. These are:

- Product brand
- Line brand
- Range brand
- Umbrella brand
- Source brand, and
- Endorsing brand

Each of these branding strategies has its usual advantages and disadvantages which we will discuss in subsequent sections. Organizations follow different strategies depending on their own perspective, vision, potential, and strategic objective the brand is expected to fulfill. While taking decisions on branding strategies, brand marketers have to think through which strategy really suits his organization's immediate as well as long-term objective. Also for various product categories there can be different strategies.

Product Brand

This branding strategy suggests that one brand will be assigned to one and only one product and it will have exclusive position in the market. Each product gets its own brand name that belongs to it. P&G adopted this strategy as their brand management philosophy. Thus we can see Camay (a seductive soap) and Zest (soap for energy), although both belong to soap category.

Product brand policy allows corporations to take risks in new market since each brand is independent of others and thus failure of one of them will have no risk of rebounding on the others. Besides, one can preempt specific positioning options by the competition. One can cover all possible positioning options in a product category and compete in the entire spectrum if one wants to become a dominant player in the category. But this is a costly proposition.

Advantages:

- Consumers perceive product differences better
- Product can achieve its natural potential
- Marketers will have lot of flexibility in terms of developing brand marketing strategy and plan
- Failure of the brand will not have any negative rub-off for the parent brand

Disadvantages:

- Very costly proposition to market
- It takes longer time to market a new brand
- Failure rates will be higher being a new brand

Range Brand

The range brand strategy bestows a single brand name and promotes through a single promise a range of products belonging to the same area of competence. In range brand architecture of products guard their common name. We can take examples from various product categories, such as food (Kissan, Dabur), Luggage (Samsonite), Equipments (Godrej, Voltas, Whirlpool). A number of products are covered under one core concept to which they belong.

Advantages:

- A brand can easily distribute new products that are consistent with its mission and fall within the same category
- Avoids a random spread of external communication by focusing on a single name
- Generic communication helps to develop unique brand concept
- Less costly proposition. Cost of such new launches is very low

Disadvantages:

- It can create identity crisis at it grows
- Problem in realizing the products' full potential
- There is an issue of brand opacity as it grows

Line Brand

The line brand strategy attempts creating a line of products out of a successful product or brand. For example, Christian Dior: Capture antiaging liposome complex for skin, Capture eye shaper, lip shapers, etc; Reckitts: Dettol including Dettol antiseptic liquid, Dettol soap, Dettol liquid handwash, etc., thus creating a line of products out of a single brand name. A product line created out of a single brand name can create a strong brand image.

Advantages:

- Reinforces the selling power of the brand and creates a strong brand image
- Leads to the ease of distribution for the line extension
- Reduces the launch cost

Disadvantages:

- One should not forget that line has a limit. Therefore, line cannot be extended to any extent
- Should include product innovations that are very closely linked with the existing one
- Inclusion of a powerful development could slow down its development

Umbrella Brand

The umbrella brand strategy extends the same name (and very often a successful name) to a wide range of products. For example:

Canon: Same name has been used to market camera, photocopying machine, office equipment

Yamaha: This brand is used to market motorbikes, pianos, and guitars

Philips: Used for lighting, hi-fi TV, electric bulbs, computers, electric shavers, and appliances

Advantages:

- Capitalizing on one single name helps to get economy of scale on an international level
- High level of awareness
- High degree of awareness helps to build instantaneous goodwill

Disadvantages:

- All products do not attain or realize their full potential
- An overstretched brand can have rubber effect (Ries and Trout 1987)
- It basically stems from the failure to appreciate its demand

Source Brand

Source brand strategy is identical to umbrella brand strategy except for one key point that the products are now directly named and they are no longer called by one generic name such as eau de toilette and eau de perfume but each has its own name as well. For example, Poison, Opium, and Nina. This is also a two-tier brand structure, also known as double branding.

Advantages:

- Its ability to provide two tiered sense of difference and depth
- The parent brand offers its significance and identity, modified and enriched by the daughter brand in order to attract a specific customer segment
- It is difficult to personalize an offer or a proposition to a client without any personalized communication

Disadvantages:

- Lies in the necessity to respect the core, the spirit, and the identity of the parent brand

- Only the names that are related to the parent brand's field of activity should be associated with it

Endorsing Brand

The endorsing branding strategy strongly relies on the support and promise of the endorsing character. Brand endorsement can be indicated in a graphic manner by placing the emblem next to the brand name. For example, Tata's salt where Tata is the endorser. However, endorser has to have strong presence and goodwill for the endorsing to have any value. Endorsers immediately provide some guarantee of quality and performance.

Advantages:

- Least expensive way of giving substance to a name to achieve a brand status
- Provides greater freedom of movement
- Provides indirect guarantee of quality and promise

Disadvantages:

- Too much proliferation will lead to dilution of identity
- Product gets dependent on the endorser's strength and image for performance.

The branding strategies presented here are various models. In reality, however, one will still find a mixed bag of all types of branding strategies in the same organization's product portfolio.

CHOOSING APPROPRIATE BRAND STRATEGY

Without a name product has no real existence. Once branded it has a life. As discussed above, each branding strategy has its advantages and disadvantages. Which branding strategy will work for the business has to be decided with great care and the decision has to be based on the capitalization of long-term potential.

In 1981 at 3M 244 new brands were created and registered. In 1991 only four brands were created. In 1991 in Nestle 101 new products were created but only five new brands. The age of brand proliferation seems to be over now because it is too costly and risky to introduce, support, and promote a new brand to success. 3M has 60,000 products, 1,500 brands, is 29th in Fortune 500 list but is still a relatively unknown company.

Choosing the right branding strategies is, therefore, critical to the success of business in today's competitive environment. If we carefully examine the product portfolio of any company we will find that only a handful of brands constitute over 80 percent of the company's business. This is a clear indication that not all brands that were launched have great potential and only a few brands are of significant value to the businesses compared to the other brands that they have. Thus there is a need for preferential resource allocations to the few well-performing brands over others. Businesses are even seen to divest underperforming brands to create additional resources to support well-performing brands as a strategy. A detailed study of the product portfolio is required to take strategic decisions on branding and brand development including resource allocation.

DECISION CRITERIA FOR BRANDING STRATEGY

To develop appropriate branding strategies marketer will be required to get valid answers to a few important issues. The answers to these questions will help finding appropriate strategies for the business and the brand.

The key question—does the new product meet one or more of these criteria will really help you to decide what branding strategies to follow:

- Is it a top priority innovation
- Whether the product could be used to nurture an existing brand
- Whether the new product can provide the occasion for the creation of a new parent brand which means the new product has also many extension possibilities
- Capacity of new product to justify the creation of a new secondary brand (daughter brand)

Any innovation creates new primary brand. Therefore, a significant new innovation must be given a new brand to create a new identity, new image, and position. Also a product with very high potential should be given a new brand name. A product which has potential eventually to emerge as a global brand or can emerge as a power brand has to have a new brand name in order to have its distinctive position in the marketplace.

We will now discuss a case of creating a powerful brand in a fiercely competitive noninvolvement category to illustrate the key strategic elements which were identified to create a differentiation in a category where differentiation possibility was almost nil. The case study will help brand marketers to understand what it takes to create a successful brand.

Case Study: Mortein

This is a case of building a very successful brand in a low involvement category which also has low innovation possibilities and in a scenario where market leader controls a very high market share making the task of brand marketer extremely difficult.

Early Days

Mortein was manufactured as an insecticidal powder in the 1870s by J. Hageman, a German immigrant to Australia. Mortein is combination of two words, "mort" (dead) and "ein" (one). Hageman used crushed chrysanthemum flowers to produce a pyrethrum extract. The powder was originally sprinkled around for use. In 1920s a squeeze puffer was developed. Also in 1928 Hageman developed a liquid version. He combined this with kerosene and had a pump pack designed (the traditional flint gun) which allowed the insecticide to be sprayed into air or onto the pests themselves. Mortein was first advertised in a lengthy infomercial in 1956 and was one of the first TV commercial to be produced and aired. Hagemans' product was distributed wholesale by Samuel Taylor who ran his own business until his death in 1895. Soon after that the business went broke. In 1909, F. S. Steer and Thomas Jackson acquired the business. They revived the Samuel Taylor business and set it up as a proprietary company in 1937 as Samuel Taylor Pty Ltd. By 1953 Mortein was already a household name when the Samuel Taylor company pioneered the aerosol industry in Australia by introducing the Pressure Pak. In 1969 the Samuel Taylor company was bought by Reckitt and Coleman. Mortein was developed and made in Australia and has been the leading brand of household insecticide in Australian homes for more than a century. Mortein is the number one pest control brand in Australia and the most recognized and widely used household insecticide in Australia.

Mortein Launch in India

Household insecticide is a big category in Reckitt Benckiser's global portfolio. However, Reckitt's entry into this category was quite late. Other players were well entrenched when Reckitt was able to introduce Mortein in the market in the year 1993. Household insecticide is basically a noninvolvement category. Consumer's involvement in the buying decision is low and as long as the brand can protect them from mosquito bites or the problems of cockroaches and flies, it is okay with them no matter which brand it is. Creating a successful brand, therefore, in a category like this is always a challenge for brand marketers. Reckitt was toying with the idea of introducing a household insecticide in India from their global repository of brands and formulation. Australia was the center of excellence for Reckitt for technical and marketing support in this category of products. But in India household insecticide is a highly regulated category and, therefore, getting new active ingredients approved by the regulatory authority was a very time-consuming and cumbersome exercise. Besides, there is no legal protection of the formulations in India. Competitor can easily copy the formulation once registered by a company through repeat registration route very easily. Hence there is no competitive advantage for a company who has spent enormous amounts of money and resources to register a new active formulation generating huge amount of toxicological-and other bio-efficacy-related data because the competitor can easily copy it the moment the new registration is granted to the company. German company Bayer registered a liquid formulation for cockroach and got it registered in India and their competitor Good Knight took repeat registration after Bayer got the first registration and it so happened that Good Knight launched their product Hit earlier than Bayer could introduce their product Baygon. While Bayer spent all the money and resources to generate a new formulation, the advantage could not be derived by them.

Of late, of course, the scenario has changed and India grants product patent now but the situation was different in the 1990s.

Household insecticide category in India can broadly be divided into repellent and killer which is constituted by the following subcategories, namely,

- Mosquito repellent and killers
- Cockroach killers
- Rodent and pest killers
- Cream (repellent)

Broadly the killer category can also be divided into FIK (flying insect killer) and CIK (crawling insect killer).

Whether a product will fall into repellent or killer category depends upon the knock-down characteristics to be determined by bio-efficacy tests. Creams are normally repellent of insects including mosquitoes. The bio-efficacy and particularly the knock-down property normally depend on the type of active ingredients used and the dosage forms.

Mat, coil, liquid vaporizer, aerosol, baits, and creams are the product variants in the market and mat had the largest share followed by coil, vaporizer, liquid, and then cream. The mosquito repellent cream was a very small market then. But composition of the market has changed now and coil and liquid have emerged now as much bigger categories. The growth of coil segment was largely driven by Mortein. It can be noted that for mosquitoes we have both repellents as well as killers. For example, cream can only work as repellent for mosquitoes. The Tortoise coil which had no active ingredients like d-allethrin but had only natural extract of chrysanthemum flower having repellent property was not that effective. Mortein was the first coil with active ingredient in the market and that has worked to support the brand as the most powerful.

When Mortein was introduced there were three major players each holding significant market share in that subsegment and were the market leaders. Transelectra (owner of the Good Knight brand then) had 65 percent market share in mat segment, Bombay Chemicals (owner of Tortoise brand) had 75 percent market share in coil segment and Bayer (owner of Baygon brand) had 60 percent market share in liquid spray segment. There were other smaller and regional players also in the market. It was, therefore, not an easy task for Reckitt to introduce yet another product as a me-too product to create a success story. Dr Rajat Baisya (the author), the then vice president (business development) of Reckitt was given the challenge to decide an entry strategy in this low involvement category where product innovation prospect was nil and also where three segments of the market were really controlled by well-entrenched brands as mentioned above. All other studies done by Reckitt earlier were concluded by saying that there is no opportunity in this category in India. Initially Rajat Baisya tried to acquire brands like Tortoise and Good Knight as acquisition was thought to be the best option to get an entry into a category like this which has a dominant player in each of the subsegments. But all negotiations to buy these brands at a fair market price based on the value of those brands failed with no options left but either to not get into this category or enter it with a me-too formulation and fight it out in the marketplace. Rajat Baisya recommended that Reckitt get into this category with all three variants—mat, coil, and liquid at the same time and take a specialist position in the market—that only Reckitt can provide total solution of all insect-related problems in the household. In fact Reckitt introduced mat, coil, liquid, aerosol, and liquid vaporizer. For vaporizer a unique machine was designed for which the mould was developed in South Korea which could serve both as liquid vaporizer as well as heater for mat as a two-in-one machine.

Tamil Nadu was the single largest market in India and also a stronghold of all the leading players in the market. Rajat Baisya took the decision to test launch the product in Tamil Nadu. He worked very closely with the advertising agency Ogilvy & Mather represented by late Achin Ganguly and also Sumitomo Corporation of Japan, the world leader in the manufacture of active ingredients. Sumitomo supported this business of Reckitt by offering a special price for the active ingredient d-allethrin and worked closely with Dr Baisya to help create a success story. It is Sumitomo who predicted a great success in coils and used to argue that because of limited availability of power, coil has to grow faster in India and used to advise us to focus on coil. It is on Sumitomo's insistence that Dr Baisya undertook a study tour to Thailand and Malaysia to see the coil market and manufacturing practices. In later years coil manufacturing plants were imported from Malaysia by Reckitt to set up their own manufacturing operations close to their R&D unit at Hosur, Tamil Nadu. Packaging of Mortein was designed to give the effect of strength and efficacy of the product and the product was launched with the claim that it comes from the house of a specialist and has more strength and power than other brands in the market supported by heavy advertisement and promotional budget. The product pack design and color scheme gave a powerful look with the use of strong colors like red and black. And it worked. The projected performance which was targeted to be achieved within six months was actually achieved within three months. And within next three months the Mortein brand was rolled out to rest of India in a phased manner. Coil was a remarkable success but liquid vaporizer and mat also did well. Today Mortein is the largest brand in Reckitts' portfolio in India. Shortly thereafter, Sara Lee launched their global brand Raid in the market but did not succeed.

Brand Launch History in India

- Mortein launched in 1993 in South; national rollout completed in 1996
  - Launched coils, mats, aerosols, and liquids
  - Vaporizer launched in 1999
  - Rat killer added in 2000. National rollout in April 2001
- The opportunity in the coils category
  - Low category penetration
  - One local player (Tortoise) with a product which was not rated very high on efficacy
  - Inadequate supply, particularly in peak mosquito seasons
  - No big investment on brand building at the initial stage
- First coil to use an active ingredient in prescribed dosage and to be advertised heavily on efficacy
- The product found instant favor with consumers on efficacy and power
  - Initial copy focused on powerful action of the coils
  - Supported by a highly successful disease prevention social awareness infomercial in association with Indian Medical Association
- Mortein's entry led to growth in the coil market and the mosquito repellant and killer market as a whole.
  - Sales grew explosively in the first 8 years post launch due to coil. CAGR during 1994–2000 was 66 percent.
- In 2000, new brands (Good Knight and Maxo) entered the coil market
- Reckitt Benckiser, as the market leader in coils faced severe competition for the first time
  - Reacted with heavy promotion spending
- The lack of any other format (mats, aerosols, vaporizers) in which Reckitt had a large business made it worse
  - Coil contributed to 86 percent of the category in 2000.

- The failure of triple coil in 2002 and its subsequent withdrawal from the market made matters even worse
- From Q4 2002, strategy changed to media plus trade led
  - Share has risen steadily since then
- Aggressive share gain strategy on other segments:
  - Power Booster Coils in 2004
  - CIK (crawling insect killer) Launched in 2004
  - Rat 2 bait launched in 2004
  - AIK (all insect killer) in 2005
  - Small AIK in 2006

Brand Positioning Statement: Is a powerful, efficacious brand that guarantees quality and hygiene by keeping your home free from all types of household pests offering a total and reliable solution for you?

Brand Mortein has attempted to occupy a unique position and to build a strategy to deliver that stated position which can be stated and summarized as:

- Positioning: Trusted protection from pests
- Strategy: Maintain dominance in coils and increase share in aerosols and vaporizers
- Key Strategic Pillars: Superior Products supported by cut-through communication and activation support in trade

Its sole reason for existence in the market is the omnipresent mosquito, which makes life excruciatingly difficult for the average Indians during summer and monsoon months. In many ways the primary factor fuelling the explosive growth of this market, characterized by low brand loyalty and low product involvement has been the availability of cost-effective mosquito repellents. The night long noisy humming of mosquitoes that disturbs our sleep is music to the ears of the ₹1,100 crore (USD 100 billion) mosquito repellent industry. The various segments in this industry are coils, mats, vaporizers, aerosols, and creams. The two new segments are personal sprays and gels.

Product Packaging

To project the brand Mortein as powerful the packaging design and color scheme were chosen in a manner to create that impact. Black and red colors used in the design signify strength. The packshot and logo of the brand had significant shelf throw and dominant presence in the retail outlets. Mortein logo also gives similar image as shown in Figure 5.3.

Figure 5.3   Mortein Logo

SOURCE: Reckitt Benckiser.

Figure 5.4   Mortein Power Booster Coil 12 Hours

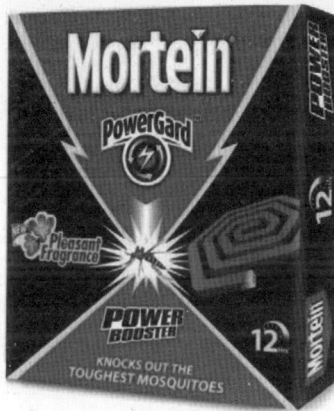

SOURCE: Reckitt Benckiser.

Figure 5.5   Mortein Max Power Jumbo Coil

SOURCE: Reckitt Benckiser.

Figure 5.6 Mortein Natur Gard Combi Pack

SOURCE: Reckitt Benckiser.

Category-wise Market Shares

Coils command nearly 50 percent of the market share, vaporizer refills at 20 percent, with mats at 10 percent, followed by aerosols at 9 percent and the rest shared by creams, heating devices, and other products.

Segment-wise Market Share

The market for insecticides and repellents has grown by 20 percent in 2003–2004 and is estimated to grow at about 20 percent even now. The rural market for mosquito repellents is reckoned at around ₹173 million (USD 3.5 million) against a mere ₹79 million (USD 1.6 million) in urban centers. The market leader of the industry is Godrej Sara Lee Ltd with brands like Good Knight, Jet, and Hit enjoying a market share of 40 percent.

In spite of the pervasiveness of the mosquito problem, the use of repellents in India is fairly low. It is estimated that only 16.4 percent of the households in all urban areas and 22.6 percent in the metros use mosquito repellents. The figure for the rural areas is even lower, at only 6.9 percent. In terms of value, the mat segment was the largest (51 percent), followed by coils (21 percent) and vaporizers (7 percent).

Coils were the first mosquito repellents to be introduced in the Indian market. The first brand of coils was Tortoise, launched by Bombay Chemicals Ltd (BCL) in the 1970s. Until 1994, Tortoise remained the market leader in its segment, with a 67 percent market share. Other significant players emerged over the years, offering products in many segments: Bayer with the brands Baygon Spray, Baygon Power Mats, and Baygon Knockout; Balsara Hygiene with a repellant cream, Odomos; and Tainwala Chemicals with the Casper brand of mats and coils. Besides these large players, a number of local brands were also available across the country.

In the latter half of 1990s, the market became much more competitive, with the entry of GSLL (Godrej Sara Lee Ltd), Reckitt & Coleman (R&C, now Reckitt Benckiser) and HUL. GSLL launched an array of brands (all coils) one after the other—Jet Fighter (1997), Good Knight Jumbo (1999), Good Knight Instant, Good Knight Smokeless, and Jet Jumbo (2000). The company's other brands included Banish (mats), Hit (aerosols), Hit Lines (chalks), Mosfree (lotion) and Hexit (spray). The Jet brand was extended to coils and sprays. R&C also launched its range of mats and coils—Mortein, Mortein King, and Mortein Red while HLL (in association with S.C. Johnson) launched Raid and Attack. It can be noted here that whereas Reckitt's competitor like GSLL resorted to launch and support many brands, some of those like Good Knight, Jet and Banish were acquired. Reckitt consistently focused on one single brand, Mortein, and put heavy resources to support the brand in media as well in various product forms and quality and that has helped them very well in terms of performance.

These new entrants resorted to heavy advertising and aggressive sales promotion tactics. GSLL soon emerged as the market leader in the mats segment with a 68 percent share in May 2000. R&C quickly became the second largest player in the coils segment, next only to Tortoise. (Refer to Tables 5.3 and 5.4.)

Major Players (Competitors)

- Karamchand Appliances Private Ltd.: All Out
- Godrej Sara Lee Ltd: Good Knight, Jet, Banish, Hit
- Jyothy Laboratories: Maxo
- Tainwala Personal Care Products: Casper
- Bombay Chemicals: Tortoise

Company's Share (Segment-wise)

Mosquito Coil Market:

Market leader: Mortein (35 percent)
   Market challenger: Good Knight with a share of 30 percent
   Market Follower: Maxo from Jyothy Laboratories is rapidly increasing its share

Vaporizer Fill Market:

Market leader: All Out brand (65 percent).
   Market challenger: Good Knight and Jet from Godrej Sara Lee Ltd together account for 24 percent of the vaporizer segment.

Market follower: Mortein Vaporizer by Reckitt Benckiser has a market share of about 5–7 percent.

Mats and Aerosol Categories:

Market leader: Godrej Sara Lee leads the market with its brands Good Knight Silver mat and Hit (aerosol) (68 percent).
Market follower: Mortein's share in mats is estimated at roughly 15 percent.

Mortein: The Brand

₹158.5 billion (USD 3.15 billion) Reckitt Benckiser in India is high-profile particularly because it has a range of popular products. Reckitt launched mosquito repellent coils and mats under the brand name Mortein in 1993. Mortein is also available in liquid and aerosol spray forms. Mortein is the number two pest-control brand in the country. Mortein sales grew by 9.2 percent in the Financial Year 2012, Quarter 1, as against market growth of 9 percent. Mortein Coil sales grew by 14.5 percent despite stiff competition in the category. For Mortein the strategy is to increase penetration of coils, enhance brand salience of other variants, and tap niche segments through a stream of innovations. Mortein's share in mats is estimated at roughly 15 percent.

MORTEIN–The Brand Architecture

- Brand Essence: Powerful trusted protection
- Brand Values: Protection, family health, integrity
- Personality: Powerful, approachable, expert, smart, and intelligent
- Capsule: Protect the family with the power of Mortein
- Brand Positioning: To mothers, concerned about their family's health and well-being
- Brand Identity: Pest-control brand
- Function: Protects the family from disease-carrying pests
- Benefits: Powerful trusted products that have long-lasting effects

Reasons for Success

Mortein has performed remarkably well because of the following reasons:

- The first brand which was introduced containing active ingredients in required dosage forms
- The first brand to have launched all variants offering a total solution to all kinds of household pests
- The first brand which guarantees high performance and high efficacy

- Focused resources behind one brand Mortein whereas competition like Godrej had many brands and hence fragmented resources
- The first brand which has been very actively promoted through all kinds of media options
- The first brand to occupy a unique value proposition in the customers' mind
- The first brand which has demonstrated many innovations in the category
- The first brand to have been supported by huge advertisement spend
- Mortein entered with a superior product-efficacy proposition
- Entry backed by a high investment on TV and other brand-building activities
- Continuous pipeline of innovations to maintain dominance. Hexagonal shape coil—unique shape and claim led to increase in share by 900 bps within 2 years.
- Combination of high media investment plus trade spends

Brand Performance

Mortein has steadily increased its brand share in coil and enjoys above 30 percent market share. And on all pests segment it has a share of above 20 percent by volume. The once market leader Tortoise from BCL which enjoyed over 75 percent market share in coil segment in early 1990s is nowhere to be seen now.

The category which falls into a noninvolvement category of products where consumers have no apparent brand loyalty and the decision of buying is taken as an impulse purchase decision where any brand is good enough as long as it works.

Table 5.2 gives the brand's performance criteria for over a period of last 3 years. The high pitch advertisement spend has helped the category to grow at about 18 percent consistently over the last three years.

Table 5.2   Indian Pest Control Market

The Indian Pest Market is estimated at 367MGBP; growing at 18% (3 YR CAGR)					
	Value off take in MGBP				
Category	*FY 08*	*FY 09*	*FY 10*	*Contri.*	*CAGR*
Coils	133	153	173	47%	15%
Aerosols	26	32	40	11%	28%
Vaps	71	81	98	27%	19%
Rodenticides	4	4	6	2%	27%
Mats	8	8	9	2%	2%
All Pests	**268**	**310**	**367**	**100%**	**18%**

SOURCE: Reckitt Benckiser.

Figure 5.7   Product Category Penetration: Market Penetration Trends for Mosquito Repellent Category

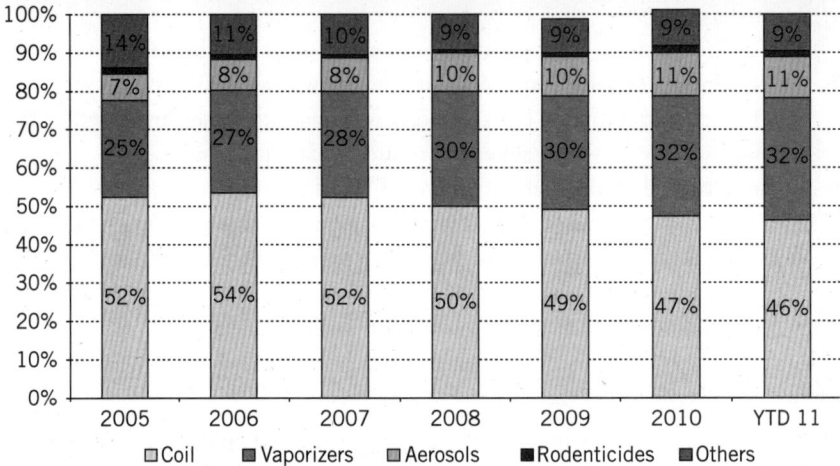

SOURCE: Reckitt Benckiser.

Box 5.1

- Coils contribute to a lion share (47%) of the pest market and growing at 15%.
- Aerosols is growing the fastest at 28%.
- **Around 84% of Pest market in India is Mosquito Centric.**

SOURCE: Reckitt Benckiser.

As shown in Figure 5.8, category penetration is close to about 77 percent for household pests and at above 50 percent for coils. The vaporizers seem to be the growth opportunity now having a penetration at about 43 percent where Mortein has about 12 percent market share. In aerosol category Mortein is the second largest player with 19 percent market share.

Mortein as a brand has led the growth through coil having over 63 percent of the total brand's contribution as will be revealed from Figure 5.9. Reckitt had very weak competition in coil from BCL offering a quick growth opportunity for an organized player like Reckitt Benckiser.

Reason for low share in aerosols and vaporizers:

- Late entrant in the segment. Let the local players (All Out, Hit) pioneer these segments
- Entry into the segment with undifferentiated products

Figure 5.8 Category Penetration Trends

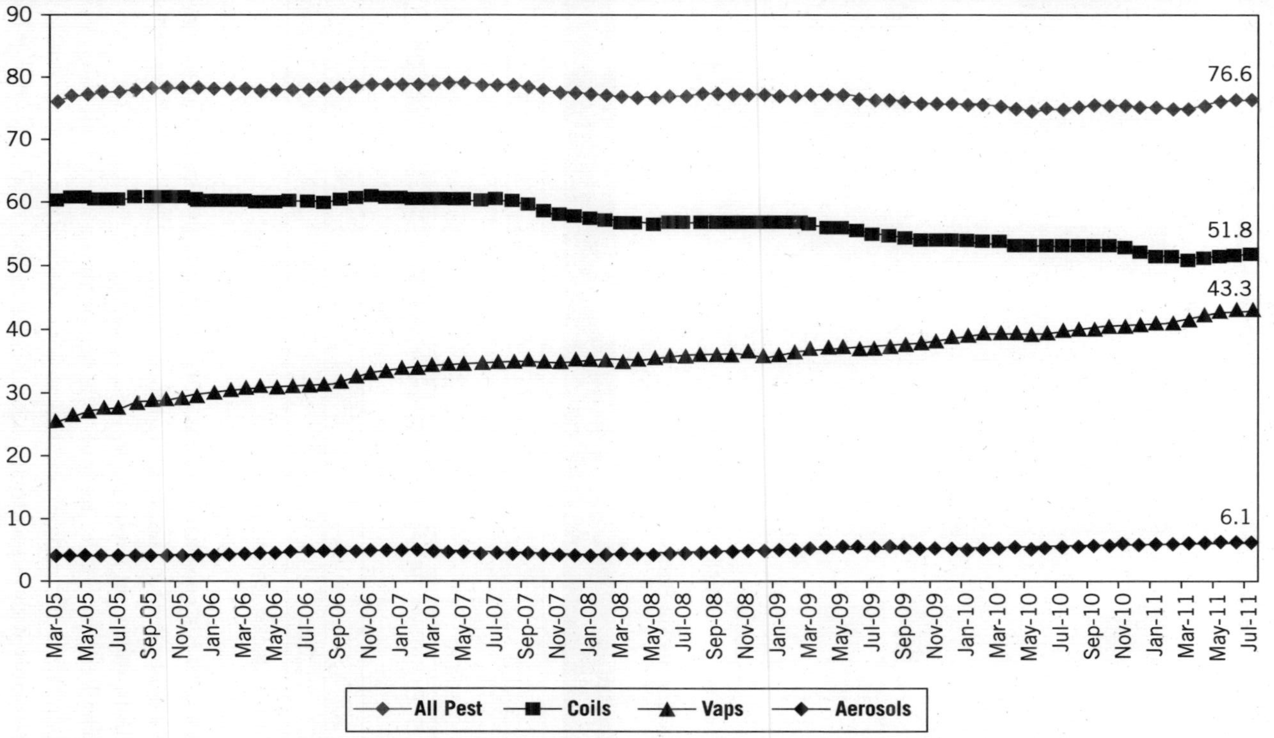

76.6

51.8

43.3

6.1

Legend: —◆— All Pest   —■— Coils   —▲— Vaps   —◆— Aerosols

SOURCE: A. C. Nielsen Data provided by Reckitt Benckiser.

Figure 5.9 Mortein Portfolio Evolution Stack—Contribution Increasing for Vaporizers and Aerosols, but Coils Contribution Still High at 63 Percent

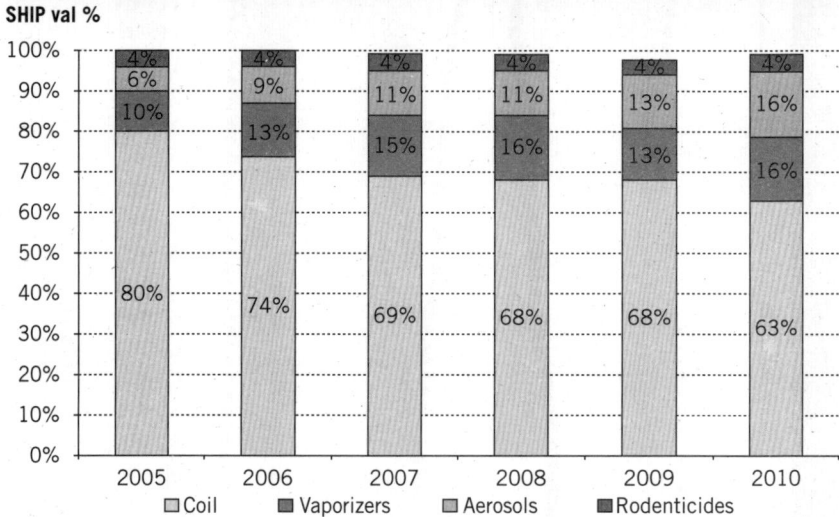

SHIP val %

SOURCE: Reckitt Benckiser.

Table 5.3 Market Share—Coil (Value)

Value Share	2002	2003	2004	2005	2006	2007	2008	2009	2010
RECKITT BENCKISER	28%	29%	34%	37%	36%	36%	34%	32%	30%
GODREJ SARA LEE LTD	34%	34%	31%	31%	30%	28%	31%	28%	29%
SC JOHNSON	5%	3%	3%	2%	2%	1%	2%	2%	2%
JYOTHY LABS	19%	22%	22%	19%	19%	21%	21%	21%	22%

SOURCE: Reckitt Benckiser.

Mortein is a remarkable success story of a brand that started its journey in the year 1993 by having a test launch in the southern market in Tamil Nadu and then gradually rolled out nationally by the year 1996. Today it represents 20 percent of Reckitt Benckiser's sales revenue totaling approximately a value sales of ₹5,000 million (USD 100 million) and still growing. Reckitt has never experienced such success story with respect to any other brands in spite of the fact that it has in its portfolio powerful brands like Dettol, Cherry Blossom, Disprin, etc.

Figure 5.10 Mortein Share Beginning to Revive in 2011

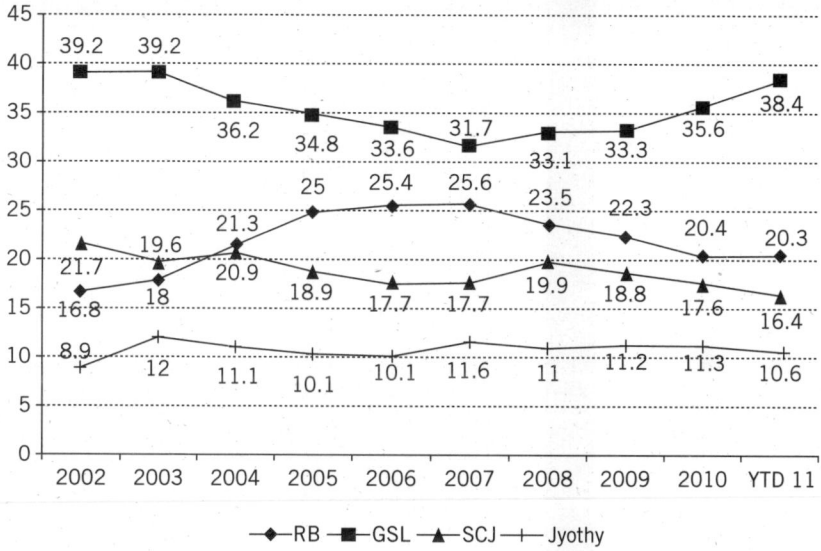

SOURCE: Reckitt Benckiser.

Figure 5.11 Mortein Segment-wise Shares

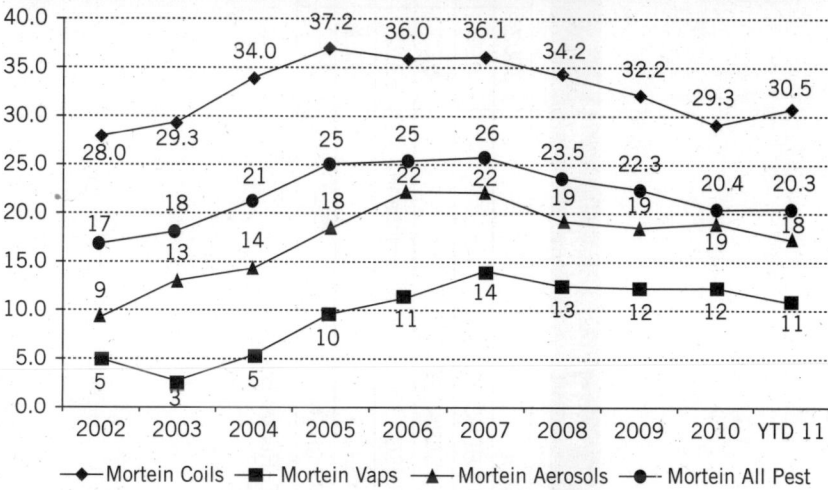

SOURCE: Reckitt Benckiser.

Table 5.4 Market Share—Vaporizer (Value)

Value Share	2002	2003	2004	2005	2006	2007	2008	2009	2010
RECKITT BENCKISER	4.9%	2.6%	5.3%	9.6%	11.3%	14.0%	12.6%	12.5%	12.6%
GODREJ SARA LEE LTD	30.9%	30.6%	30.9%	31.4%	30.4%	28.4%	29.2%	33.2%	36.3%
SC JOHNSON (Including Karamchand)	63.3%	63.6%	60.7%	55.8%	54.7%	52.9%	54.0%	50.4%	45.8%
JYOTHY LABS	0.2%	1.6%	0.4%	0.1%	0.2%	3.0%	3.2%	3.0%	4.0%
BOMBAY CHEM				0.0%	0.4%	0.1%	0.0%	0.0%	0.0%

SOURCE: Reckitt Benckiser.

Table 5.5	Market Share—Aerosols (Value)								
Value Share	2002	2003	2004	2005	2006	2007	2008	2009	2010
RECKITT BENCKISER	9%	13%	14%	18%	22%	22%	20%	19%	19%
GODREJ SARA LEE LTD	58%	66%	65%	59%	56%	57%	58%	60%	64%
SC JOHNSON	29%	18%	16%	18%	17%	14%	15%	13%	11%
JYOTHY LABS	0%	0%	0%	0%	0%	1%	1%	1%	1%

SOURCE: Reckitt Benckiser.

The Future

According to industry reports, the Indian mosquito repellent and killer market was expected to grow rapidly in the early 21st century. Analysts said that with improvement in literacy and health consciousness in rural areas, the use of mosquito repellents was expected to increase substantially in these areas. As the per capita usage of repellents was very low in the country, there was considerable scope for the market to expand. However, increasing concern over the harmful effects of the chemicals in mosquito repellents on the health of human beings was expected to hamper growth. Allethrin, the chemical used in most of the repellents, was reported to be very dangerous, being potentially harmful to the eyes, skin, the respiratory tract, and the nervous system. A study done on rats by the Industrial Toxicology Research Center showed that the rats suffered brain, liver, and kidney damage after prolonged exposure to liquid mosquito repellents. Research in Sweden and the USA had also shown that long-term and persistent use of products containing allethrin could cause brain cancer, blood cancer, and deformity of fetuses. There were also doubts about the efficacy of mosquito repellents. In 1998, studies conducted by the Malaria Research Center found that none of the leading brands provided 100 percent protection against mosquitoes. Also, in the 653 households surveyed in eight cities, 193 people complained of various health problems linked to mosquito repellents. They suffered from breathing problems, headaches, eye irritation, skin rashes, suffocation, itching, bronchitis, cold and cough, asthma, nausea, and throat and ear pain. Of the 286 doctors questioned, 50 percent reported cases of acute toxicity following the use of these repellents or killers.

Therefore, it's clear from the above data that use of repellents or killers are not recommended by the doctors also. So to avoid the above mentioned situation or harmful side effects the repellent companies should come together and work for a solution. Any company who makes the first moves regarding the removal of the toxicity from the repellents enjoys the first mover advantage in the market which should reflect in increased sales performance of their products.

CHAPTER SUMMARY

This chapter deals with the branding, brand-building strategies, and strategic alternatives that marketers can decide to opt for. Creating a new brand is increasingly becoming a difficult and costly proposition. All businesses, therefore, have to carefully examine how to build a portfolio of the brands and business and which brand to support and which to divest. The failure rates of new brands is very high nowadays and almost 95 percent of the new launches ended up in failures in many markets which has forced the businesses to think new branding strategies and alternative routes to branding. This chapter brings in many examples to understand the potential of a brand and brand development strategies to decide on issues like when to go for a new brand and when is it better to opt for extension in order to minimize the risks associated with the new launch and the consequent impact on the business. The chapter discusses the advantages and limitations of brand extension and also narrates the various branding options and strategies with examples. The chapter also includes various brand extensions and branding alternatives and their advantages and disadvantages and what it takes to build a brand that stands out in the clutter and still performs significantly better than competition. The chapter explains the decision criteria with respect to developing brand-building strategies when there are a number of brands in the portfolio and limited resources for allocation to support those brands in a competitive business environment.

Finally, the chapter discusses the case of an important and well-known brand Mortein which was built to become a big success story in a highly cluttered market with many brands in low involvement category like household insecticide. Mortein has done exceptionally well and this case study will help to understand the key elements of branding strategies in a fiercely competitive market.

CHAPTER 6

Designing Marketing Programs to Build Brand Equity

Because of fierce competition, companies are required to have a shift in strategic orientation from being product-focused to increasingly being market- and customer-focused. They are now required to build, measure, and manage brand equity and customer equity in a highly complex and competitive environment. The key challenges in front of FMCG global brand marketers lie in how they can make their brands stronger in a highly cluttered environment since strong brands (with unique benefits) in conjunction with sound business strategy can only deliver sustainable competitive advantage and both top line and bottom line growth in line with expectation.

Global FMCG brand marketers need to stop pursuing consumers through indiscriminate promotions and also need to tailor their value chains employing very unique and innovative methods. Corporations are required now to build brands and build strong collaborative strategic relationships to cope effectively in a very competitive business environment. CEOs and top management teams these days acknowledge that globalization is the most critical challenge they face and accordingly they need to formulate customized strategies for key emerging markets keeping the indigenous factors in consideration. The face of communication is changing and is being geared toward more interactive marketing. There is more and more clutter on TV and there are separate sets of challenges for rural market in India. Marketers will have to try out many alternative avenues of growth and not simply follow the traditional rules of the game. For example, the solution may even lie in more one-to-one marketing and in creating consumer experience environments rather than in going for mass marketing route. Global marketers operating in India in FMCG sector will have to deal with competition from multiple fronts, namely, competition from other global marketers, competition from regional brands, competition from national Indian brands, and competition from emerging store label or private label brands. Even small local brands are creating local competition and it is not always easy to fight them. In order to survive in this competitive environment, marketers will have to achieve higher levels of operational efficiency and also higher efficiency on their marketing investments. Every rupee or dollar spent on the brand will have to be utilized effectively. Only those marketers will prosper in this competitive environment who are master brand-builders and who are seen to be responsible to all their stakeholders through collaborative relationships. Depending on the environment, competitive strengths and weaknesses as well as the opportunity and potential that exist for exploitation, brand marketers are designing specific marketing plan following a strategic route to build or to make the brand even stronger. Global marketers are thus taking many new initiatives which are being discussed in this chapter.

ABILITY TO SERVE THE BOTTOM OF THE PYRAMID AND DRIVE PENETRATION AND CONSUMPTION

"CEOs and top management teams of large corporations, particularly in North America, Europe, and Japan, acknowledge that globalization is the most critical challenge they face today" (Khanna et al. 2005). Success in emerging markets requires a different type of mindset. Prahalad (1998) indicated that as businesses are in search for growth, MNCs will have no option but to compete in the big emerging markets of China, India, Indonesia, and Brazil. Global businesses and western executives, therefore, need to explore how these markets will transform businesses themselves. To be successful, businesses will have to rethink every element of their business models and companies will need to undergo a fundamental rethinking. This involves rethinking on price/performance equation, rethinking on brand management, rethinking the costs of market building, rethinking the product design, rethinking packaging, and rethinking capital efficiency. The attraction for global marketers in these markets is the large aggregate buying power of poor communities and possibility of rapid revenue growth for corporations entering these markets has advocated that the world's most exciting, fastest growing market is in the least expected places, i.e., at the bottom of the pyramid in places like India, Peru, Mexico, Brazil, and Venezuela (Prahalad 2004). He has advocated driving radical innovations within the business to profit from them and also demonstrated how those innovations will make the companies more competitive everywhere in diverse categories.

Keller has also tried to understand the reasons why the comparative performances of powerful brands such as Coke, McDonald's, etc., in developing countries have not been very impressive (Keller and Moorthi 2003). Many of these marketers have inadequate reconciliation of the realities in the emerging markets and, therefore, there is a need to be aware of the limitations of the value dysfunctionality and image dysfunctionality in order for the managers to avoid the pitfalls.

Key challenges (and reasons for failure) for the global marketers lie in the fact that there are so many institutional voids in most of the developing countries. American corporations since 1990s have performed much better in home environment than they have in foreign countries, especially in emerging markets (Khanna et al. 2005). This indicates that global marketers have to understand the merit of each market on a case-to-case basis and employ customized approaches in dealing with different markets in conjunction with possible scope for some synergies wherever applicable.

In India, a few of the more established global marketers like Kellogg's, Coke, etc., have not been very successful in business operations as yet. Other giants like P&G over the years have been very cautious in terms of expanding their brand portfolio. Companies like McDonald's have stabilized a bit after facing initial hiccups in operations. The answer to this relatively low success rate and slow progress lies in the fact that many of the global marketers are experimenting about how to be successful in a very diverse, complex, and vast developing market. These global players have encountered problems like introducing products that do not necessarily serve an immediate mass need, providing wrong price–value proposition, or being unable to configure a proper distribution network in early stages, etc. In India, an effective growth strategy must address the needs of rural India, home to around 70 percent of the country's population. The other key aspect that global marketers need to address is that on infrastructure front there are challenges which require long-term planning. Inadequate infrastructure, for example, leads to 40 percent of perishable food produced in India rotting during transportation due to a lack of refrigerated distribution networks or cold chain (Kearney 2005). This throws up new challenges to product distribution and operational planning.

VANISHING MASS MARKET AND NEED FOR EFFECTIVE SEGMENTATION AND MICRO-MARKETING

The mass market is gradually vanishing in more developed markets like the U.S. The mass market is also vanishing in developing markets but at a lesser pace, courtesy highly fragmented media, new technology, and more products in the market trying to exist by creating differentiated position. One of the key strategies marketers are adopting to fight stagnant growth scenario is by undergoing a paradigm shift in strategic focus from mass marketing to micro marketing (Bianco 2004). The TV audience internationally and also now in India is fragmenting at an accelerated rate. In the way that network TV's dominance of media is eroding, advertising's dominance of marketing is also diminishing.

CHANGING FACE OF COMMUNICATION, MEDIA FRAGMENTATION, AND MARKETING EFFECTIVENESS

The face of communication is changing and is being geared toward more interactive marketing. There is more and more clutter on TV as an average urban consumer is exposed to 350–400 advertisements in a week (Banga 2004). The challenges in rural India are somewhat different as neither print nor TV reaches around 40 percent of the population. One-to-one marketing is creating challenges and promising to increase the value of the customer base by establishing a learning relationship with each customer (Peppers, Rogers, and Dorr 1999). The challenge for marketers is how to effectively integrate telemarketing, direct mail, e-mail, in-store displays, and other forms of closely targeted, non-media spending targeted to an increasingly diverse marketplace instead of relying primarily on one-to-many communications like advertising.

In 1994, 90 percent of major global marketers like P&G's global spending on advertisements was on TV; however, in recent times, launch of Prilosec OTC in 2003 was one of the most successful brand launches in P&G's history and by allocating only around 25 percent spend on TV (Stengel 2004). Brands are built by performance, not by advertising only. The dependence on advertising is going down and dependence on non-advertising brand-building parameters is on the rise (Ries and Ries 2002). Al Ries and Laura Ries also argued that the rising costs (far in excess of inflation), declining credibility, and decreasing media audiences for advertising are all valid points for brands like Starbucks to eschew traditional advertising and still be able to soar to the top through the savvy use of public relations (Ries and Ries 2002). Al Ries and Laura Ries believed marketers should allow public relations to run their course before using advertising (Ries and Ries 2004). Similarly, advertising's role is questioned these days because it is dominated by overly creative television advertisements that entertain and win awards but don't generate sales (Zyman 1999). Money spent on advertising must show a clear measurable return. The key challenges before the marketers are the ability to have tools and benchmarks to understand the effectiveness of its entire marketing spending and also to develop detailed understanding about the effectiveness of various types of media multiplier effects.

ABILITY TO CREATE EXPERIENCE ENVIRONMENTS AND TO ENGAGE THROUGH 360-DEGREE APPROACH

Prahalad has explored why despite enormous opportunities for innovation, companies still can't satisfy consumers and sustain profitable growth (Prahalad and Ramaswamy 2004). The role of the consumer these days has evolved from passive recipient to active cocreator of value. Firms can no longer autonomously create value, as value is not embedded in products and services per se and products are but artifacts around which compelling individual experiences have to be created through brilliant interactive marketing programs. Consequently, the focus of innovation is shifting from products and services to experience environments that individuals can interact with to co-construct their own experiences. These personalized cocreation experiences are becoming the source of unique value for consumers and companies alike. Marketers have to come up with innovative solutions to create consumer experience environments the way the pioneering trend has been started by Barista in India.

COMPETITION AMONG GLOBAL MARKETERS

In India in recent times different global marketers are aggressively fighting for more market position. A few of the relevant examples of intense competition are: between HUL and P&G in laundry and shampoo markets, between HUL and Colgate Palmolive in toothpaste market, and between Coca-Cola and Pepsi in soft drinks market, Nestle and Cadbury (now Kraft Foods) in chocolate market, etc. Global marketers will have to customize many of their more established international brands in Indian market to achieve higher market share position. And this is now being done by these global players. Even advertisement messages and languages of communication used by these global players have significant local and ethnic component now. This trend of localization of the marketing communications so that consumers correlate better is a phenomenon we are witnessing post liberalization.

PRICE-LED COMPETITION FROM REGIONAL BRANDS AND MENACE OF DUPLICATE BRANDS

Down trading in most FMCG categories has created opportunities for regional brands. The success of Ghari, CavinKare, Anchor, Wagh Bakri, and Society (in detergents, personal care, toothpaste, and tea business, respectively) is well established. Regional brands are growing in local pockets (mostly limited scale players) primarily due to competitive pricing. Groups like Adani (manufacturers of Fortune Brand of edible oil) are great followers of high volume, low margin strategy. These brands are very active in rural markets. These brands are turning out to be major competition for global marketers in specific pockets, though the competitive dynamics with respect to regional brands now may go through a transformation given the recent introduction of value added tax and planned abolition of central sales tax when regional players may lose some of their competitive cost advantages mainly arising out of tax advantage. The fact that media segmentation has become much easier these days is also helping regional brands to effectively compete with global brand marketers by leveraging the explosion of local and regional television channels.

Additionally, there is the menace of duplicate, imitation, and low-cost Chinese brands that are not sparing even global giants like HUL and Coke and are thriving in the absence of stringent law enforcement.

MANAGING ORGANIZED RETAILER–MANUFACTURER RELATIONSHIP AND THREAT OF STORE BRANDS

Managing the relationship with large organized retailers is critical for global marketers for building international infrastructure as for the top five retailers 33 percent of the sales come from international markets and for top 10 retailers the corresponding figure is 27 percent (Kearney 2005). The underlying requirement for the organized retailer from the marketer is that of a highly responsive partner who offers brands and products that keep shoppers coming back for more. Historically, because of growing retail trade consolidation, major FMCG giants have faced key challenges from the bargaining clout of organized retailers in developed markets like Western Europe and U.S. global marketers have devoted significant attention to manage this changing manufacturer–retailer dynamics and to handle the growing demand of retailers to provide more favorable trade terms. Many brand marketers have been negatively affected by change in policies of retailers in terms of trade inventory levels, access to shelf space, or even in store promotional support, etc. PepsiCo sales incentives worldwide to various organized retailers and consumers (accounted for a reduction of sales) totaled USD 6.6 billion in 2004 (22.6 percent of its total net revenue in 2004).

In India also retail trade consolidation has started happening in recent times, though it is in a relatively nascent stage now. The Indian organized retail industry is just 3 percent of the country's total retail pie (moneycontrolgroup.com 2005) though growing at a fast pace and presently it is about 6 percent. India has been ranked Number 1 in terms of attractiveness in global retail development index among the top 30 emerging markets in 2005 (Kearney 2005) and it has moved to the top spot from its ranking of number 2 in 2004 in the same survey. India's USD 330 billion retail market has grown by 10 percent on average per year over the past five years (A.T. Kearney survey).

In a short time, Pantaloon Retail has raced to be amongst the front-runners in the Indian retail sector. Success of other key organized retailers like Big Bazaar, Food Baazar, Food World, etc., has encouraged a plethora of corporate groups to enter the organized retailing sector. The entire manufacturer–retailer dynamics has started to change in many consumer product categories. Very recently Pantaloon Retail chain has been acquired by Aditya Birla Group because of the synergy that they found in market of branded garments from Coats India. Organized retailing may get a fillip as the government is looking at a model for allowing foreign direct investment (FDI) in retail and finally single brand retail is cleared with some preconditions attached. Store brands from many of these retailers like Big Baazar, Food Baazar, Food World, etc., have already started competing with the brands of many of the reputed marketers. Lot of consolidation, restructuring and reformatting of stores is happening in organized retail. Indian organized retail industry still going through the learning phase.

COMPETITION AMONGST NATIONAL INDIAN AND GLOBAL BRANDS

Many of these global marketers are facing competition from leading Indian national brands like Tata, Nirma, Godrej, Fevicol, Dabur, Amul, Bisleri, Parle, etc. Some of them are formidable competitors and focusing more on the high margin businesses and trying to move upwards in the value chain. The global marketers have to engage with Indian rural audience the same way ITC is now engaged by leveraging information technology through its trailblazing e-Choupal initiative that is already benefiting over 3.5 million farmers. Similarly, global marketers need to take into account the actions of many smaller national marketers (for example, Godrej Consumer Products selling soaps) who have started exploring rural markets, not through their own network (expensive affair) but through other larger companies who have created such networks (for example, ITC e-choupal network).

Kotler argues that the two key challenges facing Indian companies are the capability of Indian companies to defend their market against the growing invasion of foreign global brands and their capability to develop strong global brands (Kotler 2004). This process has already started as acknowledged by ad guru Ian Batey (Bhusan 2003) in Ad Asia 2003 who opined that FMCG brands from ITC, Ranbaxy, Old Monk rum, Nutrine may propel Brand India onto the global map (along with other very well-known Indian IT, manufacturing, and service brands). These marketers are in their own ways becoming formidable competitors of global marketers.

NEED FOR COST-SAVING STRATEGY

Many of the FMCG marketers' margins are under pressure because of rising prices for many commodities. Companies like Colgate Palmolive have been hit by rising oil prices. Sara Lee estimated a dramatic incremental increase of more than USD 300 million in commodity costs in fiscal year 2004 involving key inputs to its products like cotton, meats, and energy. There have been high input cost escalations, particularly in chemicals and packaging, which has impacted categories like laundry. Marketers will have to constantly manage and monitor their cost reduction programs that will require the consolidation and integration of facilities, functions, systems, and procedures. Cost savings generated through operational efficiency can to a large extent offset the escalating costs of key inputs and oil for many marketers. As cost advantage can offer significant competitive edge organizations are seen to be very careful about any possibility of cost increase which they would like to neutralize by implementing effective cost reduction or cost saving programs or even still better cost prevention programs.

CREATING COLLABORATING RELATIONSHIP WITH ALL STAKEHOLDERS FOR CO-CREATION

All stakeholders (shareholders, employees, customers, consumers, creditors, suppliers, society, and government) have a stake in a company and together shape a company's value and reputation in the market. Shareholder value can be delivered on a consistent basis only when a company is responsible to all its stakeholders.

The biggest challenge before global marketers is achieving sustainable development. Most corporations are now required to work with a vision that through their operations, technologies, products, and services, people's lives (the consumers, employees, and the communities where they operate) will be better. Corporations need to build social, environmental, and economic sustainability into their businesses strategy. Though 94 percent of companies believe the development of a corporate social responsibility strategy can deliver real business benefits, only 11 percent have made significant progress in implementing the strategy in their organizations (Ernst & Young Survey 2002). Major global marketers need to follow the lead given by corporations like P&G who has reduced its use of packaging by 25 percent, has saved USD 500 million over a six-year period by designing waste-out, and bringing worker safety to its best ever performance levels (Carpenter 2003). And most importantly companies will have to involve its customers and trade partners in the process of development of new products as well as for improving the service quality to ensure sustained growth.

ABILITY TO BENCHMARK MARKETING CAPABILITIES

Market-based organizational learning may be an important source of sustainable competitive advantage. Businesses are required to constantly benchmark the key operational parameters with their nearest competitors as well as with the industry leader to help them constantly upgrade and improve their performance on the identified criteria where they are underperforming in relation to their own competitive set. Marketers have identified eight marketing capability areas: pricing capabilities, product development capabilities, distribution capabilities, marketing communication capabilities, selling capabilities, market information management capabilities, marketing planning capabilities, and marketing implementation capabilities for benchmarking as these are associated with business performance. Global marketers need to analyze and benchmark on a consistent basis to build and enhance marketing capabilities (Vorhies and Morgan 2005).

STRATEGIC MARKETING FOR GLOBAL FMCG BRAND MARKETERS IN A COMPETITIVE ENVIRONMENT–CRITICAL SUCCESS FACTORS

Business environment internationally and in India in recent times is going through rapid transformation. The competitive environment is not sparing even the major fast moving consumer goods (FMCG) brand marketers like Unilever which in recent times has failed to adjust its plans quickly enough to react to a more difficult business environment and in the process, has failed to achieve sustained top-level growth internationally and also in India. These brand marketers and their brands now have to be alert all the time as the technology is changing very fast and there is a plethora of new product introductions all the time in the market. The number of trademarks and patents is increasing and consumers are getting fragmented. Category definitions and competitor sets are changing rapidly like when HUL realizes that rather than competing in the shampoo category (where it has market share of 50 percent) only, it is competing in the much broader hair wash category (where it has a market share of only 6 percent). Automatically the marketing challenge and the task in front of the marketer change its orientation significantly. In this environment, marketing must become the driver of business strategy and companies need to adopt a more holistic view of the marketing challenge (Kotler 2004). Companies need to change orientation from a product-focused to a market- and consumer-focused organization. They need to build, measure, and manage brand equity and customer equity. Most products need to create and maintain differentiation and can't graduate to a brand unless they are offering some unique value proposition.

As traditional marketing programs are not delivering the expected performance and majority of these programs are resulting into declining brand equity and market share and also as most of the sales promotion activities are becoming unprofitable there is a need for the marketers to come up with customized strategies that will help their brands to break the clutter in the marketplace and enter the consumer's mind space. Marketers need to find ways of creating and sustaining more successful brands. Worldwide brands like Starbucks have provided superior delivery of desired benefits on a consistent basis. The strongest brands provide both use value and purchase value. Internationally, Nestle not only sells baby food, but also provides free dietician phone line at Nestops along the highway. These are the critical success factors that the global FMCG marketers are focusing on in order to build and sustain winning brands in the marketplace internationally and also in India. In the process, some product or business ideas are becoming powerful, connecting emotionally to the target audience and building winning brands with the support of consistent levels of communication in a changed business environment. HUL has recently embarked upon a unique way of communicating by stamping the millions of *chapatis* (*rotis*) served to devotees in Kumbh Mela in Allahabad with the message "have you washed your hands with Lifebuoy before eating." Their ad agency Ogilvy & Mather coordinated with all food vendors in this mega mela where even students from Harvard came to study how such a mammoth event is organized.

Major global marketer P&G underscores three strength areas for itself: branding, innovation, and scale (Jim Stengel, P&G Chairman 2003). In India, global FMCG marketers have to build their core competence keeping in mind that FMCG market has slowed in 2000 after growing at almost 15 percent per annum in the 1990s. This has been caused by the diversion of consumer incomes to other spending avenues like monthly installments for consumer durables, mobile usage, and spending on entertainment and travel. This along with factors like poor monsoon and low agricultural growth (in rural areas) and regular monthly budget allocation for health, education, and utilities (in urban areas) has led to downtrading, whereby consumers have started looking for more value for money and sometimes cheaper products. The key global marketers in India have to concentrate on critical success factors to counter this downtrading process and build real value (more in terms of benefits rather than price-centric value only) in their offerings. The potential is enormous in some categories for increasing penetration and consumption as India's per capita income increases.

FOCUS ON INNOVATION AND PRODUCT QUALITY

Nowadays companies are vigorously focusing on building customer share. They are also moving to customer lifetime value thinking. Products are functionally equivalent in many categories and with the shortening of new product development cycles innovations are getting imitated in many categories. Yet continuous innovation resulting in a more contemporary brand is essential for brands to remain on top of consumer's consideration set. Many global marketers are proactively investing behind brands through innovation and quality improvement. Major marketers like Reckitt Benckiser and Colgate Palmolive get 40 percent of their revenue from new products launched within the last three to five year's period (three years for Reckitt Benckiser and five years for Colgate Palmolive). Technology leadership is the crux of Gillette's ability to create superior and distinctive new product platforms like the

Mach3 family, which contributes significantly to its top line and to operating margins. For a company like Gillette unmatched global ability to trade up consumers to higher performance products accrues from its technological leadership.

Similarly, after relatively stagnant sales in the 1990s, in recent times P&G under its CEO A. G. Lafley has reengineered itself as a master brand builder and a model growth company through enhanced focus on innovations (Fortune Innovation Special 2004). P&G has around 7,500 researchers working on 20 technical centers on four continents. Olay is a good example of how P&G surrounds consumers with innovation that delights them. P&G has made it a billion dollar brand and through Olay Regenerist in recent times P&G has delivered to the world one of the very best antiaging technology in the world. In fabric and home care, P&G has more than doubled its innovation success rate in fiscal 2004 compared to those in fiscal 2003 and has more than doubled the future value potential of the innovations in its pipeline. Also, it is introducing to the world those products that are making consumers' lives easier and building business for its trade customers.

In Colgate Palmolive, innovative products are generated by new product innovation groups, made up of collaborative teams of experts in marketing, R&D, and consumer insights. Colgate is very focused on new product innovation in its core categories and prepared to spend aggressively to continue to support the global brands. Product innovation is an important growth driver for Cadbury also in the beverage and confectionery markets. In 2004, Cadbury Schweppes has invested in a new consumer segmentation study across its major markets around the world, which has provided valuable insights for the innovation platforms, which the group has chosen to pursue globally. It has also used proprietary software to increase the focus on discovery of ideas to feed the group's innovation pipelines. In Danone, innovation means being open to opportunities, which include research, health, nutrition, management, and expansion into new geographical markets. Similarly, Unilever has filed a total of 370 new patent applications in 2004 to keep its innovative edge intact in many categories. Overall, many major global marketers are spending significant amount like 2–4.3 percent of their revenue on R&D spend. In India, HUL's investment in product quality alone has been over ₹4 billion (USD 80 million), or 5 percent of sales, in the last three years in addition to the cost of defending market position.

BRAND-BUILDING CAPABILITY

Brand-building capability is very critical given the abundant choices consumers have in different categories and with the growing clout of organized retailers. Leading consumer goods marketers are trying to grow sales, market shares, and profits on their leading brands, in biggest markets, in growing distribution channels and trying at winning retailers. P&G's key strength comes from the fact that eight of its sixteen USD 1 billion plus brands are leaders in their categories or in its own segments. In India, Colgate has been ranked as India's most trusted brand in 2003 (ETIG Survey with A. C. Nielsen ORG/Marg) and it has also been ranked as the Number 1 brand in India across all categories in eight out of nine years since 1992 in the surveys done by Advertising & Marketing in conjunction with MODE (Bharat Patel, Colgate India Chairman 2004).

ROLE OF PROPER SEGMENTATION AND CONSUMER INSIGHTS

In today's environment if a brand has to enter consumer mind space, it has to understand the functional, the psychological, and the emotional gratification that the consumer craves for. HUL in recent times has used its consumer insights to reposition Lux from the soap of the stars to a soap that brings out the star in a person. Through this initiative, it has gone beyond the functional benefits and has captured emotional and psychological facets also.

FOCUS ON CORE BUSINESS

Over the years P&G has steadily expanded its share in all its core businesses (its foundation is household products) of baby care, fabric care, feminine care, and health care (categories in which P&G is number1 in global sales and market share). Gillette has extensively focused on its core business of blades and razors that contributes to about 40 percent of its net sales. A highly focused organization like Kellogg's sells only cereal and wholesome snacks in its international business. Similarly, in recent times Diageo has focused on its core business of premium drinks only and has divested its noncore Pillsbury food business to General Mills in October 2001 and acquired related Seagram spirits and wine business in December 2001.

EXPAND INTO OTHER RELATED PROFITABLE SEGMENTS

Core brands also may generate new avenues of growth like what Coca-Cola is doing through its focus on related diet and light products. Beverages major Coke and Pepsi have introduced fruit drinks and packaged drinking water. Fruit-based beverages in ready-to-serve category are now driving the growth. Similarly, Cadbury (now Kraft Foods) entered into specialty biscuit by introducing cream biscuit under the brand name Oreo and ITC, Smith Kline Beecham (makers of Horlicks), and HUL have now introduced instant noodles, a sector which was earlier dominated by Nestle's Maggi.

VIBRANT BRAND IDEA AND CONNECTING WITH TARGET AUDIENCE

Brands also need to have simple, attractive ideas and catch phrases to enter into consumer's mind space (for example, "Gillette, The Best A Man Can Get"). A few of the appropriate examples from Indian scenario include Mountain Dew—"Cheetah Bhi Peeta Hai," Coca Cola—"Thanda Matlab Coca Cola," or "Paanch Matlab Chotta Coke," Horlicks—"Taller, Stronger, Sharper," and Vicks Cough Drops "Khich Khich Door Karo." Pepsi and Coca-Cola have also been successful on the communication front since they have identified themselves with the culture and its people. Pepsi has been successful internationally and in India because from time to time it has been successful talking the lingo of the youth ("Yeh Dil Maange More").

BRAND PORTFOLIO RATIONALIZATION AND NEED FOR COHERENT BRAND PORTFOLIO STRATEGY

For Unilever, nearly two-thirds of the turnover in 2004 came from brands which had sales in excess of Euro 0.5 billion. For P&G about 60 percent of the turnover in fiscal 2004 comes from its 16 brands with more than USD 1 billion turnover. Six worldwide corporate brands of Nestle (Nestle, Nescafe, Nestea, Maggi, Buitoni and Purina) contributed to about 70 percent of the group's sales in 2003 with the Nestle brand contributing about 40 percent. For Reckitt, 53 percent of net revenues in 2004 came from the top 15 brands compared to 40 percent in 2001 for the same. In 2004, concentrates and syrups for beverages bearing the trademark of Coca-Cola or including the trademark of Coke have accounted for approximately 56 percent of Coca-Cola's total gallon sales. This skew toward the sales of largest brands brings about the need to allocate adequate resources to these brands. This in turn is prompting top corporate executives in biggest FMCG organizations to lean toward the concepts of power branding and rationalization of brand portfolio.

From a careful analysis one can conclude that most brands don't make money for companies (Kumar 2003). Businesses earn all their profit from a small number of brands—smaller than even the 80/20 rule of thumb suggests. For Diageo, eight of its 35 brands provide the company with more than 50 percent of its sales and 70 percent of its profits. For Nestle, around 2.5 percent of the company's portfolio contributes to bulk of the company's profits. For P&G, 4 percent of its portfolio accounts for more than 50 percent of its profits and 66 percent of its sales growth between 1992 and 2002. Similarly, 25 percent of Unilever's brand portfolio contributed to 90 percent of its profits. Companies like Unilever and Electrolux have been able to increase both profits and sales by systematically killing their own low performing brands (Kumar 2003). Therefore, rigorous economic analysis and strong insights into consumers can help marketers clarify the competitive positioning of their brands, avoid offending core consumers of repositioned or discontinued ones, minimize cannibalization, and seize growth opportunities.

In recent times, Reckitt Benckiser like other FMCG manufacturers is also putting more focus on power brands and these brands are being rolled out in more number of countries. For example, Veet was available in 51 countries in January 2005 as compared to 26 countries in 1999. Similarly, Sara Lee in fiscal 2004 has adopted a new brand segmentation strategy that concentrates its financial and management resources behind its most powerful brands. To drive overall top line growth, it has identified one of four strategic roles for each of its brands. It is also progressively shaping its portfolio of brands by this brand segmentation strategy, which is helping it to identify some businesses for divestiture. In India, HUL has scaled down from a portfolio of 110 brands to 35 power brands across 20 categories in recent times. The focusing of portfolio has resulted in the share of non-FMCG business reduced from 24 percent to 8 percent of business. HUL, backed by appropriate technology, has strengthened the power brands by ensuring that they offer better value and play a bigger role in consumers' lives. Wherever necessary, HUL has reduced prices to make the brands more affordable, and launched several low unit size and price packs to make them more accessible and affordable.

Aaker has also argued about the need for a company to have a coherent brand portfolio strategy which specifies the scope, roles, and interrelationships of the portfolio brands with the goal of creating synergy, leverage, and clarity within the portfolio and having relevant, differentiated and energized brands (Aaker 2004). In India Brooke Bond (India's single largest tea brand) is a good example of a brand that is brilliantly using sub-brand strategy and building four powerful sub-brands (based on local tastes and flavors), namely, Brooke Bond Taj Mahal, Brooke Bond Red Label, Brooke Bond Taaza and Brooke Bond 3 Roses.

CREATING MORE TOUCH POINTS TO DELIVER CONSUMER EXPERIENCE

These days consumer's direct experiences drive brand perceptions more than traditional advertising. As functional benefits get replicated more often, process and relationship benefits increasingly drive purchase decisions, word of mouth communication, and loyalty. The ability of a firm to create and maintain relationships with the most valuable customers is a durable basis for competitive advantage (Day 2000). A firm has to master the three elements of market-relating capability—a relationship orientation, deepening of the knowledge of the customers, and internal integration of key processes. Internationally, Starbucks has used experiential marketing to build relationships with consumers and to grow the consumer base.

These days there is an ever-growing need to bring a brand to life via activation. There are fast changes in the lifestyles and buying habits of India's burgeoning population. In the new brand paradigm brand essence is focused on a set of touch points through which the brand can deliver a consistently distinctive and inspiring consumer experience (Court, McLaughlin, and Halsall 2000; Eccleshare et al. 2001). This increase in touch points creates opportunities and challenges for branding. Ensuring consistent delivery of the brand promise across touch points is a challenge and accordingly, successful brands these days focus on key touch points where they can create distinctive propositions that meet or exceed consumer's expectations. Also, these days brands are concentrating on surrounding the consumer with superior market experience. Market presence is beneficial because of the image benefits of being seen everywhere and the power of word-of-mouth communications. Brands are also creating total brand presence through innovative approaches like using new media, word-of-mouth viral marketing, guerrilla marketing, alliances, and customer's in-store experiences.

Making products online is becoming a key success mantra in many markets. In the U.S. research shows, on an average, people now spend more time online than time spent on reading magazines and newspapers combined. To capitalize on this, an Internet component is now built into many companies' advertising and media plans. Porter has argued about using Internet for creating strategic positioning and differentiation using its ability to support convenience, service, specialization, customization, and other forms of values that justify attractive prices (Porter 2001).

Consumer insights help Colgate identify and target its messages (case in point being the success of Colgate Sensitive toothpaste in Western Europe). The company is trying similar strategy for Sensitive toothpaste in Indian market as well. HUL in recent times has shifted emphasis from mere reach or availability to a 3-way convergence of product availability, brand communication, and higher levels of brand experience (Banga 2004). HUL has developed an Internet-based system that will bring the power of net to rural India. The algorithms developed as part of this project are more widely applicable as a tool for consumer dialog.

STANDARDIZATION VERSUS LOCALIZATION AND NEED FOR BRAND CUSTOMIZATION

It is possible for many companies to adopt a unified marketing program because of shared universal needs and desires of the target segment. From a consumer standpoint, consumers' needs are similar in many categories due to constant exposure to media and technology (Levitt 1983). There is, therefore, a need to have standardized product and at the same time incorporate some local needs based on local consumer insight. Rather than ignore the global characteristics of their brands, it is critical for firms to manage those characteristics, because future growth for most companies is likely to come from foreign markets.

High quality and similar portfolios of products provide Kellogg's a key standardization benefit. They allow it to effectively spread advertising and promotional ideas from business to business and across borders whereas many other FMCG majors have done a lot of localization in their product and communications. Glocal strategies now rule marketing and many companies are making necessary adaptations on a country/region basis. Coca-Cola, the most recognised global brand in the world, recorded radio spots in 40 languages with 140 different music backgrounds (Coca-Cola Annual Report 1999). Local adaptations many times have to take indigenous condition into account. On the innovation front, Surf Excel Quick Wash is powered with a path-breaking technology that reduces water consumption and time taken for rinsing by 50 percent. It is a significant benefit given the water scarcity in most parts of India. Fair & Lovely's formulation contains a unique fairness system that consists of a combination of active agents and sunscreens and its sunscreen system is specially optimized for Indian skin. McDonald's, in line with its philosophy of being global but acting local, has transplanted itself successfully into a number of different cultures, including China. Its India strategy has been formulated based on the findings that the people here wanted McDonald's to serve something that is not available anywhere else but at the same time is also distinctly Indian in terms of taste. Since Indian society is family-oriented, McDonald's has positioned itself as a family restaurant. In contrast, a reputed marketer like Kellogg's has faced many hurdles because it has not been able to break the Indian local food habit.

APPROPRIATE PRICING AND IMPACT ON CONSUMPTION

Consumer value is also being provided through strategic pricing. Colgate internationally is making products more affordable for consumers through smaller sizes, refill packs, and low-cost formulas. A key to its growth strategy in emerging markets is supporting the brand with educational and consumption building programs that increase product usage. P&G has repositioned itself globally from its premium-tier focus strategy to become a true mass player with quality (by incorporating mid-tier consumers also). Evidence of this is manifest in its aggressive pricing strategy in many categories like detergents, etc., in large emerging markets like China and India to combat Unilever and many of the very strong regional brands. It is satisfying more number of lower income consumers with unique product designs and marketing programs. It is building unique activity systems that integrate product design, manufacturing supply chain, and customer distribution systems to keep its costs competitive with local, low cost competition.

HUL is also following strategic pricing through increasing accessibility, driving affordability through lower price points, and strategic price reductions.

Coca-Cola also has learnt with experience that price is a strategic weapon in India where many people found a bottle of Coca-Cola to be an expensive proposition earlier. In 2000, Coca-Cola conducted an experiment by introducing a 200 ml bottle priced at ₹7 (14 cents). The volumes went up by 30 percent demonstrating the importance of consumer affordability. The 200 ml pack, priced at ₹5 (10 cents), was rolled out countrywide in January 2003. The advertising campaign (shot in rural background) highlighted the affordability (lower price). Appropriate pricing (value packs, etc.) is very critical for FMCG marketers to be able to synchronize their efforts in rural India in line with the budgetary incentives that the Union government is giving in recent times to increase social investments and to stimulate rural demand. Rural investment in agricultural sector will increase the rural consumers' purchasing power and consumption level and gradually will provide larger market for FMCG marketers. However, key marketers in this context need to keep in mind the fact that they should earn market share by offering unique value proposition and not buy market share through mindless promotions and freebies. When both Coke and Pepsi reduced their prices, volume went up significantly because of expansion of rural market but for obvious reasons profit from this low-price strategy has also drastically reduced. It is, therefore, necessary that price reduction be supported by equivalent cost reduction. Otherwise, such strategy will not be sustainable in the long run and that is exactly what had happened to both Coke and Pepsi which forced them to withdraw from this strategy. Later on, both Coke and Pepsi introduced smaller bottles, which is actually a reversal from 250 ml to 300 ml per bottle to 200 ml per bottle per serving now in order to make the proposition affordable. Both Pepsi and Coke are now are available in 200 ml glass bottles.

THE ROLE OF INTEGRATED MARKETING COMMUNICATION

Increasing need is being felt these days to use integrated marketing communication in brand building by using alternative ways like advertising, sponsorship, event planning, promotions, PR, etc., to break out of the clutter in the marketplace. Costs, market fragmentation, and new media channels that let customers bypass advertisements seem to be in league against the old ways of marketing. Relying on mass media campaigns to build strong brands may be a thing of the past and several companies in Europe, making a virtue of necessity, have come up with alternative brand-building approaches (Joachimsthaler and Aaker 1997). The various campaigns shared characteristics like senior managers getting closely involved with brand-building efforts, the companies recognizing the importance of clarifying their core brand identity and making sure that all their efforts to gain visibility are tied to that core identity. Table 6.1 provides a summary of innovative brand-building approaches followed by some of leading global brands successfully in a competitive environment.

Table 6.1 Innovative Brand-Building Approaches

Brand-Building Tool	Brand
Clubs (Programs)	Nestlé's Casa Buitoni Club
Company Visits	Cadbury's Theme Park
Distribution Outlets	Haagen-Dazs Parlors
Public Facilities	Nestle Nestops
Social/Environ. Causes	The Body Shop

SOURCE: Joachimsthaler and Aaker (1997).

GLOBAL SCALE DEVELOPMENT

There is a need to have a scale of operations to be effective in the marketplace. And there are ways for building that scale. These are:

- **Need for Focused Acquisitions**
  Scale is so important for viability of a global marketer that a profitable, dominating marketer like Gillette had to allow itself to be acquired in 2005 by P&G as management decided this was the best option for long-term survival and profitability given the difficulty in waging an effective battle with much larger sized competitors with greater sales, reach, and resources (Gillette Annual Report 2004). Acquisition is a key strategic tool for marketers for scale enhancement. It may involve the scope of getting both synergy and complementary product range (like Gillette offering to P&G) or scale enhancement in the same product category. Similarly, Thums Up has contributed significantly to Coke's strategic plan and business in India.
- **Need for International Infrastructure**
  Many global marketers in recent times are building international infrastructure by trying to build leadership in fast growing developing markets. HUL for long is the giant among the FMCG marketers in India and it is virtually impossible for smaller FMCG marketers to effectively match the distribution prowess enjoyed by it especially in rural markets. Internationalization

is a big challenge because either the good markets are overcrowded or the poor markets have no money and marketers need to exhibit real analytic and decision-making skills to decide which markets they need to focus upon.

For Unilever, about a third of its turnover comes from developing and emerging countries whereas for P&G 20 percent of the revenues come from developing countries. For P&G, organic volume in developing markets is growing more than 50 percent faster than in the developed markets. Building international infrastructure requires time and resources like the Coca-Cola system investing more than USD 1 billion in India over the last decade (Coca-Cola is one of India's top international investors) or Kellogg's taking around 20 years to be successful in Japan.

- **New Businesses For the Future**

  HUL has also begun to nurture new businesses and new ways of engaging with consumers for the future. It has entered into water purifiers, with Pureit. In urban India, Hindustan Unilever Network is HUL's direct selling initiative (new channel), which reaches 1,400 towns through a consultant base of 330,000. Its rural marketing project Shakti is doing rural selling through self-help groups (SHGs) in 12 states currently. The program covers 60,000 villages and touches 75 million rural lives. It plans to cover additional 100,000 villages touching 100 million more rural lives. Simultaneously, it is providing a sustainable source of income to underprivileged rural women, HUL's partners in this initiative.

ACHIEVING INCREASED OPERATIONAL EFFICIENCY AND EFFECTIVENESS

- **Streamlining Supply Chain**

  In Colgate, increasing efficiency has begun with supply chain and now reaches all functions worldwide. The savings generated are reinvested into new product development and marketing activities that fuel further growth. Colgate is moving toward a global supply chain with fewer and more sophisticated global and regional state-of-the-art manufacturing centers. Business support functions will be centralized into regional and global shared service centers with larger and more effective sales and marketing organizations in key markets. With toothbrushes, for example, Colgate has reduced the number of suppliers by 30 percent over the past years. Other initiatives include reducing the number of SKUs, generating savings through purchasing efficiency and finding new lower cost sources for high-quality raw material in countries such as China and India. Colgate is also reaching more and more consumers across the world by building and expanding its national distribution network in emerging markets around the world.

In India, through 22 members of Efficient Consumer Response (ECR) India, the FMCG sector has taken industry-wide initiative for collaboration in logistics (Ambwani 2002). The initiative includes all the key FMCG players like HUL, Nestle, P&G, Colgate Palmolive, Cadbury, etc. HUL in recent times has reinvented the management of distribution channels and customers, who are now being serviced on continuous replenishment. It is leveraging scale and building expertise to service modern trade and rural markets. Its sales force has been de-layered to improve response times and service levels. IT tools have been deployed by HUL for connectivity across the extended supply chain of about 2,000 suppliers, 80 company factories, 45 clearing and forwarding agents (C&FAs), 7,000 stockists, and a direct coverage of 1 million outlets. Its back-end processes have been combined into a common shared service infrastructure and it has made necessary changes in its system to gear the organization toward the opportunity for food revolution (by focusing on the supply chain for agricultural products).

In India, companies now will need to proactively think on their distribution structure given the recent introduction of value added tax (VAT) and planned phase-out of central sales tax (CST). India is truly becoming a common market and companies will have to go through a rethink on location decisions of warehouses and key mid-country locations are likely to gain more prominence.

- **The Role of Restructured, Empowered Organization in Value Creation**
  Gillette has cut its overhead costs by 3 percent point of its sales. Nestle's factory efficiency program, Target 2004+, was successfully closed at the end of 2004, achieving savings of over CHF 3.2 billion. The key enabler for Nestle's efficiencies is the GLOBE program (Global Business Excellence), which is expected to enable Nestle to combine complexity with operational efficiency. Its three objectives include implementing best practices, data standards, and standardized systems. Similarly, P&G these days is able to capture the benefits of focused, smaller companies through dedicated global business units (GBUs) while capturing the go-to market capabilities and strengths of a USD 51 billion giant. Also, the organization has been reengineered to ensure seamless integration of commercial and technical evaluation. P&G has drastically restructured its sales and distribution system creating large distributors in states and putting smaller distributors under the large distributors (mega distributor—one in each state) to streamline and simplify the delivery points. They also have been able to reduce large numbers of sales force for

direct employment and put them under the focused large distributors. This was implemented by P&G under the project named "Golden Eye." This project is based on the principle of 80/20 and they focused on 20 percent of the distributors who contributed to 80 percent of the sales which has reduced the complexity and cost of distribution significantly. Unilever has been restructured with its eight profit centers being integrated into two divisions of Home & Personal Care and Foods. It is a simpler and leaner organization, less hierarchical with fewer levels and greater empowerment. This has eliminated complexity and sped up decision-making. P&G now even in discussion with potential investors for divesting its stackable potato chips brand Pringles. Sara Lee's "Functional Excellence" program focuses on improving its effectiveness in key areas as well as increasing its overall operational efficiency in order to enhance its competitiveness in the marketplace and reduce costs.

BUILDING STRATEGIC ALLIANCES

Organizations are increasingly seen to join hands with other players where synergies can be derived for common good and growth in the name of strategic alliances—a move that helps faster capturing of local opportunities.

- **Alliance Between Key Marketers**
  Coca-Cola produces, distributes, and markets Bacardi tropical fruit mixers (manufactured and marketed under a license from Bacardi & Company Ltd). Beverage major Coke partners worldwide, Coca-Cola's 50 percent owned joint venture with Nestle markets ready-to-drink coffee and tea in certain countries. Coca-Cola is the exclusive master distributor of Evian bottled water in the U.S. and Canada. In addition, CCDA Waters, L.L.C. (CCDA), a 51 percent owned consolidated subsidiary, manufactures and markets Dannon, Sparkletts, and other water brands in the U.S. under a license from Group Danone. Similarly, the joint venture between Unilever and Pepsico, the Pepsi Lipton International partnership, helps Unilever to extend the reach of its brands through a distribution network complementary to Unilever supply chain network. Schweppes Cottee's (part of Cadbury group) has a license to manufacture, sell, and distribute Pepsi, 7 Up, Mountain Dew and Gatorade. Among the brewers, in Italy, Anheuser-Busch International has a Budweiser license partnership with Heineken Italia SpA (number 1 brewer in Italy)—that is the first partnership between Anheuser-Busch and Heineken

in the world. In India United Breweries Ltd sells Heineken beer in India which is a joint venture partner in the company holding equal shares. Starbucks has extended its presence in more consumption occasions through its alliance with companies such as Barnes & Noble, United Airlines, and Ben & Jerry's.

In India, cooperation between global marketers exists like the tie-up between HUL and Kimberly Clark Ltd. However, global marketers need to extend beyond short-term promotional tie-ups more often. They need to have more strategic tie ups the way Barista chain of coffee and espresso bars has recently announced a strategic tie up with Indian Oil Corporation Ltd to open outlets at select petrol pumps within metros and mini metros located on highways (Express Hotelier & Caterer 2005).

- Partnership with Organized Retailers

Developing worldwide relationship with global organized retailers is very important for global marketers as 15 of the top 20 retailers operate globally (Kearney 2005). P&G is growing volume and share at 9 out of 10 of its top 10 retail customers. It is developing highly collaborative relationship with organized retailers by leveraging its strengths on shopper understanding, innovation, and supply chain efficiency. Sales to Walmart (and affiliates) represent approximately 11 percent and 13 percent of PepsiCo's and Gillette's total net revenue, respectively, in 2004. PepsiCo's top five retail customers currently represent approximately 27 percent of Pepsico's 2004 North American net revenue, with Walmart representing approximately 14 percent. Sara Lee has initiated significant projects in recent times with mass retailers such as Walmart, Target, and Carrefour to better apply its brand power and value-added product development skills toward building sales.

- **Partnership with Experts, Industry Bodies, and Academic Institutes**

One key aspect of Colgate's growth strategy is continuously strengthening and building upon company's close partnership with dental profession. Methods range from distributing samples of Colgate products and supporting educational programs to participating in dental conventions and creating alliances with dental schools—all activities that bring Colgate closer to dental care professional. Unilever oral care brands have signed a partnership with World Dental Federation that will focus on providing improved oral health. Also, Unilever brand Becel/Flora continues to work with the World Heart Federation. PepsiCo participates in research-based programing like the partnership Gatorade has with University of North Carolina's School of Public Health for preventing childhood obesity.

Consumption building activities especially in emerging markets are building key Colgate brands. In India, Colgate has established a productive partnership with Indian Dental Association and its members. Colgate in association with Indian Dental Association commenced oral health education program in schools in 1976 and so far this program has covered over 30 million school children across the country. In India, on academic collaboration front, P&G has recently donated USD 100,000 to IISc Bangalore to foster collaboration in the area of modeling for chemical and formulated systems (*Business Standard* 2005).

- **Partnership with Society: Ethical Business Practices and Social Responsibility** Global branding has lost some aura recently because transnational companies have been under siege, with brands like Coca-Cola, Starbucks, and McDonald's becoming hot targets with antiglobalization protests. McDonald's has found its fast food outlets attacked all over the world as the brand has come to symbolize globalization and the increasing might of the multinational giant. In India in recent times there has been lot of consumer and political outcry against Coke and Pepsi based on the publication of the pesticide content report by Center for Science and Environment (CSE) in August 2003. Sales of these brands also got affected in the short term. Similarly, Cadbury India also suffered from worm controversy at the end of 2003.

These incidents highlight the need for global marketers to participate in responsible social and environmental causes (including green marketing) that may result in social and consumer level uplift and may provide the brands consumers' respect and goodwill. Eighty-six percent of institutional investors across Europe believe that social and environmental risk management has a significantly positive impact on a company's long-term market value (Nelson 2001). Porter has argued that environmentally sound management can be beneficial for both the environment and the business (Porter and Van Der Linde 1995).

Marketers like P&G especially in the last decade or so have enhanced consumer goodwill significantly for their brands by coming up with more and more eco-friendly versions of their products. P&G has delivered bottom line savings through eco-efficiency (Carpenter 2003). P&G and United Nations Children's Fund (UNICEF) also have formed an alliance to provide safe drinking water for millions of families and schoolchildren in India, South America, and the Caribbean. P&G through its Safeguard brand, working in developing countries with local health ministries, has created awareness about the importance of hygiene and the combined effort is showing how public–private partnerships can reach far more people with health messages than what either the ministry or P&G could do individually

(Carpenter 2003). Similarly, as a socially responsible organization, Starbucks gives all its employees who work more than 20 hours a week stock options and health care benefits.

P&G with Child Rights and You (CRY) and Sony Entertainment Television has launched "Shiksha," a program to help educate underprivileged children across India. The company in the past has also supported other social responsibility initiatives like Peace, Future Focus, Project Drishti, Project Open Minds, and Project Poshan, etc. HUL on its part has initiated quite a few projects on this front. Lifebuoy Swasthya Chetna Program is the biggest rural health and hygiene program ever undertaken in India. The goal of the program is to help educate people about basic hygiene habits and HUL is working with parents, health educators, teachers, community leaders, and government agencies to spread the message. In 2004 the program covered 18,000 villages and reached 70 million people. Reckitt has built on its social program with Save the Children, supporting projects in Bangladesh, Kenya, and India.

All these initiatives from large corporations have a positive business side also. Seventy percent of European consumers say that a company's commitment to social responsibility is important when buying a product or service and one in five consumers would be very willing to pay more for products that are socially and environmentally responsible (CSR Europe/MORI 2000). Ninety-four percent of company executives believe that the development of a CSR strategy can deliver real business benefits (Ernst & Young survey 2002) and one out of three international executives think that social responsibility initiatives will increase sales (Hill & Knowlton's Corporate Reputation Watch 2002).

EMPLOYEE DEVELOPMENT AND TRAINING

One of the key pillars of success for global marketers has been installing a corporate culture that promotes capable employees and supports the strategy of the organization. Global marketers share strongly embedded values of achievement, commitment, teamwork, and entrepreneurship. In Colgate Palmolive more than 150 global training courses are offered and the company has created Colgate Leadership Challenge program for identifying, developing, and retaining future leaders. Reckitt Benckiser has a truly multinational team where a dozen nationalities are represented in its top 40 managers alone. In India in recent corporate history, marketers like HUL, PepsiCo, Cadbury, etc., have consistently promoted local managers to CEO positions.

MONITORING NEEDS

Maintaining Brand Report Card

Marketers need to continuously monitor their operations to understand the health of their brands. They need to take necessary actions so that their brands emerge stronger in the process. Brand health also may be monitored by using well-known methodologies like brand asset valuator from Young & Rubicam which is to diagnose a brand's health and examine four primary dimensions and their relationships, namely, differentiation, relevance, esteem, and knowledge that determine the brand's health.

CATERING TO EMERGING NEEDS

Focus on Fast Growing Segments

There are several consumer subsegments that need to be addressed by the marketer with segment specific strategies. No uniform strategy will work for all. Key growth subsegments would require focused attention for faster growth and development.

Focus on More Convenience and Shopping Experience

Sara Lee's Senseo coffee system (launched in some key markets in fiscal 2004) is catering to today's busy coffee lover. Marketers in India also have to focus on more convenience products as housewives' desire for spending time with children and for leisure increases. Also, growing proportion of working women is increasing the need for convenience. In India, with the advent of organized retail phenomenon in recent times consumers have started craving for shopping experience also.

Focus on Health, Nutrition, and Beauty

Both personal care and food companies are making significant expansion to cater to the booming health care market. P&G in health care has strong, growing franchises in Crest, I ams and Prilosec OTC. Major food marketers like Nestle, Kraft, Unilever, and Danone are investing heavily to come up with new products catering to health conscious people. Worldwide beauty care is another fast growing, higher margin business in which marketers like P&G are emerging as global leaders. It provides a huge market and is more than four times the size of the fabric market with no dominant leaders. P&G has a low share of about 10 percent but it is developing the capabilities to grow rapidly through its brands and new capabilities added by Clairol and Wella. For catering to health and beauty needs, HUL has pioneered two concepts in India: Lakme Salons and Ayush Therapy Centres.

PRICING STRATEGY

Pricing is a very critical marketing mix. It has been said that about 14 percent of the products fail because of wrong pricing (R.G. Cooper). Product generally has to be priced just below the perceived value of the product. Some marketers believe that if the best product is available at the least cost then success is assured. But product has to be sold at a price so that it can generate healthy profits which would enable the product to be supported in terms of media and promotion that it requires and also for future innovation. In competitive business environment one can follow the leader strategy and price the product at par with the market leader. It is also possible to follow price leadership strategy or even preemptive strategy. To gain market share a lower price below competitive level helps. To get an entry into the market, marketer can even consider predatory pricing to ensure almost forced trial. The Times of India group followed predatory pricing strategy to establish its daily newspaper in all the major cities very successfully. When price of the newspaper can hardly cover the cost of the newspaper and when advertisement tariff depends on circulation volume this is indeed a very good strategy to enter the market and increase circulation which in turn can improve advertisement revenue. The pricing objective can be different for different organizations for a given product. These could be: survival, maximize current profit, maximize current revenue, maximum sales growth, and maximum market skimming or product quality leadership. Broadly, therefore, pricing objective could be profit oriented, sales oriented, or even status quo oriented to stabilize the prices or even to correct the competition.

The pricing strategies will largely depend on the product positioning, objective, current market standing, product types, and more importantly the current stage of product life cycle and brand strength in the current competitive environment. However, in the longer run, brand must make a healthy bottom line.

The price of a product should reflect the product's perceived value by the target consumers. The value perception has several components, namely,

- products utility
- delivery mode and convenience
- quality promise it fulfills
- needs it satisfies
- brand value which is a function of advertisement and communication

Determining perceived value is not easy and it is subjective although pricing research is normally done before taking a final call on the price.

As more and more brands are introduced in the market and all talk about the same end benefits delivered through same technology, consumers have difficulty in choosing the right product. Pricing then becomes a very important criterion for selection. Wrong pricing, therefore, can ruin the product's prospect totally. In a me-too product category in a competitive scenario parity pricing is an option. If, however, the company wants to maintain the desired price level, high ad spend will be an imperative. The choice between the two options will be dictated by organizational policy, marketing skills, and ability to fight competition, financial resources, and sustainability of the corporation.

CHAPTER SUMMARY

Marketers these days face a plethora of challenges. The brand value of top global brands is more or less stagnant. Markets are becoming more and more complex and competitive. The number of brands in the market is increasing, though only 10–20 percent of the new product introductions in most categories are surviving. Markets and media are getting fragmented and consumers are becoming more and more selective. The effectiveness of marketing programs has been under the scanner.

Marketing paradigms worldwide are evolving. Consumers are in control of their destinies and in order to be successful in the new-age business environment, marketers will have to build sustainable competitive advantage and excel in a few critical success factors as discussed in this chapter. Marketers will have to continuously invest in R&D and there should be steady investment behind brands through focused integrated marketing communication to reach consumers at multiple touch points. Marketers need to be more proactive and change their business models in order to be successful in emerging markets like India. They will need to build alliances at multiple directions and reengineer their organizations to build more efficiency and effectiveness. Value-for-money brands focusing on quality and on interactive marketing will be able to create consumer experience environments and will be the winners. However, these brands need to provide unique value propositions and earn market share instead of mindlessly compromising with their bottom line. Finally, marketers will need to monitor the health of their key brands on a regular basis and will have to proactively embrace new age marketing concepts. Product price is a very important marketing mix and must be decided with great care depending on the pricing objective and current standing of the brand in the competitive environment. The chapter discusses the criteria of deciding the product price with examples.

CHAPTER 7

Managing Brands over Time and Building Equity through Relationships

M arketers' actions and promotions can change the consumer response. Anticipating the future consumer response now is not that easy a task. However, marketers must actively manage brand equity over time by reinforcing the brand meaning and by making adjustments as necessary to the marketing programs by identifying new sources of brand equity. The most important considerations in reinforcing brands are the consistency of the nature and amount of the marketing support the brand receives. Inadequate marketing support will dwarf the brand over time and when it is combined with the price increase it is dangerous. Being consistent, however, does not mean that marketers should avoid making any changes in the marketing program. In fact, managing a brand with consistency might require numerous tactical shifts and changes to maintain the strategic thrust and direction of the brand. In reality it can be seen that prices move up and down, product features are changed, advertisement campaigns followed different creative strategies, and different extensions were carried out or even withdrawn over time. But despite these changes the strategic positioning of many leading brands remained remarkably consistent over time. Unless there is change with respect to the consumers and competition, or current position has become very weak there will be little need for any change in the successful positioning of the brand. Over time, a brand may also need to be revitalized by making it more current and contemporary which happens if the brand loses its original sources of brand equity which need to be recaptured and reinforced. Managing brand transition is important in rapidly changing technologically intensive markets.

Brand revitalization strategies would mean both refreshing old sources of brand equity as well as creating new sources of brand equity and expand both depth and breadth of awareness and usage of brand. This would need creation of more occasions for the consumer interface with the brand.

NEED FOR INNOVATIVE MARKETING PRACTICES IN UNCERTAIN TIMES

Uncertainty is the greatest driver of organic growth and innovation but is also the most difficult variable in decision-making. Desperate times call for desperate but appropriate measures. In the midst of today's global economic crisis and downturn that the organizations are facing, it is not just the largest, the strongest, or the leader that would survive but it is the one that predicts and adjusts to the situation at the earliest. It becomes imperative for all firms to innovate, adapt, evolve, and revolutionize their marketing efforts to ensure their existence.

Uncertainty

Uncertainty is omnipresent in every walk of life and business is no exception. In business it comes at three levels, i.e., company, industry sector, and economy. Firstly, company-specific uncertainty deals with the micro-economic decision variables that are in-house to the organizations and relates to its functioning and survival. Secondly, at the sector-specific level uncertainty is inherent to the various firms catering to similar types of consumer needs. Finally, economic uncertainties exist at the macro level and fuels growth and innovation at global level. Country-level economy- and sector-specific uncertainty variables impact the corporation equally but responses and strategies at firm level can greatly change the performance of individual organizations.

Uncertainty is an inbuilt variable in the outcome of any decision and it increases greatly in times of recession and economic meltdown. With rising inventories, falling demands, and pressurized bottom line, when technological innovation is unable to sustain a firm's profitability, the only solace lies in looking toward innovations in marketing. Though long-term sustainability undoubtedly depends on constant innovations in products, processes, and technology, in the short term profitability depends solely on the marketing efforts undertaken by a firm.

It is against this backdrop that brand marketers should look for better avenues for reaching and addressing their target markets by way of employing innovative and novel marketing strategies that should essentially lead to faster payoffs.

Some of the strategies in times of distress firms should look at these options more intimately and their relevance in a given scenario.

CHALLENGES OF GLOBALIZATION IN BRAND MARKETING

The forces of globalization have diffused the trade boundaries and the whole world is gradually emerging as one homogeneous market. The evolution of a global market led to the emergence of global customers with universal mindset. Goods and services are being designed to meet the expectations of global customers. Organizations which are not viewing the whole world as one market and creating a global mindset will be increasingly marginalized. Even small and medium enterprise (SME) sectors need to focus on extending the geographical boundaries and build collaboration and strategic alliances with the partners in other countries to ensure survival. Definition of marketing still remains same whether an organization chooses to market products domestically or internationally. However, scope of marketing is broadened when the organization decides to sell the products across international boundaries. This is primarily due to the fact that complexities and challenges increase in a global marketing environment. The reason for this complexity largely arises from language barrier, a legal framework which is country-specific as well as other customers' specific requirements which goods and services have to satisfy including the environmental and larger social issues. Global marketers have to integrate all these diverse issues and find a place in the market. In addition, there is a need for faster flow of goods and services to face the global competition. Organizations thus will be required to build competitive advantage by managing knowledge and technology better than competition. Therefore, traditional marketing model is not going to be effective any longer. Marketers will always be in search of more efficient and functional business model to deliver the competitive edge. In this chapter various marketing models in networking environment are discussed with a case of how a company can gradually emerge as a global player with very limited resources which a traditional business model requires.

TRADITIONAL MARKETING MODELS WILL NOT WORK

Global marketing is characterized by the key imperative:

- Global product (acceptable to wider market segments represented by various countries targeted)
- Fast to act (speed of action)
- Cost competitiveness
- Reaching out directly to customers instead of going through channels

Traditional marketing model will not be able to deliver these key concerns. Mainly because:

- Traditional marketing is highly resource-intensive. To reach the end customers requires huge manpower and funds to market the firms' products. Evidently it is not the most cost-effective method of marketing a firm's product.
- Traditional channel structure is long and hence it takes longer time and higher cost to take the product and services to target consumers.
- Traditional marketing model reaches out to consumers through indirect means and thus lose out on knowing the customer requirement better.

These inherent limitations of traditional marketing model have forced market-ers to constantly search for alternative and better marketing method to overcome these difficulties using the available technologies.

ALTERNATIVE MARKETING CHANNELS

Internet is a very powerful medium to reach out to target audience at the lowest or even at no cost. Businesses are happening online and consumers are increasingly be-coming comfortable buying online. For certain kind of goods and services booking or buying online is much easier and even hassle-free. For example, books or even certain branded goods whose quality is assured by the brand marketers. Youngsters are seen to prefer this mode of shopping. With increased Internet penetration and growing comfort levels among consumers to shop online consumer durable retailers are now seen to log back into e-commerce.

Some of the large consumer durable retailers are taking this route to boost up their sales. For example, Mumbai-based Vijay Sales Corporation and Chennai-based Vivek Sales are among those kick-starting e-commerce operation this year. While Vijay Sales is planning to take plunge in six to eight months, Vivek is expected to soon start selling goods online. In next three to four years e-commerce will be big in electronic goods—expect owners of the large multi-brand consumer durable retail-ers. Vijay sales started as a small television store at Mahim (in Mumbai) in 1967 and has come a long way since then and today it has clocked a turnover of ₹1,250 crores (USD 250 million) in the year 2010–2011. Vijay Sales has rapidly expanded its pres-ence outside Mumbai covering Delhi, Pune, Surat, and Ahmedabad. It has 17 stores outside Mumbai; however, over 65 percent of its sales come from Mumbai where it has 12 stores. The company feels that there is a potential of garnering 10 to 15 percent of total sales, contributed by e-commerce during the next two to three years. Growing at about 10 percent annually this retailer has projected a sales turnover of ₹1,750 crores (USD 350 million) in 2011–2012. Trust and service quality will play a critical role to gain consumer confidence in this mode of purchase which will actually drive the growth of e-commerce.

For Vivek, e-commerce is a mode of business one can no longer ignore. But you need to have an excellent supply chain management practice in place that will ensure the delivery in time as well as service as and when required. Otherwise, this initiative will not deliver results. To begin with, Vivek is planning south-centric portal as Vivek has a strong presence in south India and hence it makes good sense to start the new initiative first in south. Some of the manufacturer marketers still feel that this is an early stage until entire payment structure is set up and working. If e-commerce picks up there is nothing like it. But even if consumers are becoming net-savvy they are still hesitant to purchase on the net just because they fear whether what they buy and what they order are really the same and assured of what has been promised on the net. While these fears are valid, they will gradually disappear. E-bays business model is working fine and soon other consumer durable manufacturers and distributors will have to consider e-commerce opportunity more seriously. Available information suggests that even today consumer durable manufacturers do about 10–12 percent of their business through e-commerce route.

Premier, a Chennai-based brand that manufactures appliances and cook-wares is very keen to go the e-commerce way in about three months' time from now and by the time this book will be released they would be already on line. To avoid e-commerce is foolish according to the CEO of Srinivasan Group which owns the Premier brand. And like Vivek, Premier will also initially restrict its online sales only in south from the point of view of supply chain management constraints. However, they think of going national in about two to three years' time.

Mobile phones and laptop sales are growing online but some experts still question whether consumer durable sales will pick up that fast. It is seen that women are still not very comfortable with Internet and they are the key decision makers. Women still prefer a demonstration and a touch-and-feel experience. The scenario will soon change. LCD, LED TV sets, and DVD players are likely to do well in online counters. In spite of all skepticism the ₹35,000 crores (USD 700 million) consumer durable industry is expecting 15 percent growth this year driven by a rise in disposable income.

It has been said that e-commerce sites are having a field day in Gurgaon (in national capital region, NCR). During the past one year online shopping portals across all sectors ranging from fashion and food to home decor, travel, and electronics have witnessed a 15–20 percent growth in their business from the city of Gurgaon which is one of the biggest corporate hubs in the country with double-income working couples who are credit card owners and savvy with transacting on the Internet, make it the most receptive to the concept of online shopping. Zomato. com, an online food guide and restaurant directory which boasts of over 70,000 visitors every month from the NCR township and whenever the site connects a customer to a restaurant, it charges the restaurant a fee which is typically 15 percent of the customer's value of transaction in the restaurant. Some portals offer specialized goods and services. A small group of IITians have started a portal for selling sports goods and sports accessories quite successfully.

Sky-shopping is another model fast catching up. Flipkart is being seen doing extensive promotion on television where you can buy anything by placing an order on phone and deliveries are made to your home. There are television channels promoting imported equipments showing demonstrations of the product and promoting the products using foreign models. These advertisements promise a great deal of convenience of performance of their products and follow through the endorsement route of the users of the product. While there is no estimate available of how much business they do but it looks to be growing seeing the amount of money they spend on television promotions alone.

MARKETERS EXPLORING NEW MODELS FOR ADVERTISEMENT AND PROMOTIONS

The utility of television advertisement seems to be reducing because of too much of clutter and too many channels to select from and also because of too many media options that marketers can choose from. The task of advertisement and promotion seems to be becoming an increasingly complex exercise and marketers are constantly evaluating the cost benefit of the financial resources allocated to the specific brands and products. The stringent laws, food safety guidelines, and enforcement as well as the relentless campaign of nutritionists and consumer activists are the additional considerations for advertisement and promotional strategies for food products. For most of the food products, the target audience are children. Children are now technology-savvy. They are more intelligent, smart, and are more knowledgeable with diverse involvement and attractions. The effectiveness of traditional media has reduced also because of numerous activities involving target audience happening these days. Cricket is now being played throughout the year. Promoting an event or even a part of the event and putting up visual signs, banners, etc., provides much better opportunity for the marketers than simply putting commercials in television channels. Spending the resources and every advertising rupee (money) judiciously is, therefore, key to the marketing effort of the today's business.

Food companies in USA and Europe target the young via online gaming these days. This has become a concern for the authorities. Federal Trade Commission has undertaken a study of food marketing to children while White House task force on childhood obesity said one reason children are overweight is the way junk food is marketed. Critics say the ads, from companies like Unilever and Post Foods, let marketers engage children in a way they cannot do on television, where rules limit commercial time during children's programming. With hundreds of thousands of visits monthly on these sites, the ads are becoming part of children's daily digital journeys.

Food marketers have, therefore, got so much access to the children practically bypassing the parents totally. Major food companies including General Mills, McDonald's, Pepsi, Coca-Cola and Burger King have taken a voluntary pledge to reduce marketing of their less nutritious products to children. But all food companies may not follow the same guidelines. These opportunities have widened the scope of food marketers to reach the children who are their primary target segments. World Cup win for India, for example, has encouraged lakhs (one lakh is one hundred thousand) of virtual Sachins and Yuvrajs to keep the scoreboard ticking in the online world. This translates into big bucks for online gaming sites such as Indiagames, Games2win.com, Dream11.com, and Zapak.com which are offering cricket games and applications. Big advertisers and leaders in food marketing like HUL cannot ignore the burgeoning traffic in online gaming after the world cup win and are making sure that they are visible in this segment.

It has been observed that children have moved out of even popular cartoon films to cricket. Online mobile traffic has increased from 12 million a year ago to about 30 million this fiscal. If 30 lakhs (3 million) children were playing online sometime back, about 60 lakhs to 1 crore (6 million to 10 million) are expected to play now and a significant part of this—up to about 40 percent—prefer cricket. Gamers on Games2win.com have increased since world cup and according to company sources the site gets about 2.5 lakhs (0.25 million) gamers per day. Seeing the opportunity Perfetti and Frito-Lay are queuing up for ad space on the website. This gives much focused advertisement and promotional opportunities for the businesses.

Social networking sites like Facebook and Twitter have opened up other opportunities for the marketers to advertise. Facebook, which was created by a 26-year-old student, has now been valued at 50 billion USD. The social networking sites are very powerful not only for advertisement and promotion of the products but also for initiating a discussion around the product and even generating feedback and opinion including expert opinions and customers' feedback which are very useful information for the marketers in terms of developing marketing and promotional strategies for the brand as well as getting ideas for improvement and development of new products. On social networking sites we have witnessed things have spread like wild fire sometimes and brand marketers can derive tremendous mileage for the small amount of money that they spend in advertisement on those sites. Besides, there are methods of search engine optimization to give even better and preferred recall for the brand and the product so advertised.

Online marketing, Internet marketing, telemarketing, catalogue marketing, direct marketing, multilevel marketing, etc., are other models marketers are trying depending on the product types and opportunities that exist. Mobile penetration is increasing at a phenomenal rate and that opens up other opportunity to communicate. Mobile messaging is as cheap as a few paise to send the message across. There are agencies that will take your communication mail and message it across a large database taking a small sum of money. These companies are coming up every day. Consumers are getting bombarded everyday with so much information and communication that effectiveness of such communication is a big issue.

NEED FOR INNOVATIONS FOR SUCCESS: THE NEW SOURCES OF EQUITY

An idea when pursued with passion can create a success story. Everyone of us get ideas—good, bad, or indifferent. Few can pursue an idea and can give it a shape. And still fewer who can commit himself to the idea and become passionate about it and finally pursue to create a success story. Seldom can you find people willing to fund just an idea, a sapling which may or may not succeed. People only invest in success or in an idea that is proven in the market already. Idea Cellular (An Aditya Birla Group mobile business) has a long running campaign—"An Idea can change your life"—and it is very much true although all ideas cannot be converted into success. A few instances as mentioned below will illustrate the point.

A popular saying is: "Necessity is the mother of all invention," but for some it is personal passion that has created significant success. For example, Sony's late president, Norio Ohga, who died recently, drove Sony's famous world-beating foray into the music market. Ohga, himself a music connoisseur and trained opera singer, insisted that the CD be designed at 12 centimeters in diameter or 75 minutes worth of music to enable him to store his beloved Beethoven's Ninth Symphony in its entirety. The music CD was thus born and still remains in use today. Ogha's own passion perfectly matched or married with his company's drive for profit.

Ogha's example will prove that the best CEOs will normally be seen to pursue their personal passion to product's success.

Back home, Ajit Nambiar, BPL Telecom chairman and MD, has also done exactly the same thing. His interest in music began in the 1980s while watching the BBC's Top of the Pops and Neil Peart, drummer of the band Rush. He said, "I saw him live and I said I want to do that," and he did and today he plays the percussion and drums. He further said, "I feel music speaks to the heart and soul no matter where people live or what language they speak." Nambiar's passion translated into Pro FX, a high-end audio venture. In the 1990s, it was almost impossible to purchase a good music system in India and that was when he realized that an organized, niche retail business would work with music lovers. The company partnered with global giants and today, Pro FX with its 10 stores is into home theatres, multi-room AV solutions, 3D projection theatres, home automation solutions, and acoustics. This is still a small business but growing rapidly.

Mumbai-based Vishal Gondal's passion for computer games started at 13, when his parents presented him with a computer. By the time he was in class X, Gondal had started teaching programming to other children, earning about ₹5,000 (USD 10). At 19, at the height of Pepsi–Coke war, he made a game where Pepsi bottles shot at Coke cans. And he forced the head of Pepsi to watch it. It was a hit. "I love India," a Kargil game was another hit, with close to one lakh downloads within a month. Soon venture capitalists (VCs) approached him (He did not know even what VCs were at that time) and in 1999, ₹3.5 crore (USD 7 million) were invested in his company. Today, Indiagames works across various platforms—the Internet, PC, broadband, mobile phones, consoles, and so on. "Making money was never my aim, I just followed my passion," says Gondal (*Sunday Times of India* 2011).

To build a brand over a period of time some radical approaches to marketing program are required. These are:

Holistic Marketing

Kotler talks about replacing the old marketing with new marketing that is holistic, technology enabled, and strategic. Marketing must become strategic and drive business strategy (Kotler 2004). The companies need to take a more holistic view of the target customer's activities, lifestyle and social space, the company's channels and supply chain, the company's communications, and the company's stakeholders' interests. HUL in recent times has become more holistic and it is touching consumers in multiple ways at the point of purchase and creating opportunities for its consumers to receive brand messages and experience its brands (Banga 2004).

Permission Marketing

Marketers like P&G (Stengel 2004) are trying to ensure that all marketing is permission marketing (Godin 1999). It is trying to ensure that all marketing is so appealing that the consumer wants the marketer and the brands in his/her life. Mobile marketing using permission-based marketing methods promises the advent of a new marketing channel interconnected with the Internet and the television and complementary to traditional marketing channels. P&G is using mobile marketing in U.K. (telecomsinfo.com 2005). Similarly, Nestle Nesquik has planned to deliver an integrated mobile marketing promotion by combining gaming, mobile phones, and music affinities to engage teens and young adults in an instant-win game (m-qube. com 2005). Recently, L'Oreal has relaunched its sunscreen moisturizer Synergy Sun Control, with the help of an SMS-based campaign in India. The campaign, launched with the objective of creating excitement around the relaunch, educated consumers about the new product and its new properties (agencyfaqs.com).

Return on Investment (ROI) Marketing

Low level of effectiveness of various consumers and B2B marketing programs gives rise to a situation where with increasing precision, marketers need to measure the impact of ill-defined targeting, weak positioning, mediocre advertising, pedestrian products and services, giveaway promotions, and poorly allocating spending (Clancy 2005). This is the reason why beyond the classical methods and media, marketers like Nestle are looking to improve the pay back or efficiency from their spendings. In this context the importance of three critical levers for increasing marketing spending efficiency and effectiveness: the need for strategic sourcing, focus spending on the most valuable segment bottlenecks and the need to incorporate focused analytic rigor in the process can be emphasized (Singer 2002).

BUILDING EQUITY THROUGH FORGING RELATIONSHIP

The ultimate key in building brand equity is to build a permanent relationship with the customers. Kevin Keller model described in details the four steps of building brand equity and ultimate relationship will be a measure of the equity. Performance of the brand also depends on the service efficiency and effectiveness. These days everything is considered as service. The products are also designed in a way to better serve the customers. The customer relationships are also built by knowing the customers' needs and behavior better. Brand is built by creating loyal sets of customers and, therefore, effective management of customer loyalty program is very important. Treating each and every customer for their life time value to the business will help in creating program for effective management of customers' expectation which will help in creation of loyal set of customers for the brand.

WHY IS CUSTOMER LOYALTY IMPORTANT

Customer loyalty is important to survive in business because these days products and services of one firm are not much differentiated from the products that competitors offer. Improvements in existing product lines are quickly copied by competitors and even innovations are also copied in short time due to technological advancements. Growth in business nowadays is achieved by eating into market share of others. As switching cost is decreasing, businesses have to protect or shield their market share aggressively and on the top of all these there is rising level of expectations from the customers. As customers have many choices they are now most demanding and discerning. The key benefits that arise out of an efficient customer loyalty program include lower customer price sensitivity, reduced expenditure on attracting new customers, improved organizational profitability, and building of brand equity. Customer loyalty leads to increased shareholders' value. As we deliver higher customer value we get more satisfied customers which will help build a relationship with the customers resulting into patronage and increased purchases leading to higher shareholder value.

In a survey conducted amongst CEOs in banking, financial, and service sectors to understand the concerns of theirs in terms of managing the challenges of the new competition it was found that most of the CEOs (almost 100 percent) mentioned that attracting and retaining the loyal customers is the most challenging task for them. Increasing the market share featured only next to this (Gary Cokins).

BUILDING CUSTOMER LOYALTY

Oliver (1997) defines loyalty as "A deeply held commitment to re-buy or re-patronize a preferred product or service consistently in the future despite situational influences and marketing efforts having the potential to cause switching behavior." A satisfied customer does positive and favorable publicity to four customers and an unsatisfied customer will do negative publicity to 9 customers. And for negating a bad experience 16 good experiences are needed. It is generally said that if you want to add a customer quick, focus on price but if you want to add customers forever focus on customer loyalty.

BRAND EQUITY THROUGH CUSTOMER LOYALTY

Customers now look for total solution. Not simply a product. Products are thus marketed these days with support of service to provide solution. Look at the way Unilever advertises for Dove which has crossed one billion USD in sales. Every product pack now displays customer care details. Brand marketers will have to delight customers at every interface and that is how brand is build.

The concept of customer loyalty is over 100 years old. For customer loyalty the focus during 1960s to 1980s was on the product. During 1990s the focus shifted to service and in 2000s the focus is on providing complete solution to customers' need and problems which means more holistic view is now taken. This is shown in Figure 7.1.

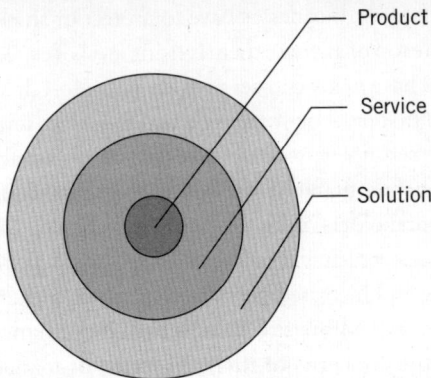

Figure 7.1   Evolution of Focus on Customer Loyalty

Product

Service

Solution

Primary task for managing the customer loyalty program will start after identifying right customer segment according to your business objectives and then focus on the customer needs in each segment, allocate costs and then link to processes for better results and then implement at every customer interface and touch points and maintain both vertical and horizontal consistency.

There are many barriers to customer loyalty program which include bad management practices, too much dependence and arrogance about successful strategies in the past, inertia or resistance to change, intrinsic or either organization driven or product driven approach, failure in creating customer driven culture and customer driven strategies.

The CRM strategy has changed over the years from attract, develop, and then retain customer to retain customers, then attract new ones, and develop both. For managing customer loyalty one needs the use the right research approach to understand the customers well. Primarily it is necessary to segment the customers according to company's objectives and then focus on that segment's needs and then to allocate resources (cost) and link to processes. As loyalty program is designed for better business results, it is effective implementation at touch points to delight customers is a key imperative. Also there should be both horizontal and vertical consistency in implementation. Companies spend a huge budget for building customer loyalty giving promotional offers and loyalty discounts. Benefits that a customer should get from implementation of such program are better buying experience, personalized attention.

DRIVERS OF CUSTOMER LOYALTY

There are three key drivers of customer loyalty, namely, Calculative Commitment, which is the rational and economic decision-making after reviewing the cost of products and services and the commensurate benefits. Commitment to the current brand or service, in this case, is due to lack of choice for similar products or services or may be high switching costs.

Affective Commitment is a warmer and emotional factor based on trust and commitment which normally arises out of emotional bondage and association customers develop over a period of time to some products or brands.

And lastly Overall Satisfaction which is described as a post-consumption experience which compares perceived quality with expected quality.

Products are introduced to satisfy an identified customer needs. If the products meet the expectation there will be a satisfied customer which will trigger repeat purchase. But a satisfied customer does not automatically convert into a loyal customer. Customer experience has to go through a phase and only when a customer receives and perceives more than expected from the product and service offered by the marketer he or she is likely to become loyal. Each satisfied customer helps create shareholder value.

Buying decisions are based on the judgments formed by the target customers about the value of the product and services after being exposed to total marketing offers. After experiencing once it is then dependent upon past buying experiences judged against expectation. In today's context most successful companies attempt to raise customers' expectation and then trying to deliver to match. This is how expectation barriers are raised. As said earlier, customers' satisfaction not necessarily can deliver loyalty. There is an underlying difference between the two. Customer satisfaction actually measures how well a customer's expectations are met. Whereas customer loyalty measures how likely customers are to return and their willingness to perform partnership activities for the organization. Customer satisfaction, therefore, is a prerequisite for loyalty.

TYPES OF CUSTOMERS

Customers can be grouped under various types based on their behavior and attitudes toward product and services available in the market to select from. These are:

Captive

Those who continue to purchase or use a product or service because they have no choice (behavior) or are even neutral to the brand which does not cause them to perceive the brand in a negative light (attitude). Examples are car owners and mobile service providers as switching cost is high.

Convenience Seeker

Includes those often associated with routine, low involvement purchases and engages in regular repeat purchase transactions associated with the brand (behavior) or even having no particular attitude to the brand except that some brands may be associated with convenience (attitude), for example, super market location, parking convenience in a store or particular timing suits the customers.

Contented

Those who are happy but hold no involvement and hold wide range of portfolio. These types of customers normally evaluate products on their merits, but previous and existing engagement with the brands is an opportunity for the brand owner to build the relationship with the customer (behavior). They have a positive attitude in relation to the brand which may be shared with acquaintances, if their advice is requested.

Committed

Those who are delighted and involved to improve. They rarely consider other brands and is prepared to 'add value' to the brand, perhaps through participating in supportive customer-to-customer interaction (behavior). They engage in positive delighted word-of-mouth (WOM) exchanges with other customers or potential customers (attitude). It is this committed lot who helps get new customers. Dove advertisement directs its communication toward that.

For managing the brand over time brand marketers have to ensure that their committed customers are always delighted to help them get more and more new customers.

THE CUSTOMER LOYALTY GRID™

Products are introduced to satisfy identified customer needs. If the products meet the expectation there will be a satisfied customer which will trigger repeat purchase. But a satisfied customer does not automatically convert into a loyal customer. Customer experience has to go through a phase and only when a customer receives and perceives more than expected from the product and service offered by the marketer he or she is likely to become loyal. Based on this understanding how customer expectations influence satisfaction to finally loyalty is better explained by the Customer Loyalty Grid as shown in Figure 7.2.

Figure 7.2   Customer Loyalty Grid

	EXPECTED	UNEXPECTED
STATED	Zone of Satisfaction	Zone of Delight
UNSTATED	Zone of Indifference	Zone of Loyalty

SOURCE: Affinity Consulting 2000–2001, www.affinitymc.com.

Each satisfied customer helps create shareholder value. But it goes and goes through an interactive process which can be explained by a diagram (Figure 7.3).

Figure 7.3 The Interaction between Customer Loyalty–Relationship and Shareholders Value

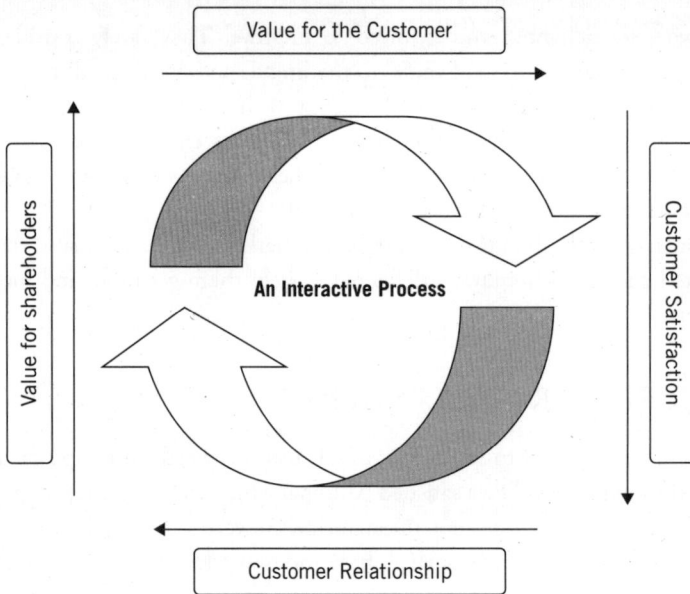

SOURCE: Metacase Asia Pte Ltd.

CUSTOMER VALUE MANAGEMENT

This would involve:
- Plan and build customer data repository
- Measure customer value
- Manage Customer segmentation
- Manage customer value
- Customer Value Management can have many dimensions, namely, Current customer Profitability, Customer Life Time Value, Predictive Analytics and Forecasting, Acquisition Cost Evaluation, etc.

Although service products and retailers have active customer loyalty program but these days product and brand marketers also spend huge resources in implementation of customer loyalty program and customer value management. In service products relationship management serves a very important purpose of building brand equity. The following examples will prove the points:

EXAMPLES AND CASES

Canon

- Canon has launched its exclusive customer loyalty program in geographies like North America and Europe
- The loyalty program covers three product lines: digital cameras, printers, and scanners
- The program offers the customers to upgrade to a refurbished, newer model at a price that is usually considerably less than repairing of their old, outdated and broken products
- Refurbished cameras are returned by customers who simply didn't want them and met the seller's return criteria
- The company offers six months warranty and technical support on new products
- It helped the company to increase its sales by 15–20 percent

Hindustan Unilever Ltd

- Ninety percent of HUL customers pay with cash. This fact prompted the behemoth to come up with a pilot of a loyalty program to drive consumption and build relationships with customers in this category. HUL test marketed the program in Southern India with plans for expansion.
- The program will allow customers to earn points for all HUL products purchased with cash. The points can then be redeemed for rewards including HUL's own products, electronic items or travel tickets. The program will allow the company to track the buying habits of its cash customers, a technique crucial to maintaining market share by targeting low value transactions.

Case Study: Kingfisher Beer Brand

There are a few Indian brands which are trying to create a global footprint by expanding into other geographic territories. Kingfisher beer brand is one of them. There are other businesses in India which are nurturing global ambition and in that list we can mention the name of Tata, Godrej, Mittal. In consumer branded products Godrej, Dabur, etc., are also trying but the route that is being followed is acquisition. There are many acquisitions happening overseas by Indian companies. Kingfisher not only formed a joint venture with Heineken in India but also extended the brand in many other countries. It is thus an Indian global brand although sales outside India constitutes only 2 percent of the total sales. In domestic market it is the leader in the category and in an environment where lot of restrictions and controls exist for the promotion and advertisement of alcoholic beverages, the case has attempted to show how the brand Kingfisher is trying to keep ahead of race in a highly competitive brewing industry in India. This is an ideal case to understand how brands are built through relationships and by providing unique experience through every touch points of consumer interface.

Kingfisher Beer from UB Group: The Early Days

The history of beer which is a fermented alcoholic beverage produced from barley malt is not very old in India. It was in the late 19th century that we had beer in Indian market. Beer was delivered in bullock carts in casks called "hogsheads." Consumers earlier were mostly defense personnel and select British officers working in India. Over hundred years have passed and beer now is produced in modern breweries and bottled in glass bottles and distributed widely. Kingfisher beer from United Breweries is now delivered all over the world, catering to the needs of consumers across generations and continents. From a modest, local beginning UB's Kingfisher beer now gradually is emerging as a global brand challenging SABMiller.

The Castle Brewery which dates back to 1857 (the year of the Indian mutiny) was set up for the European planters scattered over the Nilgiris. So was the Nilgiris Brewery Company. The British Brewing Corporation set up in Madras (1902) catered to the elite of the port town of Madras while the Bangalore Brewery Company had been supplying beer for the troops stationed at Pune and Bangalore since 1885.

United Breweries Limited (UBL) was founded on March 15, 1915, in Madras by Thomas Leishman, a Scotsman, also its first Managing Director. UBL manufactured and sold only bulk beer in casks for troops during World War I and II. Beer production technology was, therefore, taught to Indians by British. Indians were introduced to this exotic brew by British but today Kingfisher beer dominates the UK market and also available in many other countries.

UB's Long History of Brewing

The Company's brewing tradition has a legacy of nearly 130 eventful years. Along its journey through all these years, UBL has consistently attempted to influence consumer buying behavior, beer-drinking habits and conventional mindsets for drinking alcoholic beverages. One man played a pivotal role in shaping up the UBL's brand and business was Late Vittal Mallya, father of the company's current chairman Mr Vijay Mallya. Vittal Mallya got elected to the Board of Directors of UBL in 1947 at the young age of 22 and a year later became its Chairman. Company's lead brand Kingfisher was a leading brand but initially Mohan Meakin's Golden Eagle was the Number 1 brand and Kingfisher in reality had a regional presence then. Bangalore has been at the core of UBL's existence. The Registered Office of UBL was shifted to Bangalore in June 1952, into the spacious 22 acre factory of the Bangalore Brewery Company. The Bangalore Brewery buildings, dating as far back as 1885, have since given way to newer construction. The only relic that still stands is the present warehouse adjacent to the newly constructed UB Towers building, which earlier housed the bottling cellars, pasteurizing and packing departments. The five acres of land across the road donated to the Jesuit Society now forms the campus of St Joseph's Indian High School.

UB Group Today

United Breweries Group, in subsequent years diversified into many other related as well as nonrelated activities and thus changed the name of the group from United Breweries Group to UB group. This has happened in the early part of 1980s during Vijay Mallya's time who was nurturing ambition to enter into many other diversified areas including aviation. Earlier the group was known as United Breweries Group and subsequently became UB group. Not all diversification ventures of UB group succeeded and there was a time in early part of 1990s when UB group was in financial difficulty forcing them to withdraw from some of those diversified businesses to consolidate the position and focus on their core business—beer and spirit. While UB group has seen ups and downs in post-liberalization days but its Kingfisher brand in beer segment was always the leader. UB has many other beer brands but notably among those is Kalyani Black Label in Strong beer segment. UBs strong opponent and rival in both beer and spirit segments was Shaw Wallace which has a brand called Haywards as lager beer and Haywards 5000 in strong beer in competition against UBs Kalyani Black Label and Kingfisher Strong. Shaw Wallace was also originally a British company having its headquarter in Calcutta (now called Kolkata) which got acquired by Late Manu Chabbria of Jumbo Electronics in Dubai and then subsequently got acquired again. Shaw Wallace's beer business was acquired by SABMiller, global giant in brewing which has grown predominantly through acquisition globally. In India also SAB acquired beer business of Shaw Wallace to enter the market. The spirit business of Shaw Wallace was acquired by UB group which is now under the fold of UB Spirit. The popular Royal Challenge Whiskey of Shaw Wallace is thus now under UB fold.

Although UB group is now in various other businesses their flagship business is still beer and liquor. The only other high-profile diversification of UB Group is Kingfisher Airlines which has entered the category with a big bang offering—"Five star flying pleasure at affordable price"—but accumulated loss already has crippled the operations of the airlines business running now only a skeleton services and withdrawing from major routes which may have some impact on the Kingfisher brand equity. Since October 2012, Kingfisher Airlines is totally grounded and all efforts to bring in collaborator to raise capital to restart this huge debt ridden airlines has so far not yielded any result which has a significant negative impact on the brand Kingfisher. UB group's diversified business has been summarized below:

Table 7.1   UB Group Companies

Group Company	Activities
UB Holdings Limited	Holding company of the UB Group
United Spirits Limited	United Spirits Limited (USL) is the largest spirits company in the world by volume, selling 114 million cases for the fiscal ending March 21, 2011 and enjoys a strong 59 percent market share for its first line brands in India.
United Breweries Limited	Number 1 Beer company in India with over 54 percent market share. Key brands are Kingfisher Blue, Kingfisher Strong, Kingfisher Premium, Kingfisher Ultra, Kingfisher Draught, London Pilsner, Kalyani Black Label, Kalyani Black Label Premium
Kingfisher Airlines Limited	Kingfisher Airlines Limited is India's largest airline operating more than 400 flights a day and having a wide network of destinations, with regional and long-haul international services. This Company has now withdrawn all its services and is burdened by heavy debts.
Mangalore Chemicals & Fertilizers Limited	Mangalore Chemicals and Fertilizers Limited (MCF), with a turnover of over ₹2,077 Crore or USD 415 million (FY 2009-2010), is the only manufacturer of chemical fertilizers in the state of Karnataka.
UB Engineering	UB Engineering—the UB Group's Engineering Division.

SOURCE: http://www.theubgroup.com.

United Breweries Ltd

UBL is the market leader with a market share of over 54 percent in the category.

UBL has an association with brewing, dating back over five decades, starting with five breweries in south India in 1915. From bullockcart–loaded barrels or "hogsheads" of frothing ale, the beer business has gone on to become the undisputed "king" in the Indian beer market today.

UBL today boasts an impressive spread of owned and contract manufacturing facilities throughout the country. Quality and hygiene are the key elements of the United Breweries' manufacturing philosophy. To this end, the Central Technical Centre (CTC), headquartered at Bangalore, sets standards for all its breweries. Quality Management Systems laid out along the lines of ISO 9000 are strictly adhered to controlling quality at every stage of production, from raw materials to the end product. Also, besides controlling the production process, the CTC analyzes the Company's beer taken off the market shelves all over the country, the competition's beers and beers across the world. These beers are tested as per the standards laid down by the European Brewery Convention on 40 different parameters. By these standards, United Breweries' beers, as they claim, don't just equal, but even surpass several Dutch and American beers. Focus on quality and standards to meet consumer taste across many countries have helped them get entry into those markets. Globally, a few markets are attractive for beer. These include mostly Brazil, Russia, India, and China (BRIC). Although Kingfisher is a globally recognized beer brand but so far only 2 percent of its volume contributed by overseas market and rest 98 percent of the business comes from domestic market.

Its flagship brand "Kingfisher" has achieved international recognition consistently and has won many awards in international beer festivals. Kingfisher Premium Lager beer is currently available in 52 countries outside India and leads the way amongst Indian beers in the international market. It has been ranked amongst the top 10 fastest growing brands in the UK.

UBL–Heineken Deal (Strategic Alliance with Heineken N. V.)

Heineken Group (Heineken) has acquired equity shares in United Breweries Ltd The alliance is said to be offering consumers the best portfolio of national and international brands in India, including Kingfisher, the number one Indian brand, and Heineken, the leading Global beer brand. UBL's outstanding skills as India's leading brewer and Heineken's global best practices are expected to provide further strength to the business.

Innovative, creative, and aggressive marketing is complemented by a strong distribution network. A management focused on building brand equity on one hand and exploiting it to the hilt on the other with concerted emphasis on quality.

- Heineken holds a 37.5 percent stake in UBL and has a shareholder's agreement with UBL based on which Heineken will be active in India solely through UBL and will be working toward creating a unified structure, and realize synergies.
- Heineken will be produced in India by UBL. UBL will now have an access to Heineken's distribution and manufacturing facilities in the international markets, which UBL is currently catering through exports. Heineken beer is produced in horizontal beer still as against vertical fermenters used in case of Kingfisher. Heineken beer was initially imported into the country but now being produced in Mumbai. Heineken beer from local production in green-bottle was rolled out in India late 2011. Recently Charlene Lucille de Carvalho-Heineken, scion of the Heineken brewing dynasty, along with

her investment banker husband Michel de Carvalho and Heineken CEO Jean-Francois van Boxmeer, made a visit to India to strengthen the ties between the two groups who equally control the Indian beer market.

Late Vittal Mallya believed in having close control on the business but his son Vijay Mallya has resorted to diluting the holding also to generate cash to support his other ambitions and involvement. In UBL, although UB group has still significant holding but it is lower than what it used to be during 1980s. The shareholding of UBL at present is as given in Table 7.2.

Table 7.2 Shareholding of UBL	
Category of Shareholder	Shareholding (%)
Promoter and Promoter Group	74.05
FIIs	14.45
Individuals	5.22
Others	6.28

SOURCE: UBL.

Currently both Heineken and Mallya Group hold equal share (37.5 percent each) and rest is public. The Dutch Brewer Heineken and UB group now jointly owns almost 54 percent of the Indian beer market. Heineken's ownership in United Breweries came through the global acquisition of Scottish & Newcastle which held 37.5 percent stake in United Breweries.

UBL Beer Brands

The Beer brands manufactured and marketed by UBL have always been recognized for their international quality which possibly explains its brand equity and the reason why Kingfisher is getting acceptance in other markets, even in the developed world. The largest selling beer in India, Kingfisher commands a market share of over 54 percent in the country. With one out of every three bottles of beer sold in India being a Kingfisher brand, UBL controls close to 54 percent of the total beer market in India. It is also available in 52 countries across the globe. A name synonymous with beer in India, Kingfisher stands for excitement, youth, and camaraderie. The beer brands from UBL with many variants of Kingfisher include:

- Kingfisher Premium
- Kingfisher Strong
- Kingfisher Strong Fresh

- Kingfisher Draught
- Kingfisher Ultra
- Kingfisher Red
- Kingfisher Bohemia
- Zingaro
- UB Export
- UB Export Strong
- London Pilsner Premium Strong
- Kalyani Black Label Strong
- Bullet

- With close to 54 percent market share, UBL is the undisputed leader of the Indian beer industry, with over five decades of market leadership
- Sold 101 MM cases during financial year 2010
- Kingfisher is the ubiquitous Indian beer, available as Kingfisher Premium, Strong, Blue, Red, and Ultra
- UBL is uniquely positioned with manufacturing facilities in all key markets

  - Ensuring freshness of beer
  - Leveraging India's interstate tariff difference to economic advantage

The relative contribution of all these variants in the total beer business of UB is given in the following Table 7.3.

Table 7.3 Contribution of Variants of Kingfisher Beer Brand

Brand Family	Contribution (%)
Kingfisher Strong	55
Kingfisher Mild	24
London No.1 Strong	3
Zingaro Strong	3
UB Export Mild	3
Bullet Strong	2
Kalyani Black Label Strong	2
Cannon 10000	1
Kalyani Black Label Mild	1
UB Export Strong	1
Others	5

SOURCE: UBL.

It can be noted that Kingfisher contributes about 80 percent total beer sales in UBL which is positioned in premium segment competing with SABMiller's Haywards 5000 and Fosters.

Kingfisher's Unique Position

The brand's advertisements epitomize energy, youthfulness, enthusiasm, and freedom, but with a touch of professionalism. Kingfisher brand stands for fun, lifestyle and king of good things in life. Things go better with Kingfisher. Outside India, Kingfisher is well-known and is widely available in many European countries, especially those with a large Indian ethnic population like the UK.

Current Chairman (Vijay Mallya) initiated the promotion and globalization of brands from the UB stable; in particular, Kingfisher and McDowell. The Indian beer brand, Kingfisher, was the first to foray into the international arena and made inroads into the British market, so much so, that industry analysts say that "beers from the Indian subcontinent are now quite a preferred brand in Europe."

Industry Overview

Beer is the world's most consumed alcoholic beverage and the third most popular drink after water and tea. However, the consumption pattern in India is distinctly different from other countries, as alcohol consumption is skewed toward spirits. The per capita consumption of beer in India is very low—at about 1.5 liter per capita it is 5 percent of the global average. It is believed in industry that the primary reasons for the extremely low consumption of beer are the tax structure, which does not differentiate between the alcohol content of various classes of beverages, and the low penetration of outlets for the sale and consumption of beer in India. In India, spirits and beer are treated as similar alcoholic beverages and, therefore, taxed on a similar basis without taking into account the fact that beer contains about 5-7 percent of alcohol by volume, whereas spirits contain over 40 percent of alcohol by volume. The result of this policy is that the consumer price of beer is 2 to 3 times higher than that of spirits on an equivalent alcohol basis. In the context of availability, beer and spirits are viewed alike by the Excise Authorities, and the number of Points of Sale for beer is very low in the country. This too results in the suppression of beer consumption. In many parts of the country, the wholesale, and at times the retail distribution points, are controlled by the State Government. Moreover, in about 60 percent of India, the State dictates the price at which beer can be sold by the brewers. Notwithstanding the constraints mentioned above, industry believes that the future of the industry is very bright. As the economy develops, disposable incomes will keep rising and this in combination with the young demography of the country, will spur growth in the beer industry.

The size of the Indian beer industry as estimated for the year 2010–2011 was approximately 225 million cases, showing a compounded annual growth rate of around 13 percent in the past 5 years. During the year 2011 the industry grew by 18 percent. Salience of the strong beer segment continues to increase, and strong beer now accounts for an estimated 79 percent of volumes sold. United Breweries Limited has not only successfully overcome the challenges of the industry, but also outpaced several global beer brands that have entered India in the recent past. In the process, the Company has increased its market share and widened the gap with its competitors.

The Central and State governments have been considering a harmonized Goods and Services Tax (GST) regime for a number of years, but have not been able to conclude on the terms of this regime. Most notably, there is a likelihood that the alcoholic beverages industry is excluded from GST altogether. Alcoholic beverages industry strongly feels that such exclusion of an industry is against the foundation of GST and would not achieve the stated objective of creating a uniform market with uniform taxes.

Sales

The year 2010–2011 was an excellent year for UBL in which volumes grew by 23 percent, crossing the land mark figure of 125 million cases.

The net sales for the year 2010–2011 stood at ₹30,132 million (about USD 600 million) as against net sales of ₹19,975 million (USD 400 million) in the previous year, registering a growth of 51 percent. During the year, the combined national market share reached 54 percent, which is more than twice the size of the nearest competitor (SAB Miler). This is achieved through a national market share of 69 percent in the mild beer market, and 50 percent of the strong beer market. UBL achieved market leadership in the State of Andhra Pradesh for the first time, and strengthened its presence in Orissa and Uttar Pradesh.

The ubiquitous Kingfisher brand continues to be the largest selling beer brand in India, with a volume growth of 20 percent during the year. Kingfisher Ultra, Kingfisher Blue, and Kingfisher Red are the latest additions to the Kingfisher portfolio, and have been received well in the market and are being rolled out across the country.

The Company received two International Awards at the World Beer Awards 2010, as well as three national awards for excellence in packing at IndiaStar 2010. Kingfisher Premium and Kingfisher Strong received awards in Asia's Best Lager Premium and Asia's Best Lager Strong categories, respectively. Kingfisher Ultra's bottle design, Kingfisher's Premium fourpack carrier and the Kingfisher premium gift pack were awarded at the IndiaStar 2010.

Manufacturing Strategy Initiatives

Manufacturing expenses for the financial year 2010–2011 were ₹15,067 million (USD 301 million), constituting 50.0 percent of net sales, as against ₹10,088 million (USD 201 million) in the previous financial year, which constituted 50.6 percent of net sales. The beer industry depends largely on recycled bottles. An organized collection system exists for the used bottles from which the industry players buy back the bottles for refilling.

In the previous financial year, the company started the infusion of patented bottles in order to secure the availability of bottles and to obtain efficiencies in the cost of bottles. Such bottles with embossed name and logo of the company cannot be used by other brewers and are to be necessarily supplied back to the company by the bottle vendors. This strategy is showing positive results, with the cost of recycled patented bottles being significantly lower compared to similar "industry" bottles. The Company intends to complete the establishment of a patented bottle pool across India in the financial year ending March 31, 2012, and the cost associated with accelerated investment in new patented bottles is expected to be recovered in the coming years. The Company has agreements in place for the supply of malt, barley and bottles.

Figure: 7.4   Kingfisher Premium Pint 350 ml

SOURCE: United Breweries Ltd.

Figure 7.5   Kingfisher Strong Pint 350 ml

SOURCE: United Breweries Ltd.

Figure 7.6   Kingfisher Premium Bottle 650 ml

SOURCE: United Breweries Ltd.

Figure 7.7   Kingfisher Strong Bottle 650 ml

SOURCE: United Breweries Ltd.

Figure 7.8   Kingfisher Premium Can 350 ml

SOURCE: United Breweries Ltd.

Figure 7.9   Kingfisher Strong Can 350 ml

SOURCE: United Breweries Ltd.

Figure 7.10   Kingfisher Premium Can 500 ml

SOURCE: United Breweries Ltd.

Figure 7.11   Kingfisher Strong Can 500 ml

SOURCE: United Breweries Ltd.

Most of the units have installed solid fuel boilers, which has resulted in a reduction in fuel cost. In order to further reduce power consumption, the company is exploring conversion of organic waste into energy to obtain savings in electricity cost in an environmentally sustainable manner. The breweries are continuously improving efficiencies in the brewing process and in packaging, thereby containing overall manufacturing cost.

In order to keep pace with the growing demand, the company proposes to expand its capacity through expansion of its existing breweries, building new breweries, and entering into new contract brewing agreements where required. The proposed Greenfield brewery at Nanjangud, Karnataka, is expected to be commissioned in the year 2013. In view of the rapid growth, the company is commencing a Greenfield brewery in the state of Bihar. The acquisition of land for this purpose at Naubatpur, Patna, through the Bihar Industrial Area Development Authority is completed. The company has also augmented brewing capacity by amalgamations of its associate companies, namely, UB Nizam, CBPL, and UB Ajanta Breweries Private Limited (UB Ajanta) that operate in the vital markets of Andhra Pradesh, Tamil Nadu, and Maharashtra. Prior to the Scheme of Amalgamation, UBL management secured its rights over the CBPL brewery by payment of facility advance to the promoters of Balaji Distilleries Limited (now CBPL) which stands amalgamated into the Company.

While the scheme for merger of UB Ajanta is pending approval by BIFR, the Company has secured its capacity by executing a management agreement.

Personnel and Other Operating Expenses

Personnel expenses of the company stood at ₹1,441 million (USD 28.8 million) in 2011, as compared to ₹989 million (USD 19.78 million) in the previous year. This constituted 4.8 percent of net sales, as against 5.0 percent of net sales in the previous year. Other operating expenses amounted to ₹1,450 million (USD 29 million) constituting 4.8 percent of net sales. Personnel and other operating expenses were contained despite increased volumes during the year due to enhanced productivity levels.

Selling and Brand Promotion Expenses and Promotional Strategies

The company has spent 28.5 percent of net sales on selling and brand promotions in 2011 as compared to 28.0 percent of net sales spent in the previous year. The selling and promotion expenses stood at ₹8,582 million (USD 171.64 million). The company is recognized as one of the premier branded goods companies in India, and Kingfisher is perhaps one of the country's best placed and recognized consumer brands. The company allocates its brand spends largely across three properties—sports, fashion, and music—with an objective to enhance the brand equity by associating with the most valuable properties in a cost-effective manner.

In sports, the company's main focus is toward the highly popular Indian Premier League in cricket. Company's association as 'Good Times Partner' with five of the leading teams of the IPL has been very effective for leveraging the flagship brand Kingfisher. The brand also continued its association as Partner with large city-based sporting events such as the Mumbai Marathon, Delhi Half Marathon and Bangalore 10K. The company's association with Formula One has garnered tremendous popularity and has provided the company with global visibility for the brand. Company has renewed its association with United East Bengal Football Team as the official sponsor of the team.

In fashion, Kingfisher is associated with Jaipur International Fashion Week for the first time and continued its association with the premier national fashion events like Wills Lifestyle, Lakme Fashion Week, Delhi & India Couture Week, Bangalore Fashion Week, and Chennai International Fashion Week. The ninth edition of Kingfisher Calendar was revealed amidst much fanfare and a host of celebrities. Launch of the Kingfisher Calendar was preceded by Hunt for the Kingfisher Calendar Girl 2011 on national television.

In music, its main activity was the Great Indian October Fest, which was held in Bangalore and drew huge response from the visitors with a combination of famed DJs, Bollywood artists, fashion markets, and contests. October Fest has now become a much anticipated fixture in the Country's social and cultural calendar.

The Kingfisher brand is very active in new media, as evidenced by its Facebook fan page that now has a fan base of over 2.5 million. This has catapulted the brand into the top Facebook fan pages from India, and makes it one of the largest Facebook followings of any beer brand across the globe (UBL Annual Report 2010–2011).

How Is Brand Kingfisher Performing

Although SABMiller is gradually inching and increasing its brand share but it is still close to about 30 percent of the total market whereas Kingfisher is close to about 52 percent of the market. SABMiller's global acquisition of Fosters is unlikely to make any difference in Indian market as Fosters brand in India was earlier acquired by SABMiller. The relative performance of different beer brands in India in terms of volume share is as given in Table 7.4.

Table 7.4 Competitive Brands Volume Share for the Last Five Years

Brand Family	06–07 (%)	07–08 (%)	08–09 (%)	09–10 (%)	10–11 (%)
Haywards 5k	16	16	16	13	12
Knock Out	7	8	8	6	6
Thunder Bolt	3	3	3	3	3
Godfather Strong	1	2	2	2	2
Palone	0	0	1	2	2
Royal Challenge	6	6	4	3	2
Fosters	2	2	2	2	1
Budweiser	0	0	1	1	1
Tuborg Lager	0	0	0	0	1
Golden Eagle Lager	1	1	1	1	1

SOURCE: United Breweries Ltd.

The Key Milestone

The Indian beer market has seen many competitive brands in last 10 years, notable amongst which are Cobra, Fosters, Carlsberg, Budweiser, Haywards, etc. But Kingfisher beer brand kept its dominance over those brands and reported significant achievement year on year as can be revealed by the following milestones.

2005–2006

- UBL grew by 18 percent
- Sales volume of 43.4 million cases against 36.4 million cases the previous year
- Achieved overall market share of 40 percent
- Kingfisher Lager Beer sold over 20 million cases and achieved a market share of over 65 percent
- Kingfisher Strong Beer sold over 17 million cases and achieved a market share of over 19 percent

2006–2007

- Overall sales volume of over 66.1 million cases
- Achieved an overall market share of over 48 percent
- Kingfisher Lager Beer achieved a market share of over 66 percent
- Kingfisher Strong Beer achieved a market share of over 38 percent

2007–2008

- Overall sales volume of over 75.4 million cases
- Mild beer has a market share of over 64 percent
- Strong beer segment has a market share of over 40 percent
- Kingfisher Lager Beer sold over 25 million cases
- Kingfisher Strong Beer sold over 32 million cases

2008–2009

- Overall sales volume of over 82.4 million cases
- Achieved an overall market share of over 50 percent

2009–2010

- Overall sales volume of over 100 million cases
- Overall market share of over 50 percent
- Mild Beer has a market share of 63 percent
- Strong Beer segment has a market share of over 46 percent

2010–2011

- Overall sales volume of over 125 million cases
- Achieved an overall market share of over 54 percent
- Mild Beer segment has a market share of over 69 percent
- Strong Beer segment has a market share of over 50 percent
- Kingfisher Brand grew by over 20 percent on the back of additions of new brands like Kingfisher Ultra, Kingfisher Red, and Kingfisher Blue

2011–2012

- Kingfisher Beer brand crosses 100 million cases for the year

Table 7.5   Financial Performance for the Last Five Years

In ₹000's

Particulars	2006–2007	2007–2008	2008–2009	2009–2010	2010–2011
Income					
Sales and Services	14,817,978	19,802,844	24,604,481	29,558,009	45,571,227
Less: Excise Duty	4,280,190	6,112,233	7,621,772	9,583,515	15,439,160
	10,537,788	13,690,611	16,982,709	19,974,494	30,132,067
Other Income	210,950	257,948	492,991	776,834	827,841
Total	10,748,738	13,948,559	17,475,700	20,751,328	30,959,908
Expenditure					
Cost of Sales	6,596,961	8,672,344	10,472,894	12,171,636	17,958,663
Other Expenses	2,536,711	3,303,517	4,327,570	5,630,706	8,652,678
Interest and Finance Charges	279,788	428,282	896,377	555,006	781,294
Depreciation and Amortization	385,352	612,276	762,150	882,692	1,305,123
Total	9,798,812	13,016,419	16,458,991	19,240,040	28,697,758
Profit before Taxation	**949,926**	**932,140**	**1,016,709**	**1,511,288**	**2,262,150**
Provision for Taxation	299,009	307,415	391,769	541,579	789,285
Profit after Taxation	**650,917**	**624,725**	**624,940**	**969,709**	**1,472,865**

SOURCE: United Breweries Ltd–Annual Report.

Kingfisher's Brand Extension

Significant extension of the Kingfisher brand was entry into the aviation industry. The year 2005 saw the UB Group entering the airline business with its Kingfisher Airlines. UB group's original foray into airlines with the launch of UB Air in 1990 did not really take off. Subsequently the company decided to capitalize on the potential growth opportunities in the Indian airline industry through a second attempt. Noting the phenomenal rise in per capita income among the burgeoning Indian middle class, company engaged Indian Market Research Bureau (IMRB) to assess a potential slot in the aviation sector. The result recommended that there was a need for a trendy, entertaining and a premium product. Company decided to make the most of the notable status of Kingfisher and focus on young business travelers. By leveraging the brand equity of Kingfisher and the marketing skills of The UB Group, Kingfisher Airlines Limited (KAL) was launched. However, the performance of Kingfisher Airlines is very poor, incurring huge cumulative losses resulting into closing down and withdrawal from many routes unexpectedly, which may have some fall out on Kingfisher brands. Normally, brand extension is recommended for extension into the synergistic and related areas where the equity of the parent brand can have positive impact on the extended brand. One can debate on the justification of the extension of a well-known and leading beer brand to a service industry like Airlines. Actually, acquiring the low-cost airline Air Deccan was a costly mistake that Kingfisher Airlines committed. This acquisition not only weakened the financial position of the company but also did not support the stated brand positioning of Kingfisher Airlines which stands for lifestyle. The company could never come out of this shock and went gradually into deep debt trap and consequent loss of credibility as covered by press media in India, Europe, and Middle East (*Financial Times* 2011).

Opportunities, Threats, Risks, and Concerns

In terms of revenue, beer accounts only for 7 percent of the Indian alcoholic beverage market and, it is a mere 5 percent of the global average in volume terms. This low penetration in beer consumption in comparison to international level offers an opportunity for substantial growth in the coming decades.

There is a huge demographic dividend that India will reap in the next decades. The UN expects the country to overtake China as the most populous country by 2025, while its inhabitants remain very young. Half of India's population is below the age of 25, and in 2030 about 20 percent of all people below 25 years of age in the world will be Indian as compared to 11 percent from China.

On the back of solid GDP growth, income levels are expected to rise substantially and the National Council of Applied Economic Research (NCAER) estimates that today's middle class population of 160 million will grow to 547 million by 2026. This is especially significant as due to high consumer prices, beer consumption is skewed toward higher income consumers. This will also offer opportunities to further make the beer industry a premium one.

In addition, increased urbanization and evolving consumer attitudes toward alcohol consumption will provide further levers for growth. With urban consumers being more exposed to western lifestyle, there has been a positive shift in consumer behavior toward alcohol consumption. Social habits are undergoing a transformation and with further urbanization, this acceptance is only going to increase, even as we focus on responsible consumption of alcohol. The Indian beer market is one of the fastest growing markets in the world today and with the aforementioned growth drivers in place, an extended period of high growth may be expected.

Despite drivers of growth being in place, government intervention in distribution, high taxation, restricted communication, and increased cost of raw materials are some negatives that the industry faces.

The Indian beer industry is suffering from a myriad taxes and levies that vary from state to state. No two states or union territories have the same policy, and policies are generally short term in their outlook, with little or no thought to long-term interests of all stakeholders, including the general public. Changes in taxation, both on a state level and on a national level, are particularly high risks to this industry and might significantly impact profitability from time to time. There are positive trends however. A number of states, including key states such as Maharashtra and Karnataka, have taken some steps to differentiate between spirits and lower alcohol alternatives such as beer. There have been several instances where state governments have increased excise duty for spirits while maintaining the excise rate for beer or opting for a smaller increase in rates than that of spirits. Although this is far away from an alcohol content based excise policy that is prevalent in most countries, even a small differentiation between beer and spirits taxation is a good step toward delinking the two. In Maharashtra, the government improved the availability of beer through the creation of beer shop licenses, which allow the sale of only beer and not spirits. This has been a significant driver for growth in the Maharashtra beer industry and in excise revenue.

Increase in demand for malt is resulting in limited availability of locally produced barley and this shortage is anticipated to increase in coming years. Company has explored a number of avenues to address increases in cost of raw materials, and is taking measures to invest in the upstream supply chain to ensure the company continues to receive a sustainable supply of quality barley. The company has also entered into long-term contract with glass manufacturers to derive cost and supply advantages in packaging and thereby containing risk. Regulation over retail pricing in many states may create an environment where the company is unable to pass on the real escalation in cost of raw materials, which would impact profitability from time to time.

Constraints of Beer Market Growth

As discussed, the constraints for the growth of the category can be summarized as:

- Despite drivers of growth being in place, government intervention in distribution, high taxation, restricted communication, and increased cost of raw materials are some negatives that the industry faces.
- The per capita consumption of beer in India is very low—at about 1.5 liter per capita, it is 5 percent of the global average. Primary reasons for the extremely low consumption of beer are:
  o The tax structure, which does not differentiate between the alcohol content of various classes of beverages. The result of this policy is that the consumer price of beer is two to three times higher than that of spirits on an equivalent alcohol basis.
  o The low penetration of outlets for the sale and consumption of beer in India. In the context of availability, beer and spirits are viewed alike by the Excise Authorities, and the number of Points of Sale for beer is very low in the country.

- In many parts of the country, the wholesale, and at times the retail distribution points, are controlled by the State Government. Moreover, in about 60 percent of India, the State dictates the price at which beer can be sold by the brewers.
- The Indian beer industry is suffering from a myriad taxes and levies that vary from state to state. No two States or Union Territories have the same tax structure.
- Central and State Government policies are generally short term in their outlook, with little or no thought to long-term interests of all stakeholders, including the general public. Changes in taxation, both on a state level and on a national level, are particular high risks to the industry and might significantly impact profitability from time to time.

Brand Marketer thus has a task of building equity using indirect route and avenues for building relationships with the target customers which is the largely growing young population.

The Key Challenges for the Kingfisher Brand

Kingfisher, although a leader in its category and a dominant brand, cannot overlook and disregard formidable challengers in SABMiller, Carlsberg India, and ABInBev (makers of Budweiser brand of beer). Therefore, it has to maintain growth through aggressive marketing and sales initiatives. It can be noted that while Kingfisher is growing at a rate much higher than the category growth rate but in terms of market share it is going to be a big task to hold on their share above 50 percent). This means that its rival SABMiller is also growing almost at the same rate if not higher than Kingfisher. The company's key challenge would be to innovate to reduce the cost structure and to take a cost leadership over its competitors. This together with capacity expansion and increased market penetration will hold the key. Also too many brands in its portfolio is increasing the complexity and, therefore, some rationalization is also called for. Kingfisher has a dominating position as far as mild beer segment is concerned but in strong beer it is although a leader but SABMiller is a close Number 2.

Critical Success Factors for Kingfisher Beer

Kingfisher is the oldest beer brand in India and, therefore, has all the advantages of a first mover. Technically, although it is Mohan Meakin's Golden Eagle which is the first beer brand in India, today its market share is down to only 1 percent. Once a dominant player in beer market, it is now going to be almost extinct. All the other beer brands including foreign brands like Fosters, Cobra, Heineken, etc., are actually followers in the Indian market. UB group has significant control over the production capacity and efficient supply chain management system. To keep control on the production capacity group has acquired many smaller brewing plants in the country. The group has invested in innovation, and technology to remain contemporary and current with respect to beer quality and standards are concerned. Although there are lot of restrictions on direct media advertisement and promotion on an alcoholic beverage like beer, UB group has kept the brand's presence alive through innovative and indirect surrogate advertisement and promotional opportunities. The company has kept the product packaging and overall presentation always premium and kept in touch with the target segments through mailers and through organizing various activities and creating sensation around the brand, such as much talked about and published Kingfisher Calendar, introduction of Kingfisher soda and mineral water, etc. The brand has been extended to cover wide sections of the target market through introduction of beer brand variants. UB group was able to attract best professionals in beverage industry to work for the brand building and development. This was supported by latest systems, controls and management involvement which has helped the Kingfisher brand to remain ahead of others. It has done many innovations in the category. Introduction of patented bottle in the business which is very much dependent on recycled bottle for cost economy is an excellent strategic initiative.

However, it still has to go a long way to emerge as a dominant global brand although it has all the intrinsic strengths, management backing, and consumer awareness to gradually grow to that level. Kingfisher brand's presence in all sports, fashion, and music related activities and events as described in the case over the long years gave the brand a dominant position and a significant presence in consumers' mind. Whenever one thinks or talks about beer, Kingfisher beer brand becomes top of the mind response and, therefore, a preferred brand.

Global Marketing Strategy

Kingfisher is a dominant brand which has its unique position in Indian beer market. Everyone knows about the brand that stands for quality lifestyle and extravaganza. Although it was not so earlier, post mid-1980s that has been deliberately created through all forms of their marketing executions. It is, therefore, the chosen position of the UB group now. Although the brand has a dominant presence and visibility and also has all the characteristics of emerging as a global beer brand, it is yet to become a power brand in the sense that it becomes a part of the consumers' lifestyle on a global scale. Kingfisher has started its journey to eventually emerge as an Indian global brand but whether it will succeed in its attempt is yet to be seen. Currently only 2 percent of its sales revenue comes from export and, therefore, in terms of global market share it would be insignificant.

In terms of key strategic initiatives the company has set up distribution arrangement as well as production arrangement in many key markets including UK, South Africa, and China. In UK brand Kingfisher is quite well known and available everywhere where other beer brands are sold. But UK market is a different story as we have large ethnic population living there who are already exposed to the brand Kingfisher and, therefore, conversion would be much easier. In China kingfisher brand is quite well known and, doing well. But in other markets, the brand has yet to take roots.

As there are no of constraints in terms of promoting the beer in overseas market, aggressive marketing and promotion is being followed to establish the brand. The key drivers to expand the brand to exploit global opportunity are:

- Local production capacity organized through contract production as setting up company-owned production facility would be very costly
- Selectively acquire local facilities as has been done in UK and South Africa
- Creating local sales and distribution infrastructure

- Adjusting to the local taste and preferences
- Selective collaborative approach with the friendly local players (Through joint ventures Kingfisher has a presence in New Zealand and Australia now)
- Delivering greater value through cost reduction and innovation
- Aggressive promotion and media communication wherever it is justified.
- Focus on institutional segments like pubs, hotels, restaurants, and caterers which contribute large part of the market in western world

UBL has not ventured into other forms of beer like stout, portar, ale, etc., as its focus was only Indian market which is predominantly a lager beer market. But being a first mover in the market they could have developed other variants. To become a power brand one needs to be a natural owner of the category and if there is any innovation possible it should be seen as being done by the leader, which UBL has not done so far. These days, even micro-breweries are being set up. Already there are four microbreweries now existing in India including one in Gurgaon and another near Pune. While micro-breweries are combined with restaurants being run from the same premises, beer is always sold in restaurants also. People would like to drink beer and the same time eat there and in a microbrewery one has the pleasure of seeing how beer is produced. Besides, in microbreweries other types of beer such as beer from wheat and corn are also being produced and sold. While restaurants may not be the UB group's business and also microbrewery may not be economically attractive, for a leader in the category, Kingfisher's presence is a must. People otherwise will not see Kingfisher as an innovator and long-term implications may not be favorable. I visit the microbrewery located in NH8 Gurgaon quite frequently and engage myself in discussion with the brewer there who gives me an impression that it is doing exceedingly well. I also get the same feeling seeing long queues of youngsters in front the brewery waiting for their turn to get an entry. The local brewer always gives me a special treatment because when I met him first I introduced myself as an ex-employee of United Breweries having had an opportunity to work with both late Vittal Mallya and his son Mr Vijay Mallya.

CHAPTER SUMMARY

To manage a brand over a longer period marketers need to be innovative in their approach and must also use alternative approaches and take support of technology. With the disappearance of trade barriers, goods and services designed by the marketers must have global appeal and global marketing approach. The chapter explains with reasons why traditional marketing models will no longer be sufficient for building brands over a longer period of time. That is why increasingly, marketers are using alternative marketing and brand-building approaches. The ultimate key to the brand-building exercise is to build a permanent relationship with the customers. Relationship management and managing customer loyalty to realize the lifetime value of the customer is, therefore, essential to having a strong brand equity. The chapter deals with the approaches toward building brand equity through forging relationship. Kingfisher case study has been discussed in this chapter to describe how brand is built in a category where media advertisement is restricted by law and how innovative methods and approaches are taken to forge long lasting relationships with the target consumers that is nurtured over a period of time to create a permanent bond resulting in high brand equity.

CHAPTER 8

Brand Accounting and Brand Valuation

ACCOUNTING OF BRANDS

Financial valuation and accounting procedure for working out the value of a brand has become a subject matter of considerable debate as can be seen from the numerous publications and ad hoc committees that have been set up by almost all national accounting institutions. Accounting standards differ from country to country on accounting procedures for brands and their places on the balance sheet. Before 1985 there was no interest in brand valuation. The reason for sudden interest in this subject is the large increase in the number of takeover bids for brands and businesses rather than for the physical manufacturing assets.

When one company is bought by another company, there is often a huge difference between the book value of the company's assets and the price paid for the acquisition. This difference will be more for strong brands which is said to be the goodwill. Goodwill is actually a measure of the financial markets' positive attitudes to the future of the company. In all modern accounting systems and norms, goodwill must be allocated to specific items such as brands, patents, know-how, and databases, etc., that have created it. Hence it can be said that the issue of brand valuation has actually stemmed from the necessity to account for sometimes huge goodwill payments involved when major corporations were sold. Other reasons include, for example, when brands are purchased, the value of this asset must be made explicit.

Accounting is governed by the principle of prudence and its evaluation must be shown to be valid, coherent, and reproducible and that is the reason why, paradoxically, only the brands that have been bought individually, or that were included in the price paid for a company, can be posted in the balance sheet of the acquiring company. All over the world, the principle of prudence has led national and international accounting norms and standards to forbid posting in the balance sheet internally grown brands. It is, however, possible to propose brand valuations, but as long as brands have not been bought or sold, there is too much doubt about the validity of these estimates. Brands thus acquire value through market.

Accounting prudence principle suggests including only objective data and assessing only past and recorded transactions and as such only transactions involving external brands are recorded. If the internal brands were to be noted, the principle of reality would be respected at the expense of reliability and of the consistency of the accounting and in fact, what would we think of a balance sheet which was based on nonuniform and sometimes subjective method of evaluation. The inclusion of an acquired brand does not, however, violate the principle of book keeping at historical costs which is a fundamental accounting principle. How would then internal brands be valued? As we can see later, the valuation methods which are based on historical costs or replacement costs are not good enough and better methods are those which are based on projections of future income which are again highly subjective.

Accountancy, like taxation, is interested in recording of costs as expenses or as investments but financial analysts estimate the discounted value of certain assets as a function of the probability of the future income that these assets are supposed to generate. Thus there will not be one value of the brand because valuation methods depend on the goals of valuation. It is for the finance people to estimate the market value of these assets—this reasoning already exists for other physical assets such as buildings, plants, and equipments, etc., and thus also can be applied for brands.

The 1990s witnessed the concept of brand equity (Aaker 1990). The concept of brand equity represents a combination of marketing perspective with the economic and financial perspective of the brand. Earlier thought on the subject was to work out brand value taking customer's point of view. This takes the view that the value of the brand is that amount of surplus the customers are willing to pay which is greater than the cost or the utility of the products or services. However, in course of time we have several methods being used for this purpose. There are companies specialized on brand valuation and brand marketing companies make use of them to track the performance of their brand to have an idea how well they are managing their brands in terms of building incremental equity which will have a reflection on their valuation. As such periodically these companies conduct the valuation of their brands. Even companies like Young & Rubicam independently carry out such valuation of global select brands and provide those data to corporations who own those brands at a cost. In this chapter we will be discussing some of these valuation methods currently being used in the industry.

BRAND VALUES OF TOP GLOBAL BRANDS: INTERBRAND STUDY (2004)

In these days of increasing fragmented markets and fierce competition, brands are competing with each other in order to remain relevant in consumers' minds. The relationship between brands and their consumers are becoming increasingly more complex. Post Black Marlboro Friday launch in April, 1993, many of the leading brands of the world have found going really tough in recent times despite the presence of global consumer segments like MTV generation (global teenagers).

Interbrand, famous for its published list of the world's most valued brands in the *Financial Times* and more recently, *Business Week*, remains the most well-known and widely used method for brand valuation (Khermouch, Holmes, and Ihlwan 2001). Auditors and tax authorities in many countries around the world recognize Interbrand's income-based valuation methodology, which defines brand value as the net present value of future profits attributable to the brand. It appears (Table 8.1) that the top brands of the world in terms of brand value in recent times are either stagnating (Marlboro, etc.), or displaying nominal increase (McDonald's, etc.), or facing nominal decrease (Coca-Cola, etc.).

BRAND VALUATION METHODS

Primarily, valuation of brand depends on the evaluation of objectives and goals. It is generally said that the value of a brand is actually in the eye of the beholder. But still various methods are used to determine the value of the brand by brand owners for the purpose of either acquiring a brand or even for reporting brand asset in the balance sheet of the company. It also should be pointed out that the same brand can deliver different values in the hands of different companies. Otherwise, how could brands fetch different values when put on the block? The various methods used for brand valuation use various criteria such as valuation based on historical costs that helped building the brand, valuation based on present earnings or market price and still there are those which rely on the business plan and forecast. Some analysts rely on hard facts such as historical earnings or present earnings and still others rely more on estimates about the present (replacement method) or about the future earnings (discounted cash flow method). Let us now discuss each of these methods.

Valuation Based on Historical Costs

Brand can be considered as an asset arising out of the investment made on the brand over a period of time. Logical approach, therefore, would be to add together all those costs over a period of time which cover product development costs, marketing including promotional costs, advertisement and communication costs. These costs can easily be determined from past records of the business and its income statements. However, this approach needs to isolate (separability) the direct costs associated with the brand and also by attributing to the indirect costs such as the sales force and general expenses. This method, although simple and logical, raises many questions. These are:

- Time horizon: Over what period must these costs be accounted for? There are many brands which are very old or even a century old, for example, Coca Cola dates back to 1887, Danone to 1919 or Lacoste to 1933 and so on. Even in India we have age-old corporate brands like Tata, Dabur, and Godrej. Hence question arises: Should we take into account cost of building the brand from the beginning and whether past cost of advertisement has any effect today. Also a related question that arises is during which period brand growth was maximum and marketing effort has produced better result and brand performance.
- Which cost to be taken into account: Advertisement has dual purpose—one helps in generating increased sales and the other goes to build brand awareness and image which, in fact, helps in future performance of the brand and its equity. And hence there is a difficulty in attributing the costs year by year to each part and isolating only that part of the cost which has helped building the brand image and equity.
- Also there is an issue related to the diminishing impact of advertisement on the consumer's attitude toward the brand. There is always a threshold level of advertisement and exposure below which there is no impact. Also there is a level above which there is no incremental impact. It is thus not a simple addition of all costs but appropriate discount rate also should be calculated. While creating a brand a large part of the long-term investment such as stringent quality control, accumulated know-how and expertise, involvement of personnel in building brands, etc., do not involve always a cash outlay and, therefore, cannot be posted to the accounts. But all these are essential in terms of building a brand's long-term equity. The question therefore: How do we work out that part of the value which has gone into brand-building exercise? There are many brands built without any traditional mode of media advertisements also. For example, Rolls Royce did not spend any money on advertisement. Marks & Spencer's brand St. Michael also advertised very little. Hence it is difficult to establish the relationship on the advertisement spend and brand equity.
- Pricing is a strategic tool. Many new launches fail due to wrong pricing. Product pricing is thus a key strategic element. Brands are introduced in the market at a competitive price. Marketers many a times avoid taking price premium and on the contrary, sometimes best quality products are launched at an affordable price which significantly improves the product's

success. Better price–quality ratio enhances attractiveness. But this noncash expenditure will not feature in the book of accounts for building brands.
- This method, therefore, is applicable for recent brands which have a price premium and have been supported with huge advertisement budget.

Valuation by Replacement Costs

A classical alternative to historical costs is the replacement costs from the point of view that if we cannot buy this brand, then how much would it cost to recreate this again by taking various factors into consideration such as consumer awareness, percentage of trial purchases and repurchases, absolute and relative market share, brand image, distribution network, brand leadership, brand's presence in number of countries, etc. How much do we need to spend and for what period to create a similar brand? It is unlikely that we can create similar brand even if we have money and some brands may even be impossible to recreate and that is why corporations acquire brands paying astronomical sums. It is not possible to recreate because it is not simply the money spent on the brand and its marketing communication and advertisement over a period of time along with all other qualitative input in terms of product quality, performance, and service, etc., that have gone into the brand and have created today's value, most of which cannot be repeated and even if repeated may not have same impact.

- They were created in a time when advertisement costs were negligible and brand was nurtured through other modes of promotions and word-of-mouth publicity whereas in today's environment it costs huge sums to get a share of voice in a highly cluttered channel with many brands trying to attract consumer attention in the same product category.
- It is very difficult to imitate the performance level of the brand leaders and then enjoying a long-lasting competitive advantage. Challenging leaders will thus be taking enormous risk and chances of winning against a category leader are almost nil.
- The failure rate of new launches is over 90 percent these days and there is a great degree of uncertainty in the investment in building a new brand over a long period of time keeping sustained levels of marketing investment.

Brand valuation by replacement costs remains very subjective involving combined opinions of experts and ambiguous procedures. It should also be kept in mind that the objective of the brand valuation exercise is to get an idea of the economic value of the brand asset. And cost methods focus on inputs whereas economic value is based on the outputs meaning what brand produces and not what it consumes. Profit is generated through investments and also through market domination and leadership.

Valuation by Market Price

This approach starts with a question: What is the value of a similar brand in the market? This is how a real estate or property or even a second-hand cars are valued. We normally decide the price after inspection and offer a price either equal to or higher than the market price. Although this method appears to be more practical, it also has a few problems. First, comparison does not always exist for brands as brands are not daily traded like old flats and old cars. And there is a difference between a brand and a piece of real estate. Still these days we have reference points of prices at which brands were bought and sold.

In real estate, irrespective of the real use of the property, price remains the same which depends on the market trend and availability. For brands, however, buyers are the price-setters and the same brand thus fetches different prices at the hands of different business houses, which actually explains why brands exchange hands at astronomical prices. Also to use the price paid for a similar brand as a reference without knowing the specific reasons of such purchase, ignores an essential criterion or objective for the price paid for such brand acquisition. The value possibly cannot be determined by proxy. Despite these limitations, luxury market frequently takes into account recent transactions and uses a multiple of the sales. Normally one to two times the sales value or ten times the profit is often quoted for a brand.

Considering the difficulties which are inherent in the cost-based methods or in the referential methods on a hypothetical market, prospective buyers normally look at the expected profit from ownership of such brands. Cost-based method has the difficulty of separability of that amount of expenditure which can be considered as gone for brand building.

Valuation by Royalties

This approach basically can solve the issue of separability. The royalties that are receivable if the right to use the brand is licensed to a prospective user can form a means of directly measuring the brand's financial contribution to the business. This figure could subsequently be used to calculate the discounted cash flows over several years. However, in reality, companies normally use this route of licensing to reach or enter countries where brand is not currently present as a means for faster entry to those markets where business prospect is still uncertain. Global beverages majors like Coke and Pepsi often give the franchise right to the bottlers to avoid making significant investment in setting up grassroots manufacturing facilities. The company also undertakes supply of basic raw material (in this case soft drink flavor concentrate), know-how of business and services including systems and marketing support which helps the licensee to market the product and maintain the brand image. Hence it is not certain that this method properly separates the value of the brand.

Valuation by Future Earnings

Brand is a valuable asset and logically any asset has to contribute to profit if it is not an idle asset. Purchaser of a brand has the intention to make profit out of the acquisition and who has acquired the brand will decide what profit can be derived out of the newly acquired brand. Hence a global player can make bigger profits if he exploits the brand's potential globally than a local player from the same acquisition of the brand. Brand value, therefore, will change depending on who the purchaser is. This explains clearly why the stock market value of the brand and the business will always be lower than the predator's value of the branded company as market valuation deals with only the existing business taking into consideration the current performance of the brand and the business while a prospective buyer will value the brand considering the other synergies including complementarities in terms of marketing and distribution processes, strategic advantages and future plans for the brand which stock market valuation will not consider.

The valuation from the point of future earnings of the brand essentially has three basic steps as explained below:

- Separating and isolating the net income associated with the brand
- Estimating the future cash flow from a strategic analysis of the brand's prospective performance
- Choosing a discount rate and a period

This can be schematically described in Figure 8.1.

This is a classical approach of valuing all investments, both tangible and intangible, and the normal practice is to calculate the anticipated income over a period of 5 to 10 years. Beyond this period the residual value is calculated by assuming that the income is constant or growing at a constant rate. The discounted rate is taken

Figure 8.1　Multistep Approach to Brand Valuation

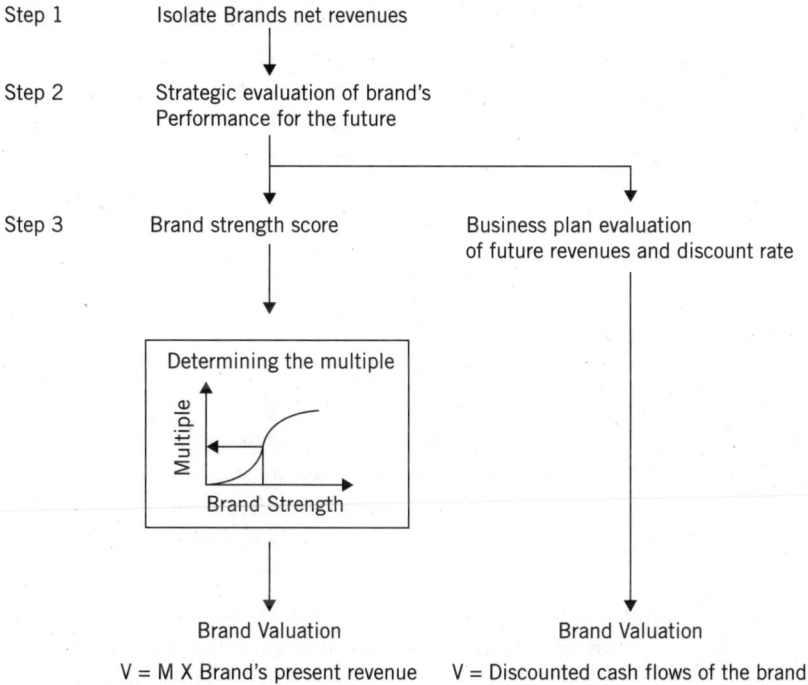

Step 1　　　　Isolate Brands net revenues

Step 2　　　　Strategic evaluation of brand's
　　　　　　　Performance for the future

Step 3　　　　Brand strength score　　　　　Business plan evaluation
　　　　　　　　　　　　　　　　　　　　of future revenues and discount rate

Determining the multiple

Multiple

Brand Strength

Brand Valuation　　　　　　　　　Brand Valuation

V = M X Brand's present revenue　　V = Discounted cash flows of the brand

as weighted average cost of the capital which is used, if necessary. The value of the brand will thus be:

$$\text{Value of the brand} = \sum_{t=1}^{N} \frac{RB_t}{(1+r)^2} + \frac{\text{Residual Value}}{(1+r)^N}$$

Where,

RB_t = anticipated revenue in the year t attributable to the brand

r = discounting rate

$$\text{Residual value after year } N = \frac{RBn}{r} \text{ or } \frac{RB_N}{r-g}$$

Where, g = rate of revenue growth

This is a classical valuation model using the discounted cash flow method. This method was used to value Cognac Hennessy at 6.9 billion Francs based on a capitalization of its net revenue over a period of 25 years at a rate of 6.5 percent

(Blanc and Hoffstetter 1990, quoted in 'Strategic Brand Management—Financial Valuation and Accounting for Brands').

Analysts have some observation to this method regarding three major sources of uncertainty (Murphy 1990; Ward 1989, quoted in 'Strategic Brand Management'). These are the anticipation of cash flows, the choice of period, and discount rate. By definition forecast is a projection based on certain assumptions and, therefore, can be uncertain even if forecast is done following a rigorous analysis of past and present trend. Similarly, discounting rates are also fixed taking into consideration hard company data and thirdly the period is normally taken 5 to 10 years because beyond that any realistic projection is not possible.

Valuation by Present Earnings

Who has seen tomorrow? And who, therefore, can predict future? How can one be so sure that the forecasts of business plan will be realized and will be accurate? In fact brand valuation process relied heavily on forecasts and business plans which were created just to attract new investors, so the founders could resell before the brand value declines. There are several instances of seller over-projecting the future of the brand just to show higher value.

To circumvent that problem, Interbrand, a major brand valuation company has promoted a specific approach. Interbrand valuation relies on just three years' performance—last year, this year, and the next year. After apportioning each year's revenue to pay for the invested capital which made the business possible and other direct intangible assets, one is left with global residues of each of these three years. These residues should then be multiplied by a figure called "the multiple," hence the name of the Interbrand proprietary method is called the multiple method. Although Interbrand seems to have now moved to the most orthodox method—the discounted cash flow but let us discuss the multiple method.

The company's stock normally is evaluated from its price earnings ratio (P/E ratio); a high ratio is indicative of high investor confidence and optimism in the growth of the future profits. Even though brand is not the company but the same reasoning can be applied:

$$\text{Firm: P/E} = \frac{\text{Market value of equity}}{\text{Known profits}}$$

$$\text{Brand: Multiple} = \frac{\text{Value to be calculated}}{\text{Net profit of the brand}}$$

For the brand there is no data on market capitalization as it does not exist and it is this we are trying to calculate. This notional market value of the equity is the price to be paid for the brand. In order to calculate this, it is necessary to determine M, the multiple which is equivalent to the P/E ratio specific to this brand.

- Calculating the applicable net profit: Interbrand actually uses the profit of the last three years (t-2, t-1 and t), thus avoiding the possibility of a typical evaluation based upon a single year. These profits are discounted to take into account inflation. A weighted average of these figures is then calculated in accordance with what we consider to be most and least important years. This weighted average after tax net profit which is attributable to the brand forms the basis of all calculations.
- Assessing the brand strength: This method uses a set of marketing and strategic criteria to give the brand an overall mark. Interbrand uses only seven of these factors and takes into account the only weighted sum of the individual marks for each factor in order to calculate the overall mark as shown in Table 8.1 (Penrose 1990).

Table 8.1 Method of Evaluating Brand Strength

Factor of Valuation	Maximum Score	Brands A	Brand B	Brand C
Leadership	25	19	19	10
Stability	15	12	9	7
Market	10	7	6	8
Internationality	25	18	5	2
Trend	10	7	5	7
Support	10	8	7	8
Protection	5	5	3	4
Brand Strength	100	76	54	46

SOURCE: Penrose/Interbrand (1990).

- Estimating the multiple: A relationship is assumed to be existing between the multiple which is an indicator of the confidence about the future of the brand and the score of brand strength. If this relationship is known precisely, the multiple would then be predicted by the brand score. For this, the multiple needs to be plotted against brand strength (S-curve). The model depends on Interbrand's examinations of the multiples involved in numerous brand negotiations over recent periods in sectors close to the one being studied. The P/Es of the companies with the closest comparable brands are used. Interbrand then reconstructed the company's profile and brand strength.

Plotting the multiples (P/E) against the reconstructed scores results in a
S-shaped curve (Figure 8.2).

• Calculating brand value: This is calculated by multiplying the applicable net
brand profit by the relevant multiple.

Figure 8.2   Brand Strength versus Multiple

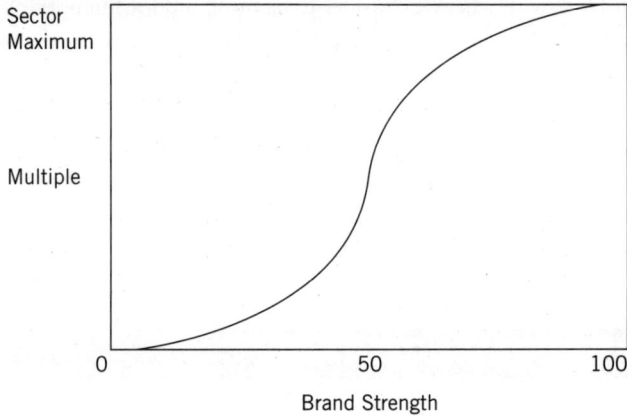

An Example: Reckitt & Colman Plc.

In 1988 Reckitt & Colman (now known as Reckitt Benckiser) valued its brands
following this method. Reckitt valued household and hygiene products where they
were the market leaders. Although they had a very limited range of food products
(for example, Colman's mustard), they were leaders in that category as well, whereas
in pharmaceutical products they had an average position. In the leadership category
Reckitt enjoyed a growing market with very few new entrants excepting where there
were distributors' own brands, world leadership, high unaided brand awareness in
UK (Airwick), brand loyalty, strong brand image but little possibility of diversification.
The company estimated that about 5 percent of the profits on these brands came
from sales under distributors' own brands. Interbrand, therefore, considered that
the remaining 95 percent was the brand's gross profit. The income generated by the
brand would then be the difference between expected return on investment and net
asset. The net revenue was weighted according to the importance of each brand on
business and discounted for last three years. The results were:

• Household and hygiene goods: GBP 53.8 million
• Food products: GBP 24.7 million
• Pharmaceutical goods: GBP 17.1 million

For the multiple to be applied in household category the multiple used by Reckitt & Colman in 1985 when they acquired Airwick was applied. A multiple of 20 thus was used for the household category of goods. A multiple of 17 was used for food products, which was based on the recent transactions at that point of time in the same category such as BSN–Nabisco takeover bid. And a multiple of 20 was used for the pharmaceutical category of business. The recent transaction in pharmaceutical industry had been using the multiple of 30 in those days but because Reckitt has a relatively weak position in this category a lower multiple of 20 was used in pharmaceutical business as well. By applying these multiples to the net revenue of these three categories as calculated above the brand values were estimated as:

- Household and Hygiene category: 53.8 × 20 = GBP 1076 million
- Food products category: 24.7 × 17 = GBP 420 million
- Pharmaceutical category: 17.1 × 20 = GBP 342 million

THE MANAGERIAL IMPLICATION OF BRAND VALUATION

Companies use brand valuation for many purposes. Although the question of valuation of brands rises whenever some acquisitions and mergers issues come up, that is not the only reason why companies use the brand valuation reports. The other purposes that brand valuation serves are:

- Financial reporting
- Strategic brand management
- Formulating corporate strategy and allocating resources
- Brand portfolio and performance evaluation
- Acquisitions or mergers
- Evaluation of managers

One of the most important implications of brand valuation is to create justification for the resources spent over a period of time to build a brand or even a portfolio of brands. For brand marketers brand is managed to improve its equity and hence for achieving higher value. Nothing gives more satisfaction to a brand manager than if he can find that his marketing plan, strategies, and creative executions are helping to deliver that incremental value as increased value will be indicative of improved brand strength, brand equity, and market share and as a result brand's financial performance will also improve. Thus brand value can also be used in managerial performance evaluation system. Brand value information alerts the management to negative as well as positive results of strategic brand management decisions. Most traditional systems of performance evaluation and reward systems are based on short-term and historically focused measures such as sales and profit. These are short-term results indicative of performance and it is possible to deliver the higher profit at the cost of the brand itself by reducing the marketing expenditure on brands which will have long-term implications of brand performance. Using brand value for performance evaluation of managers is a better way to hold managers accountable for their actions. Hence maximizing the brand value can be the fundamental operational goal of the planning process, consistent with the corporate objective of maximizing shareholders' value. When a large portfolio of products is marketed under one umbrella brand, measurement of brand value will serve as a simplified tool to evaluate the complex brand with multiple products to plan and support the brand management plan. Brand valuation is a single measure that can serve as a more integrated approach in managing and maximizing the brand's performance.

BRAND VALUATION AND BRAND SUCCESS

Continuous tracking of effectiveness of the brand performance against competition is vital to the business. There are many attributes that can be tracked to help brand managers assess how their brands are doing in the marketplace. One such measure is brand strength.

Brand Strength

The real purpose of measuring the brand strength is to know whether our customers are likely to remain with us. For many companies measuring and continuously improving the brand strength is a key goal of the business. For this, data need to be collected related to current and past behavior of consumers toward our brand. There are even models available to measure that. One such model is known as "Conversion Model™" which is a psychological analysis of commitment toward the brand incorporating measures as to how to increase commitment and exploit the weaknesses in the competition. Its diagnostic analysis helps the brand marketers to focus on key communication strategies aiming at the target consumers. This model was developed in South Africa and now licensed worldwide. This model was originally developed to track and understand religious conversion and was expanded into politics and then to business with enormous success with a variety of brands. The model determines the strength of commitment and balance of disposition and through these measurements the model gives a complete overview of a brand's position in the market in relation to its competitive set. This model is essentially predictive and it tells you in which direction your brand and your market are going and, therefore, it can predict swings in customer loyalty. The model has:

- Identified shifts in the market before they actually took place
- Rigorously validated through longitudinal studies in a variety of products and markets
- Has correctly identified which products or brands will lose or gain market share

This model clearly segments your market and classifies them into the following categories:

- The Entrenched: Highly committed segment to use the brand and unlikely to switch in foreseeable future
- The Average: Committed but not as strong as the entrenched
- The Shallow: Not content or satisfied and waiting for better alternative
- The Convertible: Discontented and actively seeking alternative brands available
- The Available: Those who are actively seeking conversion and may switch immediately
- The Ambivalent: Attracted to our brand but need motivation to switch
- The Unavailable: Not interested to switch in foreseeable future

These research data will be very useful for the marketers to identify which segments to focus on to increase sales and which brands of competition pose the greatest threat.

Asia Market Intelligence (AMI), a research agency, was founded in 1991 engaging over 900 full-time staff. AMI joined media communication specialist Aegis Plc., making it a part of global research and marketing consultancy network. The data collected in conversion model can further be interpreted using AMI approach of brand image data which provides actionable information on brand positioning and strategy by having an understanding of relative position with competition and will reveal the following:

- Relative brand image: yours versus competitors
- What images drive brand preferences
- How consumers' wants and needs are changing

AMI Pin Point™ analysis starts by grouping image attributes in terms of their relationship with the consumers and then goes to rank these image attributes in order of their relative importance in terms of driving consumer preferences. This then standardizes the image data to identify the true strengths and weaknesses of each brand in relation to its competitors. Standardized scores are calculated using prescribed formulas.

The step analyzes the true reasons for brand preference. Attribute importance measurement scores are calculated on respondent-by-respondent basis showing not only what is important to consumers but also the relative importance of these attributes. The key strategic output of this analysis is shown in the matrix in Figure 8.3 plotting relative importance of the brand to the consumer and its relative performance compared to competitive brands. An analysis of this matrix will reveal that there are several strategic recommendations and action plans will emerge for the brand managers to act upon.

Figure 8.3 Relative Importance to Relative Performance

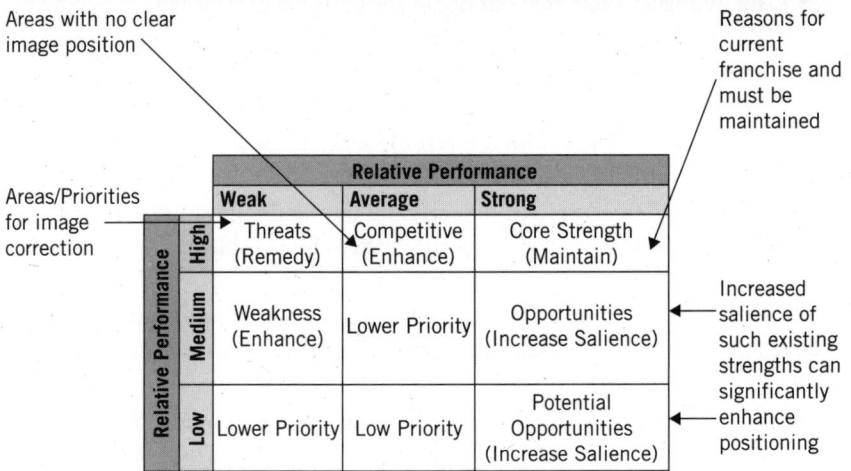

Areas with no clear image position

Reasons for current franchise and must be maintained

Areas/Priorities for image correction

		Relative Performance		
		Weak	Average	Strong
Relative Performance	High	Threats (Remedy)	Competitive (Enhance)	Core Strength (Maintain)
	Medium	Weakness (Enhance)	Lower Priority	Opportunities (Increase Salience)
	Low	Lower Priority	Low Priority	Potential Opportunities (Increase Salience)

Increased salience of such existing strengths can significantly enhance positioning

SOURCE: Asia Market Intelligence.

The output of the matrix can be interpreted into four key areas of brand management strategy. These are:

- Enhancement strategy: The brand manager might consider strengthening perceptions in the areas which are perceived as weak.
- Remedial strategy: Where image attributes are important but is not doing well and remedial actions are necessary.
- Maintenance strategy: Attributes are important and the brand is doing well in that area and it is important to maintain that level as those are the very reasons why consumers prefer your brand.

- Increase salience strategy: These are the considerable opportunity areas. Currently consumers are not considering those as important although brand scores high on those attributes but brand managers might like to take actions to make consumers feel those as important which will increase brand strength as well as improve brand positioning.

KEY LESSONS

As we can see, there are various approaches to the task of brand valuation. It is normally the basic objective of the exercise which will determine how this valuation has to be done. Some companies routinely carry out the valuation exercise primarily to understand how brand is doing and whether the incremental marketing effort is resulting into any improvement in the value previously determined. But marketers normally keep a close watch on two parameters—market share and profit from the brand. In real-life acquisition of brands one can even see at what price the brands are acquired by the potential shooter. In actual acquisition, corporations consider many other criteria besides the typical valuation of the brand as described in this chapter. As acquisition has many other considerations besides business growth, the price that is paid can be difficult to rationalize sometimes. It is because businesses have taken into consideration faster growth, eliminating a potential competitor from the market, knowledge that comes which includes both product knowledge and trade knowledge along with the brand, business synergy as well as corporation's long-term vision for the business. When a corporation wants to enter a new geographical territory, acquisition route is preferred by many companies as with acquisition, knowledge of the new territory also comes and from those considerations businesses are seen to be willing to pay much higher multiples than what would reveal in a typical valuation exercise following the methods as described in this chapter.

Let us now discuss a few cases of valuation which happened in recent past and, therefore, are still fresh in our memory. These cases will reveal how businesses are valued both from internal perspective as in the case of Godrej and Reckitt and also from the perspective of the acquirer as in the case of Henkel's brand acquisition by Jyothy Laboratories.

Case Study

A Case of Godrej

Over the years, intangible assets have gained a lot of attraction among businesses with brands increasingly playing an important role in sustaining the financial performance of the business.

A brand valuation exercise undertaken by the 114-year old Godrej Group for the first time in its life time since the inception of the business currently led by Adi Godrej has pegged the value of the master brand Godrej at USD 3 billion or ₹13,000 crores. The group whose products range from steel cupboards and consumer durables like fridge, refrigerators, air conditioners, etc., to toilet soaps, shampoos, hair colors, and other household goods had hired UK-based brand consultancy firm, Interbrand, for valuing the master brand along with the sub-brands in the group's portfolio. Although with a valuation of USD 3 billion, Godrej would not feature among the 100 top global brands which were valued by Interbrand in the year 2010, the master brand Godrej is still said to be ahead of the well-known brands like Lenevo and Nissan in the rankings. Godrej, which enjoys a consumer base of 470 million people in India, is behind the likes of Starbucks valued at 3.3 billion USD and L'Oreal valued at USD 7.9 billion.

Interbrand has submitted a detailed report of valuation of each sub-brand of Godrej recently. The key brands in Godrej portfolio include Godrej No.1, Cinthol, Good Knight, and Fair Glow. Good Knight is a household insecticide brand and has been acquired from Transelectra. For a valuation exercise the various factors that are normally taken into account are: brand values and proposition, positioning, brand's ability to adapt to market changes and its relevance with the customer needs as well as organizational internal commitment in its brand and future of the brand. The valuation exercise that Godrej Group has undertaken is expected to assist the group in developing its strategy for increasing its brand equity globally as the group is now entering new geographic areas and acquiring businesses elsewhere to create a global footprint. The group has established its presence in three continents through a series of acquisitions and collaborations and this exercise will help them to plan ahead to further on their ambition on global expansion. The group's flagship company Godrej Consumer Products Ltd (GCPL) has made seven acquisitions across Asia, Africa, and South America in the last five years. GCPL accounts for almost half the master brand's valuation. Brand valuation has other influences in a business, for example, it helps in attracting better talent; shareholders will now see better value coming through. Besides, a strong brand is a key differentiator for a consumer. A company that carries out brand valuation exercise will be able to invest better behind building and making the brands even stronger. It also assists in the process of globalization. A strong brand can fetch a premium in the marketplace.

Similarly, groups like Tata get brand valuation done annually from Brand Finance, an independent brand valuation consultancy which has valued Tata Group brand at USD 15 billion and Reliance at around USD 7 billion.

Interbrand was engaged by the Godrej Group three years back to usher in a youthful look for its logo. It had outlined four business verticals for Godrej known internally as "hero" businesses for the group; these are personal grooming, furniture, property, and aerospace. The Godrej group is a closely held diversified conglomerate with business interests in consumer products, consumer durables, chemicals, agricultural products, real estate, office furniture, locks, and foods. Since the master brand has a unifier effect on all its businesses, it was very vital for the group to renew its corporate identity (*The Times of India* 2011).

Jyothy Laboratories

Jyothy Laboratories had a very small beginning with one product Ujala which is a dye-based fabric blue. This low-technology product had really given Reckitt's Robin Blue (ultramarine) a run for their money. Reckitt ignored Ujala being from a small-time operator and technically unsound product. The remarkable success of Ujala is a glaring example of the fact that it is the perception in the consumer's mind which is important and not the product. Ujala was positioned for the "bottom of the pyramid" consumer segment and their campaign "chaar boondwala (only four drops)—Ujala" has created a history in the FMCG product category. The success of Ujala has prompted Jyothy Laboratories Ltd. (JLL) to enter into mosquito repellent and household pest control category with the launch of Maxo coil. This product, of course, did not do that well as it was not a differentiated product and fought against another formidable brand Mortein head-on with a me-too formulation. Maxo now has been relaunched and other variants such as liquid, etc., have also been introduced. The most significant milestone in JLL's history came with the recent acquisition of Henkel brands by JLL which has put JLL in league with other FMCG majors like HUL, P&G, and Godrej, etc.

In a quid pro quo deal, the board of directors of Jyothy Laboratories has approved the buyout of 50.97 percent stake in Henkel AG (a German company which has operated in the Indian market for over two decades and now decided to divest) while allowing the Euro 15 billion German major an option to acquire upto 26 percent of the equity capital of Jyothy Laboratories through either primary or secondary transactions, after a period of five years. In March 2011, Jyothy Laboratories acquired a 14.9 percent stake in Henkel from Indian promoter Tamil Nadu Petroproducts for ₹60.73 crores (USD 13 million). On May 5, 2011, Jyothy Laboratoriess said that it was acquiring 5.94 lakh (594,000 shares) equity shares of Henkel at ₹20 (40 cents) per share, aggregating to ₹118.7 crore (USD 25 million). Shares of Henkel ended at ₹32 (64 cents) down 1.18 percent on the Bombay Stock Exchange (BSE) while Jyothy Laboratories' shares closed at ₹222 (USD 4.5) up nearly 7 percent on the same day.

The acquisition, the first merger and acquisition (M&A) deal in domestic consumer goods' space in 2011 triggers the mandatory 20 percent open offer to the public shareholders of Henkel India. According to Securities and Exchange Board of India (SEBI) guidelines, Jyothi Laboratories did not disclose the price to minority shareholders, although market information is that the company would offer a price of ₹40 (80 cents) per share. Boutique investment banking firm MAPE advised Jyothy on the transaction. On this transaction Mr M.P. Ramachandran said, "This is a historic and much anticipated move from Jyothy Labs which will help us in strengthening our position in urban India. It will also give us access to any new product launches of Henkel AG in the future." Both Jyothy Laboratories and Henkel have strong synergies in various business segments such as fabric care, personal care, and household goods such as insecticides and cleaning segments and this acquisition will elevate Jyothy Laboratories to the top five FMCG players in India.

The maker of Ujala fabric whitener will refinance Henkel's debt of ₹454 crore (USD 91 million) as well as buy out the redeemable cumulative preference shares in the company held by Henkel AG. It said in a statement that Jyothy Laboratories will purchase 6.8 crore (68 million) preference shares in Henkel from Henkel AG for ₹43.9 crore (USD 8.5 million) subject to regulatory approvals. Jyothy Laboratories has lined up short-term loan of ₹600 crores (USD 6 billion) from Kotak Mahindra bank to part finance the deal. The promoters are also looking to sell a significant minority stake in Jyothy Laboraories to private equity in deleveraging its balance sheet.

With this acquisition Jyothy will add international brands like Henko, Pril, Fa, and Mr White, and Indian brands like Margo, Chek, and Neem to its brand list that features Ujala, Exo, and Maxo (*The Times of India* 2011).

Global private equity giant is likely to acquire at least 26 percent in Mumbai-based consumer products and manufacturer of Ujala brand of fabric blue, Jyothy Laboratories for about USD 150 million (₹667 crores) triggering an open offer to minority shareholders. Jyothy Laboratories which is close to buying Henkel India has discussed placement of shares at a price topping ₹300 (USD 5.0) per share. The private equity (PE) investors may acquire around 15 percent through preferential allotment and make mandatory open offer for an additional 20 percent at a similar price.

Brain Capital, Carlyle Group, TPG Capital and Apax Partners are in the fray for one of the biggest PE deals in FMCG industry. The strong PE interest comes just as Jyothy Laboratories is poised to emerge as a national player following the imminent acquisition of Henkel India. Jyothy Laboratories may partner with the PE investors for the next phase of growth as well to turn around Henkel's troubled Indian operations. The company also wants to pay off the ₹600 crore (USD 120 million) loan it has raised from Kotak Mahindra bank to clinch the Henkel India buyout. The promoters, led by M. P. Ramachandran, will hold a minimum 51 percent stake (down from 63 percent) after the PE transaction which is likely to be sealed within three to four months. The deal now has been formally sealed.

A critical board meeting of Jyothy Laboratories has discussed PE fund-raising plans besides the Henkel India buyout which is expected any time. The financial restructuring will be finalized following PE taking over 26 percent stake. Although Jyothy Laboratories has sought the all-time high stock price of ₹300 (USD 6) per share from PE investors, a deal is more likely to be sealed at around ₹300 (USD 6) per share. Apax Partners started talking to Jyothy Laboratories for a potential deal in January this year but has been challenged by its global peers with aggressive price offers. PE investment in Jyothy is an opportunity for a fairly large deal in FMCG which is rather rare. Besides, PE interest in the sector has revved up after Actis got very good returns on Reckitt Benckiser's recent acquisition of Paras Pharmaceuticals.

Jyothy Laboratories has already acquired 14.9 percent stake in Henkel India from A.C. Muthiah of Spic. It is yet to announce acquisition of Henkel AG's 50.97 percent stake at ₹20 (40 cents) per share. The deal will see Henkel AG selling its detergents and personal care brands such as Henko, Mr White, Margo, Chek, and Neem Active, while its two international brands Fa and Pril will be licensed with royalty payments. Henkel had acquired Margo soap, Chek detergent, and Neem toothpaste brands from Calcutta Chemicals which was under Shaw Wallace at that time. By this sellout Henkel AG will be divesting all its Indian brands to Jyothy Laboratories. The buyout is expected to broad-base Jyothy Laboratory's FMCG portfolio which was till recently only a single-brand (Ujala) company with a much wider basket of brands in a market dominated by MNCs like Unilever and Proctor & Gamble (*The Times of India* 2011).

Post acquisition JLL has taken many decisions to integrate Henkel's business with JLL which has a good distribution network. Company also has taken a price increase of upto 7 percent across board to improve the profit margin. These decisions include:

- Increased in the retail price of all the brands effective September 2011
- Rationalization of advertisement and sales promotion spend
- Moved from 3-tier consignment selling agent (CSA) model to 2-tier C&F model across the country
- E-sourcing with Ariba

Based on the consolidation of the Henkel business and the new initiatives supported by a new management team in place and with the distribution strength of JLL, the company is expected to emerge as a significant player in the FMCG category in India. The market analyst (SBICap Securities) has projected the business to perform significantly better in future and thus recommended investors to buy JLL stock. The projected financials is as shown in Table 8.2.

Table 8.2 Projected Financial Summary of JLL

	F 2011	F 2012*	F 2013*	F 2014*
Sales (Rs Million)	6,276	9,130	15,229	18,626
Growth (%)	4	45	67	22
EBIDTA margin (%)	12.8	9.2	12.4	13.2
Core PAT	688	446	1008	1605
Core EPS (Rs)	8.9	5.5	12.5	19.9
Growth (%)	(13)	(38)	126	59
P/E	24.3	38.9	17.2	10.8
Dividend yield (%)	2.3	1.2	2.8	3.7
RoCE (%)	10.2	9.5	24.2	33.4
ROE (%)	10.4	6.2	14.5	20.5

SOURCE: Company, SSLe.
NOTE: * Projected financials.

CHAPTER SUMMARY

The value of the brand is now becoming a part of the annual reporting on the business results and performance. As it is now recognized, brand is the most valuable asset in the business and it needs to be accounted for. The chapter deals with the concept of brand accounting and methods that can be employed to do the valuation of the brand. Numerous approaches applied to brand accounting such as valuation by replacement costs, market-price–based valuation, as well as valuation by royalties and future and present earnings are discussed. Interbrand method of Young & Rubicam, a company which regularly does the valuation of globally known brands has been discussed in details together with examples.

The chapter then deals with the managerial implications of brand valuation taking into account various key tasks that emanate from such exercise of brand valuation and how it is correlated with various elements of brand strength which need to be addressed for the brand's success. Also some of the recent valuation exercises carried out by well-known brands are discussed. Finally, a real-life case of brand valuation and divestment was discussed to explain how the method was applied to do the valuation of a well-known brand which was finally divested. The case studies will reveal how brands are valued by the acquirers to trigger inorganic growth in their business in a competitive business environment where organic growth becomes too difficult.

Candidate Measures of Brand-Building Blocks¥

SALIENCE

- What brands of product or service category can you think of (using increasingly specific product category cues)?
- Have you ever heard of these brands?
- Which brands might you be likely to use in particular situations?
- How frequently do you think of this brand?

PERFORMANCE

Compared to other brands in the category, how well does this brand provide the basic functions of the product or service category?

- To what extent does this brand have special features?
- How reliable is this brand?
- How durable is this brand?
- How easily serviced is this brand?
- How effective is this brand's service—does it completely satisfy your requirement?
- How efficient is this brand's service in terms of speed, responsiveness, etc.?
- How courteous and helpful are the providers of this brand's service?
- How stylish do you find this brand?
- How much do you like the look, feel, and other design aspects of this brand?
- Compared to other brands in the category in which it competes, is this brand's prices generally higher, lower, or about the same?
- Compared to other brands in the category in which it competes, do this brands's prices change more frequently, less frequently, or with about the same frequency ?

¥ *Source*: Working Paper Series of Marketing Science Institute, USA.

IMAGERY

- To what extent do people you admire and respect use this brand?
- How much do you like the people who use this brand?
  How well do the following words describe this brand: down-to-earth, honest, daring, up-to-date, reliable, successful, upper-class, charming, outdoorsy?
- What places are appropriate to buy this brand?
- How appropriate are the following situations to use this brand?
- Can you buy this brand in a lot of places?
- Is this a brand that you can use in a lot of different situations?
- To what extent does thinking of Coca-Cola bring back pleasant memories?
- To what extent do you feel you grew up with Coca-Cola?

JUDGMENTS

Quality

- What is your overall opinion of this brand?
- What is your assessment of the product quality of this brand?
- To what extent does this brand fully satisfy your product needs?
- Does this brand offer good value?

Credibility

- How knowledgeable are the makers of this brand?
- How innovative are the makers of this brand?
- How much do you trust the makers of this brand?
- To what extent do the makers of this brand understand your needs?
- To what extent do the makers of this brand care about your opinions?
- To what extent do the makers of this brand have your interests in mind?
- How much do you like this brand?
- How much do you admire this brand?
- How much do you respect this brand?

Consideration

- How likely would you be to recommend this brand to others?
- Which are your favorite soft drinks?
- How personally relevant is this brand to you?

Superiority

- How unique is this brand?
- To what extent does this brand offer advantages that other brands cannot?
- How superior is this brand to others in the category?

FEELINGS

- Does this brand give you a feeling of warmth?
- Does this brand give you a feeling of fun?
- Does this brand give you a feeling of excitement?
- Does this brand give you a feeling of security?
- Does this brand give you a feeling of social approval?
- Does this brand give you a feeling of self-respect?

RESONANCE

Loyalty

- I consider myself loyal to this brand.
- I buy this brand whenever I can.
- I buy as much of this brand as I can.
- I feel this is the only brand of this product I need.
- This is the one brand I would prefer to buy/use.
- If this brand were not available, it would make little difference to me if I had to use another brand.
- I would go out of my way to use this brand.

Attachment

- I really love this brand.
- I would really miss this brand if it no longer existed.
- This brand is special to me.
- This brand is more than a product to me.

Community

- I really identify with people who use this brand.
- I feel like I almost belong to a club with other users of this brand.

- This is the brand used by people like me.
- I feel a deep connection with others who use this brand.

Engagement

- I really like to talk about this brand with others.
- I am always interested in learning more about this brand.
- I would be interested to buy merchandise with this brand's name on it.
- I am proud to have others know I use this brand.
- I like to visit the website for this brand.
- Compared to other people, I closely follow news about this brand.

References

Aaker, David. 2003. "The Power of the Branded Differentiator," *MIT Sloan Management Review* 45, no. 1 (Fall): 83–87.

——. 2004. *Brand Portfolio Strategy: Creating Relevance, Differentiation, Energy, Leverage, and Clarity.* New York: The Free Press.

Aaker, Jennifer. 1997. "Dimensions of Brand Personality," *Journal of Marketing Research*, August: 347–57.

A. C. Nielsen ORG Marg Retail Audit.

Ambwani, N. 2002. "Efficient Consumer Response," *Strategic Marketing*, June–July.

Banga, M. S. 2004. "Reinventing Distribution," speech delivered at HLL AGM, June 29.

——. 2005. "Brand Power," *Business Today*, January 16: 56–62.

Bendapudi, N. and L. L. Berry. 1997. "Customers' Motivations for Maintaining Relationships with Service Providers," *Journal of Retailing* 73, no. 1: 15–37.

Bhusan, Ratna. 2003. "Building Brand India," *Hindu Business Line*, November 20.

Bianco, Anthony. 2004. "The Vanishing Mass Market," *Business Week*, July 12: 46–50.

Buell, Victor P. 1985. *Marketing Management: A Strategic Planning Approach.* International Student Edition. New Delhi: McGraw Hill Book Co.

Business Standard. 2002. "Indica Drives Tata to the Top of Indian Brands," *Business Standard Online Edition*, February 23.

——. 2005. "Fast Forward for FMCG," *Business Standard*, June 16.

——. 2005. "P&G to Fund IISc Research," *Business Standard*, June 29.

Business Wire. 2005. "NESTLE NESQUIK and m-Qube Team to Reach Target Demographic of Teens and Young Adults; NESQUIK's 'Grab. Gulp. Win!' Mobile Marketing Program Launches on 40 Million Bottles Nationwide," *Business Wire*, May 16, available online at http://www.businesswire.com/news/home/20050516005702/en/NESTLE-NESQUIK-m-Qube-Team-Reach-Target-Demographic.

Carlotti, S. J., M. E. Coe, and J. Perrey. 2004. "Making Brand Portfolios Work," *McKinsey on Marketing*, November: 1–8.

Carpenter, G. 2003. "P&G and Sustainable Development: Finding Opportunity in Responsibility," available online at www.pg.com.

"Case Studies: Mobile Marketing: Birth of a New Medium," available online at www.agencyfaqs.com.

Clancy, K. J. and R. L. Stone. 2005. "Don't Blame the Metrics," *Harvard Business Review*, June, 26 and 28.

Clifton, Rita. 2004. *Brands and Branding.* Dublin: The Economist.

CSR Europe/MORI. 2000, www.csreurope.org.

Court, David, Anthony Freeling, Mark G. Leiter, and Andrew J. Parsons. 1996. "Uncovering the Value of Brand," *Mckinsey Quaterly*, no. 4 (November).

Court, David C., Anthony Freeling, Mark G. Leiter, and Andrew J. Parsons. 1997. "If Nike Can 'Just Do It' Why Can't We," *McKinsey Quarterly*, no. 2 (August).

Court, David C., Mark G. Leiter, and Mark A. Loch. 1999. "Brand Leverage," *Mckinsey Quarterly*, no. 2 (May).

Court, D., J. Forsyth, M. Loch, and G. Kelly. 1999. "The New Rules of Branding: Building Strong Brands Faster," *McKinsey White Paper*, Fall.

Court, D., K. McLaughlin, and C. Halsall. 2000. "Marketing Spending Effectiveness: How to Win in a Complex Environment," *McKinsey Marketing Practice*, December.

Day, George. 2000. "Managing Market Relationships," *Journal of the Academy of Marketing Science* 28 (1): 24–30.

de Bono, Edward. 1992. *Serious Creativity*. New York: HarperCollins.

De Wulf, K. and G. Odekerken-Schroder. 2003. "Assessing the Impact of a Retailer's Relationship Efforts on Consumers: Attitudes and Behaviour," *Journal of Retailing and Consumer Services* 10 (2): 95–108.

Drucker, Peter. 1954. *The Practice of Management*. New York: Harper & Brothers.

Eccleshare, W., K. McLaughlin, V. Varianini, and E. Carr. 2001. "Marketing Spending Effectiveness: How to Win in A Complex Environment," *McKinsey Marketing Solutions*, July: 1–9.

Ernst & Young Survey. 2002. "Corporate Social Responsibility: Unlocking the Value," available at www.ey.com.

Express Hotelier & Caterer. 2005. "Barista, IOCL Tie-up to Start Highway Coffee Bars," June 13.

Fortune Innovation Special. 2004. "P&G: Teaching an Old Dog New Tricks," May 31, 75–80.

Gary Cokins, "Customer Value Management: The CFO's New Mission," available at http://blogs.sas.com/cokins.

Glady, Nicolas, Bart Baesens, and Christophe Croux, "Modeling Customer Loyalty Using Customer Lifetime Value," Department Of Decision Sciences and Information Management (KBI), Faculty of Economics and Applied Economics.

Godin, Seth. 1999. *Permission Marketing: Turning Strangers into Friends, and Friends into Customer*. New York: Simon & Schuster.

Heskett, J. 2006. "Beyond Customer Loyalty," *Managing Service Quality* 12.

Hill & Knowlton's Corporate Reputation Watch, 2002.

Hindu. 2005. "Govt. Looking at Model to Allow FDI in Retailing," *Hindu*, July 2.

Holt, D., J. Quelch, and E. Taylor. 2004. "How Global Brands Compete," *Harvard Business Review*, September: 68–75.

Indian Readership Survey. 2002.

Inverstors Hub. 2005. *P&G runs 2 year SMS campaign on Sunny Delight UK*, June 3, available online at http://investorshub.advfn.com/boards/read_msg.aspx?message_id=6558556.

Javed, Naseem. 1993. *Naming for Power: Creating Successful Names for the Business World*. New York: Linkbridge Pub.

———. 1999. *Domain Wars: Worldwide Administration & Registration Systems for Domain Names in over 200 Countries, Naming for the Global E-Commerce*. New York: Linkbridge Pub.

Joachimsthaler, E. and D. Aaker. 1997. "Building Brands without Mass Media," *Harvard Business Review*, January–February: 39–50.

Kapferer, Jean-Noel. 1994. *Strategic Brand Management*. New York: The Free Press.

Kearney, A. T. 2005. *Emerging Market Priorities for Global Retailers: The 2005 Global Retail Development Index*, available at http://www.atkearney.com/documents/10192/6bc59554-b251-4905-b298-25dbd2ac03c0.

Keller, Kevin Lane. 2000. "The Brand Report Card," *Harvard Business Review*, January–February: 147–157.

———. 2001. "Building Customer Based Brand Equity: A Blue Print for Creating Strong Brands," Working Paper, Report No 01-107, Working Paper Series of Marketing Science Institute.

Keller, K. L. and Y. L. R. Moorthi. 2003. "Branding in Developing Markets," *Business Horizons*, May/June: 49–59.

Khanna, Tarun, Krishna G. Palepu, and Jayant Sinha. 2005. "Strategies That Fit Emerging Markets," *Harvard Business Review*, June: 63-76.

Khermouch, G., S. Holmes, and M. Ihlwan. 2001. "The Best Global Brands," *BusinessWeek*, August 6: 50-57.

Kotabe, M. and K. Helsen. 2004. *Global Marketing Management*, 3rd edition, John Wiley.

Kotler, Philip. 1997. *Marketing Management*, 9th edition. Upper Saddle River, NJ: Prentice-Hall.

——. 2004. *Indiatimes Strategy Summit*, October 11-12.

Kotler, Philip and Fernando Trias De Bes. 2003. *Lateral Marketing: New Techniques for Finding Breakthrough Ideas*. New Jersey: John Wiley.

Kumar, Nirmalya. 2003. "Kill A Brand, Keep A Customer," *Harvard Business Review*, December: 86-95.

Levitt, Theodore. 1983. "The Globalization of Markets," *Harvard Business Review*, May-June: 2-11.

Liddell Hart, B.H. 1967. *Strategy*. New York: Praeger Publications.

Kahle, Lynn R., Basil Poulos, and Ajay Sukhdial. 1988. "Changes in Social Values in the United States during the Past Decade," *Journal of Advertising Research*, 28 (1), February/March: 35-41.

"Marketing Strategy in the Global Information Age," *Knowledge@Wharton*, July 23, 1999.

McKenna, R. 1991. "Marketing is Everything," *Harvard Business Review*, January-February, 69 (1): 65-79.

Mosad, Zineldin. 2006. "The Royalty of Loyalty: CRM, Quality and Retention," *Journal of Consumer Marketing* 23, no.7: 430-437.

Nielsen, A. C. 2001. *Reaching the Billion Dollar Mark: A Review of Today's Global Brands*, October 31.

Penrose, R. 1990. "The Nonalgorithmic Mind," *Behavioural and Brain Sciences* 13, no. 4: 692-706.

Peppers, D., M. Rogers, and B. Dorr. 1999. "Is Your Company Ready for One to One Marketing," *Harvard Business Review*, January-February: 151-160.

Oliver, R. L. 1997. *Satisfaction: A Behavioural Perspective on the Consumer*. New York: Irwin/McGraw Hill.

Porter, M. E. 2001, "Strategy and the Internet," *Harvard Business Review*, 79 (3), March: 63-78.

Porter, M. E. and C. Van Der Linde. 1995. "Green and Competitive: Ending the Stalemate," *Harvard Business Review*, 73 (5): 120-133.

Prahalad, C. K. 2004. *The Fortune at the Bottom of the Pyramid: Eradicating Poverty through Profits*. Wharton School Publishing.

Prahalad, C. K. and K. Lieberthal. 1998. "The End of Corporate Imperialism," *Harvard Business Review*, July-August: 68-79.

Prahalad, C. K. and V. Ramaswamy. 2004. *The Future of Competition: Co-Creating Unique Value with Customers*. Harvard Business School Press.

Quelch, John. 2003. "The Return of the Global Brand," *Harvard Business Review*, August: 22-23.

Raman, M. 2002. "Where Brands Fit Into Business Strategy," (David Aaker Interview), *Indian Management*, December: 20-24.

Ries, Al and Jack Trout. 1982. *Positioning: The Battle for Your Mind*. New York: Warner Books.

——. 1994. *The 22 Immutable Laws of Marketing: Violate Them at Your Own Risk*. Harper Business.

Ries, Al and Laura Ries. 2002. *The Fall of Advertising and the Rise of PR*. Harper Business.

——. 2004. *The Origin Of Brands: Discover the Natural Laws of Product Innovation and Business Survival*. Harper Business.

Rowley J. 2000. "Disloyalty: A Closer Look at Non Loyals," *Journal of Consumer Marketing* 17: 538-549.

——. 2005. "The Four Cs of Customer Loyalty," *Marketing Intelligence & Planning* 23, no. 6: 574-581.

Singer, G. and C. Halsall. 2002. "Restructuring Marketing Spending to Do More with Less: Three Critical Levers for Marketing Effectiveness and Efficiency," *McKinsey Marketing Solutions*, March.

Speisman, Stephanie. "99 Tips for Successful Business Networking."

Steenkamp, J. B., R. Batra, and D. L. Alden. 2003. "How Perceived Brand Globalness Creates Brand Value," *Journal of International Business Studies*, 34 (1): 53-65.

"Strategic Brand Management—Financial Valuation and Accounting for Brands," available at http://e-university.wisdomjobs.com/strategic-brand-management/chapter-1826-350/financial-valuation-and-accounting-for-brands.html.

Taylor Nelson Survey. 2001. "The European Survey on SRI and the Financial Community."

"The Global Brand Scoreboard: The 100 Top Brands," *Business Week* (August 2, 2004): 68–71.

Thompson, Harvey. 2004. *Who Stole My Customer??: Winning Strategies for Creating and Sustaining Customer Loyalty.* New Jersey: Prentice-Hall.

Upshaw, L. B. 1995. *Managing Brand Identity.* New York: John Wiley.

Vorhies, D. W. and N. A. Morgan. 2005. "Benchmarking Marketing Capabilities for Sustainable Competitive Advantage," *Journal of Marketing*, January: 80–94.

www.moneycontrol.com. 2005. *"Retailers Happy With New Retail FDI Rule,"* June 30.

Zyman, Sergio. 1999. *The End of Advertising as We Know It.* Harper Business.

COMPANY WEBSITES

http://en.wikipedia.org/wiki/Business_networking.

www.aa.com.

www.altria.com (Altria Group, Inc. Annual Report 2004).

www.cadburyschweppes.com (Cadbury Schweppes PLC Report & Accounts and Form 20-F 2004).

www.carrefour.com.

www.cocacola.com (2004 Coca-Cola Item 10-K Item 01, the Coca Cola Company 1999.

www.coca-colaindia.com (Coca-Cola India Web Details).

www.colgate.co.in (Colgate-Palmolive India Annual Report 2003–2004).

www.colgate.com (Colgate-Palmolive Company 22004 Annual Report).

www.danone.com (Danone 2004 Annual Report).

www.diageo.com (Diageo Annual Report and Accounts 2002).

www.gillette.com (The Gillette Company Annual Report 2004 and 2005 Proxy Statement).

www.heineken.com (Heineken N.V. Annual Report 2004).

www.hll.com (Hindustan Lever Ltd Web Details & Presentations).

www.interbrand.com.

www.kao.com (Kao Corporation Annual Report 2004).

www.kellogg.com (Kellogg Company Annual Report 2004).

www.nestle.com (Nestle Management Report 2004).

www.pepsico.com (PepsiCo Annual Report 2004).

www.pg.com (P&G Annual Report 2003, 2004).

www.pg.com (P&G Annual Report 2003, 2004, Jim Stengel Speech).

www.pg-india.com (P&G India Web Details), 99.

www.reckitt.com (Reckitt Benckiser PLC Annual Results 2004, Reckitt Benckiser Shareholder's Review 2004).

www.sap.com.

www.saralee.com (Sara Lee Annual Report 2004).

www.tesco.com.

www.unilever.com (Unilever Annual Report and Accounts 2004).

www.wikipedia.com.

www.yahoofinance.com.

www.yr.com.

Index

About the Author

Rajat K. Baisya has served as a Senior Professor in Marketing, Strategic Management, International Business, and Project Management at the Department of Management Studies, Indian Institute of Technology, Delhi. He was the President and CEO of the Emami Group of Companies and Senior Vice President, Business Development of Reckitt Benckiser India Ltd. He has also been associated with companies like Escorts Ltd, United Breweries Group, Best Food International (Unilever Group) and Parle-Bisleri Group in very senior management capacities. He was a member of Research Management Board of International Project Management Association (IPMA), Switzerland and is on the editorial board of many international journals. He is the Chairman of Strategic Consulting Group Pvt. Ltd and Frontier Agro Industries Pvt. Ltd, and also a Director on the Board of North Eastern Development Finance Corporation Ltd. He has over 300 research publications and authored five books and is associated with numerous trade and professional bodies in India and abroad. He is the Founder President of Project and Technology Management Foundation. He is a consultant to many large Indian and multinational corporations.

Professor Baisya was the recipient of Gardner Award for the year 1974 and Dr J.S. Pruthi Award for the year 2001 for significant contribution to the processed food industry in India. He received the Commendation Award of National Institute of Management and Technology for 2002 for significant contribution in corporate turnaround strategy. He has recently won the Best Professor of Marketing Management Award from Bloomberg UTV.